T0302213

BUSINESS SITE SELECTION, LOCATION ANALYSIS, AND GIS

RICHARD L. CHURCH
ALAN T. MURRAY

WILEY

JOHN WILEY & SONS, INC.

Published by John Wiley & Sons, Inc., Hoboken, New Jersey.
Published simultaneously in Canada

For general information about our other products and services, please contact our Customer
Care Department within the United States at (800) 762-2974, outside the United States at
(317) 572-3993 or fax (317) 572-4002.

Wiley also publishes its books in a variety of electronic formats. Some content that appears in
print may not be available in electronic books. For more information about Wiley products,
visit our Web site at www.wiley.com.

Library of Congress Cataloging-in-Publication Data:

Church, Richard L.
    Business site selection, location analysis and GIS / Richard L. Church, Alan T. Murray.
        p. cm.
    Includes index.
    ISBN 978-0-470-19106-4 (cloth)
    1. Industrial location–Geographic information systems.   I. Murray, Alan T.   II. Title.
    HD58.C48 2009
    658.2′1–dc22

                                                                        2008022806

10 9 8 7 6 5 4 3 2 1

To our families (Carla, Steven, and Karen, & Patty, Ryan, and Natalie)

CONTENTS

12. CONCLUSION 281

GLOSSARY 291
INDEX 301

PREFACE

Location theory is rooted in the disciplines of geography, engineering, mathematics, and economics. The science of "where should it be" is truly multidisciplinary and continues to be of interest to practitioners and researchers alike representing a variety of fields, ranging from business to operations research to computer science. The contributions of modern pioneers such as Hakimi, Vasonyi, Cooper, and ReVelle helped to expand the underlying theory, as well as to formulate relevant models for application. Since the first location algorithm was proposed in 1937 by Weiszfeld (Vasonyi), this field has relied on the computer to solve and analyze location problems. This reliance has been strengthened even more with the emergence of capable commercial modeling software packages as well as geographical information systems. We consider GIS and optimization techniques as equally important tools in this maturing field. In fact, scholars and practitioners today need an understanding of both areas (GIS and optimization).

Existing books on location tend to discuss the topic from a perspective of GIS or optimization, but not both. But the science of *where* has matured to the extent that this dichotomy is no longer ideal, so students need to be firmly grounded in both subjects. This need is what inspired us to write this text.

There is no required background for this text, simply an interest in spatial analysis. The level of discussion and technical sophistication is for both undergraduates and graduates, with all chapters including introductory and advanced material. The 12 chapters in the text can be taught over a 10-week quarter or 16-week semester.

Maintaining a reasonable length for a textbook often means that choices need to be made regarding what is covered and what is not. This book is no exception. The reader will find that all chapters, except Chapters 2 and 3, attempt to introduce location modeling as well as relevant GIS issues. Each topic is approached so that it is not necessary to have had a prior course in either area, although that might be helpful or preferable. The first three chapters are introductory and should be covered by all readers. The second part of the text is based on using models to analyze existing systems (marketing and distribution), as well as the siting of a single facility—be it point, line, or area. The third part of the text deals with the design of a system while making multiple simultaneous siting decisions. This final section addresses models for covering, dispersion/noxious facilities, and median/plant location. Although some topics were not able to be covered, such as hub location or hierarchical system design, the text is structured so that it can easily be supplemented by assigned readings associated with these more specialized topics.

Practitioners will find this text helpful as a reference given the comprehensive introductory material as well as advanced topics.

ACKNOWLEDGMENTS

This text is of our own design, and we alone are responsible for any critical omissions. We are, however, indebted to a number people and wish to express our gratitude to them for their help and support. We want to thank staff and students in the Center for Urban and Regional Analysis at OSU, especially Tim Matisziw and Wenqin Chen, and Matt Niblett (UCSB) in helping set up examples, produce figures, and proofread drafts.

We also wish to thank our wives, Carla and Patty, for their encouragement, support, and inspiration. Without their help, this book would have not been possible.

Finally, we wish to acknowledge Chuck ReVelle, Mike Goodchild, and others in this field who have both inspired and assisted us in this endeavor.

Rick Church
Alan Murray

CHAPTER 1

INTRODUCTION

1.0 MOTIVATION

Did you ever wonder why a hospital, fire station, or shopping mall was built in a certain location? Identifying the best site for a particular facility is no easy task. Planners must consider economic and demographic factors, while addressing political realities. This task is as old as our world. From early prehistoric times man has had the task of determining the best location in which to site a place to dwell, for hunting food, harvesting natural resources, and so on. As civilizations evolved, cities developed, trade routes emerged, and roads were constructed. When observing the remains of aqueducts, roads and buildings of the Roman Empire, it is easy to wonder how such systems evolved and how critical siting decisions were made. One can conclude that location decisions have always been essential. For the hunter and gatherer, a good location decision might have meant survival. Today, such decisions might not be a life and death issue, but they are nonetheless very important.

When we look at our current urban systems, we can see specific types of order and systematic arrangement. For example, older cities were located along rivers, close to the fall line—a good place to generate mechanical power and, later on, electricity. Many major cities have port facilities, as they serve as gateways to hinterlands away from the coast or navigable waterways. Some cities have developed close to major natural resources, where, for example, they can convert coal and iron ore to steel. As one looks closely at vast areas of fertile soil and adequate rainfall, a spatial arrangement of villages, towns, and cities emerges that appears almost like a regular pattern of specific geometric shapes. Christaller (1932) reasoned, "Just as there are economic laws which determine the life of the economy, so are there special economic-geographic laws determining the arrangement of towns." A contrarian might suggest that poor choices in location will be punished economically. But no one disputes the importance of location in business, manufacturing, retail, and public services.

There are three ways in which we can study location. The first approach is to *map* what we see by positioning an object's location in space by its locational coordinates. We can use such positional coordinates to accomplish tasks like navigating across an ocean, mapping all land parcels in a county, or calculating the amount of deforestation. Collecting spatial data and capturing its geographical position is an important task. The major function of **geographical information systems (GIS)** is to provide a means to collect, store, retrieve, map, and analyze such spatial data. GIS allows us to store a number of different themes of data across space, including elements such as soil type, land cover, precipitation, elevation, and so on. It is with this richness of data types and the ability to manipulate, model, and analyze spatial data in complex ways that the real value of GIS becomes apparent. In fact, it is upon this seamless fabric of multiple layers of data that today's location decisions are made. The main theme of this book involves how to integrate spatial analysis and logic with GIS.

The second approach to location analysis is an attempt to describe arrangements that have emerged and try to explain why certain decisions were made. For example, we may look for spatial clusters of a specific industry, where an individual firm appears to have made a similar siting decision based on some agglomeration property like nearness to a uniquely qualified work force. We call this a **descriptive approach**. The descriptive approach attempts to explain what emerges over time, or where a certain animal is likely to be found, as an example.

The third approach to location analysis is to identify the best location for an activity, or maybe the best set of locations for a system of activities. We call this type of modeling **prescriptive** or *normative*, in that we are trying to determine which location is best, rather than why certain location patterns have emerged. That is, the inherent feature of normative modeling is to help make decisions for the present and future. Although many models have been developed from a purely theoretical viewpoint, many others have been developed with a definite bent towards the notion of supporting a specific application, such as locating a store, locating an alignment for a road, or siting a warehouse for a distribution system.

Both pure and applied location analysis have emerged into a field called **location science**. The growth of the field of location science has occurred somewhat independent of the development of GIS. This book arises from a need for addressing specific components of location conditioned with GIS. The integration of location modeling with GIS allows one to accomplish more, do it more efficiently, produce better data and model representations, develop better solution approaches, provide new insights, and aid in the visualization of location alternatives. Our central focus will be on how practical, real-life problems involving a "siting decision" can be supported through the use of this integrated approach.

You have probably heard that there are three important issues in real estate: "Location, location, location!" There is no denying that this is true to some extent in many areas such as commerce, natural resource management and conservation, resource extraction, manufacturing, and product distribution systems, but it is important to understand that every activity has a place or location, and often it impacts the function or role of that activity. Although it is not the only consideration in the planning process, the "location decision" is obviously important, and is the central focus of this book.

In the remainder of this chapter, we will introduce what we consider to be the theoretical roots of normative location modeling, along with a set of *first principles* of geographical location theory. We also will introduce several historical developments in which modeling and quantitative assessment have become the preferred approach to resolving siting decisions. We acknowledge that some siting decisions are made in an ad hoc fashion, and they will continue to be, but as our urban and commerce systems become more complex, the ad hoc and "back-of-the-envelope" approaches fail to capture all of the important problem complexities and are more likely to fail in identifying the best alternative. Worse yet, these simple approaches may highlight or suggest an inferior alternative to what actually exists.

Within the context of spatial planning, one may well think, "There are no easy problems left." It is important to recognize that *greenfield* problems, where we start from scratch, do not exist in most applications. Often, we have parts of a system that are already in operation and we need to locate one or more facilities in order to serve or operate in conjunction with the existing elements. This fact alone demands a greater concern for characterizing what exists, as well as locating within the context of the built-up or altered landscape. Consequently, the role of location scientists must include capturing and representing relevant landscape elements, from transport linkages to sources of raw materials, so that models of location activities include all relevant features such as barriers, connections, zones of demand, and so on. It is important to handle such complexities rather than ignore them or assume they are unimportant. In fact, the merger of location science with GIS will be a necessity in order to handle the complexities of the real world.

1.1   HISTORY

Location science deals with siting one or more activities or facilities in such a manner so as to optimize one or more objectives. One of the first problems of location science was proposed by Pierre de Fermet in the early 1600s. Fermet suggested the following problem: Given three points on the plane, find the fourth point such that the sums of the distances to the three given points is a minimum. This simple, geometrically inspired problem dealt with finding a central *median* location.

Weber (1909) described a three-point problem associated with an industrial setting as follows: Find a location for a manufacturing facility that receives raw material from two point sources and ships its final product to a point-specified market. Thus, Weber's problem suggests finding a fourth point (the factory) among three points (two raw-material points and one market) in order to minimize weighted distance (see Figure 1.1). Weights here represent per-unit product amounts (i.e., the amount of raw material 1 per unit product, the weight of raw material 2 per unit product, and the weight of the final product).

The objective of the classic Weber problem is to locate the most efficient site for the factory, assuming that transport costs are a function of Euclidean (straight-line) distances. Fermet defined an unweighted problem, whereas Weber defined a weighted point location problem that represented the best location of an industrial activity. This problem is usually called the **Weber problem**, given the realistic application orientation, rather than a problem of geometrical curiosity. Weber's analysis was the first to pose a problem of industrial activity in terms of optimal placement. Weber's original work has been expanded over time in two problem domains: networks and surfaces (planar, spherical, inclined planes, etc.).

In 1826, Johann H. von Thünen proposed a model for analyzing agricultural patterns. In his explanation, he assumed that there was an isolated city surrounded by a hinterland that was uniform and unbounded in any direction. The city receives agricultural products from the surrounding hinterland only and nothing from other areas. The hinterland is occupied by farmers who wish to maximize their profits, and who adjust automatically to the market's demands. There is only one mode of transport: horse and wagon (hey, it was 1826!). It is assumed that transportation costs are borne solely by the farmers

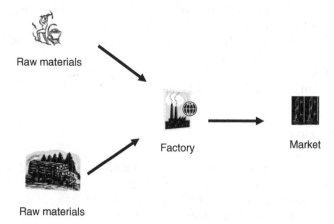

Figure 1.1 Weber's problem of locating a factory to minimize costs.

and are proportional to the distance to the market. Within this framework, von Thünen considered three interrelated factors: the distance farms are from the market (i.e., city), the prices received by the farmers for their goods, and economic rent of the land.

Land rent represents the difference between revenues obtained from the land and the costs of working that unit of land, and is the surplus left after all costs have been deducted.

Figure 1.2 depicts land rent as a function of distance from the city for two commodities. Each function is linear and decreases as a function of transport distance to the city. Notice that the cost of shipping commodity 2 is higher per unit distance than that of commodity 1. But at the market, commodity 2 commands a higher price than commodity 1. Thus, farmers near the market should plant commodity 2 instead of commodity 1. Beyond distance X, commodity 1 provides a greater net land rent than commodity 2. Thus, von Thünen reasoned that there were effectively rings around the city corresponding to different crops, reflecting the different values of uses for land. Thus, a given farmer would select those crops that would generate the greatest land rent, depending on the distance to the market and whether the demand for a given commodity has been met by farmers who are closer to the market. The von Thünen model is a simple economic construct that describes the process of land use allocation. This was the first attempt to systematically address land use allocation.

Hotelling (1929) wrote about pricing stability between two vendors of water. In his initial description, Hotelling fixed the vendors at sites of artesian wells along a linear market (see Figure 1.3). These two vendors paid nothing for the water, including pumping costs, as they were artesian sources. Hotelling's analysis showed how these two vendors would engage in **competition** for market share by setting prices, given that each attempted to maximize profit. Hotelling demonstrated that the two vendors acted like a two-person game, each responding, in turn, to the competitor's price until an equilibrium was reached. In his discussion of this model, Hotelling allowed competitors to

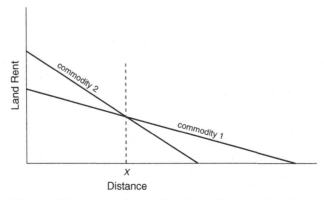

Figure 1.2   von Thünen's analysis of land rent for agricultural commodities.

Figure 1.3 Hotelling's competitive location problem.

move positions along the linear market. He reasoned that the two competitors would, in attempting to maximize profit over a series of moves, end up co-locating at the center of the market, sharing the market equally between them. Hotelling's analysis demonstrated the notion of competing retail strategies, gaming, and resulting location decisions.

In 1933, Walter Christaller attempted to describe the arrangements of the villages, towns, and cities of southern Germany. His work became the foundation of **central place theory**. Christaller's premise was that there are natural laws that could explain a systematic arrangement of towns. Christaller assumed that, given an unbounded fertile farming region, certain systematic and geometrical arrangements of retail centers would occur. He viewed the purchase of goods from retail centers based on several properties. First, all goods have a **range**, which is the furthest distance that consumers are willing to travel to buy the good. If the good is a refrigerator, for example, people are willing to travel a fairly long distance to make a purchase, because refrigerators are not purchased very often. In contrast, if the good is something like bread, which is purchased frequently, then a consumer will not be willing to travel far.

Goods with low distance ranges are classified as *low-ordered goods*, and goods with high distance ranges are *higher-ordered goods*. Christaller reasoned that centers offering low-ordered goods would be more plentiful and spread out, whereas centers offering higher-ordered goods would be less numerous.

Christaller also introduced the notion of **threshold**. The threshold is the distance from a center at which the demand for the good is large enough to satisfy the requirements for a vendor to remain in business. It is simple to see that if the threshold of a good exceeds the range of the good, at a given location, then that location is not profitable for offering that good.

Christaller assumed that each customer would travel to the closest retail center offering the good of interest, as retailers of a given type were considered to be equal in all ways. He reasoned that excess profits occurred when the market range exceeded the threshold. He further stated that entrepreneurs would attempt to compete so that excess profits would be kept to a minimum. He postulated that the ideal arrangements of centers offering the lowest ordered goods would be points on a triangular lattice, carving out hexagonal market

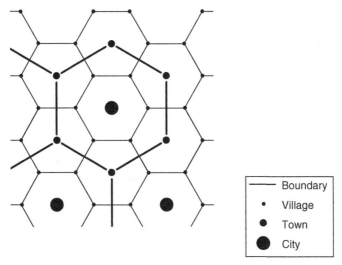

Figure 1.4   Christaller's central place hierarchy.

areas, where each customer assigns to his or her closest center. The next higher-ordered center would be located among a subset of the lowest-ordered centers. Thus, he argued that a hierarchical arrangement existed where high-ordered centers offer all goods that are offered by lower-ordered centers. Each set of higher-ordered centers, therefore, formed hexagonal-shaped market areas. A set of arrangements representing Christaller's marketing principle is given in Figure 1.4.

Geographers have had a long-term interest in Christaller's work. In the 1960s and early 1970s research focused on the geometrical arrangements reminiscent of that postulated by Christaller (Berry, 1967). Altogether, Weber, von Thünen, Hotelling, and Christaller represent founding fathers of location science, where each work laid the foundation for different areas of location research, retail competition, spatial layout, and industrial location. Much of the early work took place before computers were available. With the availability of computers, location science took a decided bent toward the use of computation and the solution of more complex location problems. Some of the leaders in the beginning of the computational modeling era of this field are Walter Isard, Leon Cooper, Charles ReVelle, Michael Teitz, and Louis Hakimi. The contributions of many of these individuals will be described at greater length in different chapters of this book.

1.2   FIRST PRINCIPLES

Some time ago, Tobler (1970) examined urban growth in an urban region. In the development of a model of population distribution, he discusses the nature of population from a global perspective. After identifying difficulties involved in specifying a model of global scale relative to impacts on a particular urban area, Tobler invoked what he termed the *first law of geography*:

> "Everything is related to everything else, but near things are more related than distant things."

With this principle, Tobler crafted a model for the urban area he was working with, Detroit, that ignored most of the world. It is important to understand that each field of science is based on a set of principles or laws, under which elements are analyzed, new laws are identified, and the field is advanced. It is natural to ask just what are the first principles of location science, and how would such principles guide us toward further study and scientific advancement?

In this spirit, we identify three **laws of location science (LLS)**. The first law of location science can be stated as follows:

LLS1—*Some locations are better than others for a given purpose.*

Even though this statement may seem obvious, the impact of this law is significant. If some locations are better than others for a stated purpose, then given a stated purpose, what is the best location at which to site a given activity? As an example, if we wish to place a fire station in order to serve a given area, it would be unlikely that the station would be located outside of the service area. Thus, one can begin the process of identifying a region, zone, or polygon within which a station should be located. The bottom line, of course, is that location matters.

A corollary to LLS1 is the following: *Efficient system locations tend to beat inefficient ones.* Holding all other factors constant, an efficient location pattern will tend to persist longer for a given use than inefficient ones. For example, if two stores are competing in a market that can support only one store, assuming that both offer the same goods and services at the same price, customers will go to the closest store. The store in the least efficient location, therefore, will have fewer customers and thus go out of business first. As a result, without other compelling factors, one should seek the best location(s) for an activity.

The second law of location science is this:

LLS2—*Spatial context can alter site efficiencies.*

Suppose you are going to locate a dry-cleaning business and you have identified an area to open a store in. The site that is the closest to your estimated customer base may not be as good as a site next to the local grocery store, as an example. That is, people can drop off their dry cleaning on their way to the grocery store, as it would be convenient and they visit the grocery store often. Even though the customer base of the grocery store may include a number of people that do not use dry-cleaning services, and that a better place to serve just those in need of dry cleaning might exist, locating next to the grocery store may be more efficient as the spatial context of other goods and services have altered travel patterns and behavior, thereby altering the landscape of efficient locations. Therefore, spatial context is important.

Often, sites where goods and services are provided tend to concentrate and build up around a given place, providing economies of agglomeration. For example, law offices are often selected close to courthouses, so that lawyers can minimize time traveling to and from the courthouse in the process of doing their business. Even though a customer base for a given legal group could be quite some distance from the courthouse, the cost of doing business may still be minimized by locating near the courthouse and ignoring the distances traveled by the clients. If a legal office is located at a great distance from a courthouse, then you will find that it tends to work in a specialty area in which the location of the local courthouse is not as important. Another example is the location of parts manufacturing in relation to assembly points for automobiles. If a given parts manufacturer only supplies parts to a single assembly plant, then the best location may well be close to the assembly plant itself. It is easy to see that the second law of location science is important in that there are dependencies between the location of other services that can be important determinants in finding the best location for a given activity.

The third law of location science is associated with investment in multiple facilities. Such problems are often termed *multifacility location problems*. Here is the third law:

LLS3 *Sites of an optimal multisite pattern must be selected simultaneously rather than independently, one at a time.*

Up to this point, virtually all of our examples have dealt with the location of a single store, office, or manufacturing location. But suppose that several locations are needed. For example, consider a simple problem of locating several pizza stores. Assume that only pizza delivery is provided, and there is guaranteed delivery of pizza in 30 minutes or less to any place in town or the pizza is free. If 15 minutes will be taken up by making and baking each pizza, this means that each area of the town needs to be within 15 minutes of at least one pizza store, or a lot of customers will be getting a free pizza.

Thus, we need to locate our pizza stores so that each neighborhood in town is within 15 minutes of at least one pizza store. Doing this means that the delivery areas of each store must be no greater in size than 15 minutes' driving time from a store, and that together the delivery areas of all stores must cover the town. Suppose that this can be achieved by the location of four pizzerias. The solution for this cannot be determined without locating the stores as a system (i.e., in concert with one another); otherwise, we risk leaving a neighborhood outside the necessary 15-minute delivery time. The third law highlights the fact that multiple facilities cannot be sited efficiently without taking into account service provided by each facility as an integrated whole. The best location of one facility is dependent on the location of others, and the best system can be found only when all facilities are located simultaneously.

The first law of location science (LLS1) easily leads us to the notion that a search for the optimal or near-optimal locations should be made. Otherwise, we risk locating in inferior places, which may lose out to a competitor's site. The second law (LLS2) means that spatial context is not only important, but that it is necessary to collect and analyze appropriate data for the purposes of making a site selection. Finally, the third law (LLS3) suggests that the search for the best pattern or configuration of sites cannot be achieved by solving a series of one-facility location problems. The impact of LLS3 is enormous, as the complexity of modeling location problems increases as the number of entities being located increases. Except in unusual circumstances, such problems cannot be decomposed into a series of simple independent problems. Thus, it is important to develop relevant multifacility location models to address complex spatial problems.

1.3   PLANNING CONTEXT

The process of planning as done by county and state public agencies and most private companies has evolved over time. For example, most public agencies now have a planning process that involves public participation. For example, in developing an *environmental impact statement* (EIS), the process starts at the outset with an invitation for the public to comment on what it considers to be elements or criteria that must be considered or addressed. Before an EIS is finally approved, the process includes a period of public review and comment, unlike master planning in the 1960s by engineers and planners with little or no public input. Planning by public agencies now includes significant public input. Such an open process requires that decisions be made with a focus on improvement, while mitigating impact as measured by metrics that communicate in a quantitative manner exactly what a project or plan is expected to produce. For example, building a county park may require a traffic study to measure the impact on local traffic levels and their impact on nearby residents, a forecast of expected attendance, a cost–benefit analysis to determine if it is economically viable, and an environmental impact review. The *do-nothing* alternative must always be considered as one possibility for final selection. Comparing alternatives, performing an EIS, and performing a cost–benefit analysis all require a quantitative framework in which to calculate metrics such as forecasted attendance and traffic flow. Some elements are not easily measured, but such intangibles (e.g., the loss of three acres of native bunch grass) need to be listed and addressed as well. With the exception of such intangibles, measuring and comparing alternatives usually can be presented in a format where each element is reported in a quantitative manner (e.g., expected attendance is 200 people per day, or traffic flows will impact traffic at the intersection of Elm and Main Streets by decreasing level of service B to C in the evening rush hour, or an additional recreational worker will be required).

It is important to note that legislation introduced in the late 1960s and early 1970s associated with the environmental movement goaded and required public agencies to be more open, involve the public, and address issues such as environmental impacts. For example, the National Environmental Policy Act (P.L. 91-190) in 1969, the Endangered Species Act (P.L. 93-205) in 1973, the Clean Water Act of 1972 (P.L. 92-500), the Resource Conservation and Recovery Act of 1974 (P.L. 92-580) and the Forest Management Planning Act of 1976 (P.L. 94-588) promulgated regulations that virtually required a quantitative approach to planning and environmental impact analysis. For example, both the Clean Water Act and the Resource Conservation and Recovery Act require that planning not be isolated and local, but that it be expanded to basinwide water management planning and regional planning for the disposal of solid waste. The cradle-to-grave requirements for hazardous materials of the Superfund Act (P.L. 96-510) require systems of quantitification, modeling, and monitoring. Thus, the era of environmentalism brought about major changes in the planning process, with a resulting need to better quantify impacts, benefits, and costs.

Another trend that emerged was the use of large-scale models called the planning revolution. In the 1960s and early 1970s, it was thought that large-scale comprehensive modeling could support and help resolve the needs of the planning process and environmental impact analysis. Although this supposition was true, there were impediments to a reliance on such large-scale models at the outset. Even though research was supported to develop large and comprehensive planning, monitoring, and management models, something was missing. That major ingredient was the technology to support such models.

First, computers were very expensive and very limited in their capability to handle large, comprehensive planning data sets. As an example, computer memory in most applications was less than 250 kilobytes, and processors were *very* slow compared to today's standards. Overall, the cost of computer use was considerably higher than it is today. The IBM personal computer was not available until 1983. Second, software for data management was limited, and GIS did not exist beyond simple raster-based applications. Software for handling spatial data was very limited, and in most instances was not sold commercially but was often written to support a specific application. Computer-driven plotters for producing maps did not exist, because most maps were produced by hand. Computer-produced maps were limited to crude shaded maps produced by repeatedly striking character keys. Color monitors did not exist, and the media for writing programs was usually limited to punch cards and paper tape. Third, inexpensive software did not exist to solve models and optimization problems representative of planning problems. Software available in the late 1960s could solve problems with a few thousand variables and constraints, but required the complete use of an expensive computer for considerable computational time. This meant that only a few agencies, such as the Air Force or companies like AT&T and Exxon (then Standard Oil), could afford to buy and apply such technology. Finally, technology to collect spatial data and store it was limited. Laser distance measures, GPS units, and satellite imagery did not initially exist. Consequently, the planning process needed technology that did not exist. But the story obviously does not end there, as improvements were made on all fronts: hardware (like computers, storage devices, monitors, plotters, etc.), database software, GIS software, modeling software, statistical software, and so on. Even new algorithms and heuristics were developed to solve model sizes that dwarfed those solved in the past.

Now it is commonplace to talk about large-scale models, such as global climate change models or large-scale models to optimize treatments within a national forest. Even linear programming software is ubiquitous; it is now a component of Microsoft Excel. Computational costs have consistently decreased over time, and now most maps are not drawn by hand but are produced using computer software. Thus, the revolution in planning, technology, and modeling has evolved over the last 40 years. We must now consider how technology can be used to support the continued quantitative revolution, supporting the planning process, optimizing the design and operations of systems involving business, natural resource management, and public services. It is with this perspective that this book has been written. Now we must, as a matter of course, consider just how to approach problems such as location modeling in an integrated manner using GIS and incorporating available census data, satellite imagery, and so on, along with data especially collected for a location model application.

1.4 ROLE OF GIS

The fields of location science and GIS have developed almost independently. The reasons for this are fourfold. First, models structured in the early period of location science were simple and structured as geometric problems (like those of the Weber and/or Fermet). Second, many models in location science utilize elements of operations research (OR). This field involves modeling for decision making where techniques are equally applicable in spatial and nonspatial domains. The field of OR has evolved since the 1940's and many of the models discussed in this text are solved using OR-based techniques. Third, the field of GIS did not develop to support location science, but, rather, because of the need to support a variety of uses and services. Geographical information systems were developed to collect, store, manage, manipulate, display, and analyze spatial data. Such systems are designed to present spatial data in the form of a map (e.g., thematic map), and are designed to retrieve data in a form that can be useful for analysis. As such, GIS was not developed per se to solve location models but to support a variety of needs, from mapping to spatial queries, and from visualizing a terrain to supplying data to models and statistical tools. That is, the goals in developing GIS transcend specific needs of location science, because the application domain is much broader than location science. Finally, the number of professionals working in both fields has been relatively small, and until now work in one area has been somewhat independent of work in the other. We can depict these three fields with a Venn diagram, as shown in Figure 1.5. Each field is illustrated as an ellipse. Notice that the ellipses overlap, reflecting that they are interdependent in some ways.

It is important to recognize that certain issues addressed in location science are actually spatial planning problems that can be resolved in GIS without knowledge of **operations research** or location science. Also, certain issues in location science can be addressed within a theoretical framework that does not involve actual data or specific techniques in operations research. However, many problems of location, from retail store siting to biological reserve site design, involve the need to characterize an application domain complete with spatial data of considerable detail (e.g., road network, census tracts, population estimates, etc.), and rely on a combination of functionality, from GIS to models and algorithms based on operations research.

As problem applications become more sophisticated, the spatial data needed in their application must be supported in one form or another by GIS. Thus, the role of GIS in location modeling ranges from central to peripheral data support, recognizing that complex spatial manipulation, query, and computation may be necessary. As an example, locating cell-phone towers requires characterizing the terrain along with characterizing surface clutter, which are elements that tend to reflect, bend, or obscure cell-phone signals (e.g., buildings and vegetation).

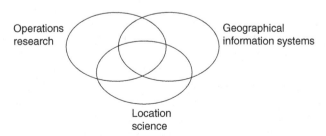

Figure 1.5 Overlapping fields of location science, operations research, and geographical information systems.

Modeling terrain is a central element of many GIS packages, and keeping track of ground cover through data attributes helps to estimate clutter height. Thus, GIS keeps track of data needed to estimate the area coverage of a potential cell-phone site. Simply put, an antenna reception model can be easily integrated with a GIS data model in order to create map coverages of potential sites, whereas such a model would require significant database development and data collection without using a general purpose GIS.

What we have attempted to show is that as these three areas of modeling have matured (GIS, OR, and location science); there is a convergence and burgeoning overlap between these fields based upon the demand for better and more accurate spatial data, the demand for better models characterizing real-landscape problem domains, and the demand to map and visualize solutions in order to support decision making across a wide-ranging set of scales, from the warehouse floor to harvest areas in a large forest plantation to the infrastructure of pipes and pumps, reservoirs, and tanks of a water supply system. Whether a water tower or a retail shop is being located, future applications are likely to be intimately linked with GIS, relying on a wealth of spatial data and spatial operations and utilizing models that characterized the problem domain in a manner that is as close to ground truth as possible. This is not only the future of business location decision making, but location science applications in general. Looking beyond theoretical location constructs and focusing on the resolution of actual siting problems will result in the production of new models, data constructs, algorithms, and theoretical principles. Hopefully, this book will be the first of many that help lead the way in this multidisciplinary field.

1.5 SUMMARY

In this chapter, we have attempted to describe the evolving fields of location science and GIS. We have also attempted to demonstrate that the future of location science and GIS will evolve and overlap, whereby many new applications and models will be developed based on a fusion of these two fields of science. This book represents an attempt to show how this fusion and integration can be accomplished. This book is meant as a textbook as well as a reference. We recognize that many students, and experts, for that matter, will understand one field and not the other. We begin with two introductory chapters: one an introduction to GIS and the other an introduction to mathematical modeling. These two chapters will form the basis of different areas of location analysis and GIS presented in subsequent chapters. Many of our examples will utilize ArcGIS, along with an optimization package called LINGO. In subsequent chapters, our examples will build on the use of ArcGIS, LINGO, and special-purpose routines.

This is not a computer programming book, but a book that presents detailed models and applications, and demonstrates how such problems can be solved with a fusion of tools, relying on concepts that fall within location science and/or GIS.

1.6   TERMS

descriptive approach
prescriptive approach
geographical information systems (GIS)
location science
Weber problem
efficiency
competition
central place theory
range
threshold
laws of location science (LLS)
operations research
planning revolution

1.7   REFERENCES

Berry, B. 1967. *Geography of market centers and retail distribution.* Englewood Cliffs, NJ: Prentice-Hall.

Christaller, W. 1966. *Central places in Southern Germany.* Trans. by C.W. Baskin. Englewood Cliffs, NJ: Prentice-Hall. Originally published in German in 1933.

Hotelling, H. 1929. Stability in competition. *Economic Journal* 39:41–57.

Isard, W. 1956. *Location and space economy.* Cambridge, MA: MIT Press.

Losch, A. 1954. *The economics of Location.* New Haven, CT: Yale University Press. Originally published in German in 1939.

Tobler, W. 1970. A computer movie simulating urban growth in the Detroit region. *Economic Geography* 46:234–240.

von Thünen, J. H. 1826. *Der Isolierte Staat in Beziehung auf Landwirtschaft und Nationalökonomie.* Hamburg: Frederich Perthes. Translated by Peter Hall as *Von Thünen's Isolated State* (Oxford: Pergamon Press, 1966).

Weber, A. 1909. *Uber den standort der Industrien* (Tubingen). Translated by C.J. Friedrichas as *Theory of the Location of Industries* (Chicago: University of Chicago Press, 1929).

1.8   EXERCISES

1.1. In your local town or region, can you list business locations that are struggling, strip malls or shopping centers that appear to have high vacancy rates, or offices with high tenant turnover? How is this explained by the first law of location science?

1.2. Give an example of how a service you rely on is well located. What about one that is poorly located?

1.3. What is a good or service that you would prefer to be co-located, or near, an activity you regularly frequent? Why?

1.4. Many towns of 50,000 to 100,000+ people have experienced growth of retail concentrated at first in regional malls, and now in "big-box" retail shopping centers. Often, such centers have decimated the classic Main Street mercantiles of town.

   (a) Has this happened in your area, or can you think of an area where this has happened?

   (b) What types of stores have moved onto Main Street after the traditional retail establishments relocated to the mall (e.g., antique stores)?

   (c) Can you estimate the threshold for a mall by observing the sizes of cities that have malls?

1.5. Classify the following goods or services within the context of order: low, medium, or high:

   (a) Plastic surgery

   (b) Convenience store

   (c) Home appliance and furniture store

   (d) Dry-cleaning shop

   (e) Videostore

   (f) Ferrari dealership

1.6. The neighborhoods depicted in the following figure indicate the number of children under age 10 in a town. Identify the best locations for two day-care centers. Why are these good sites?

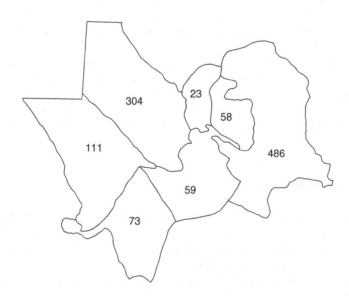

1.7. During a time of budget crunch for the city of Los Angeles, the fire department considered closing up to 10 fire stations out of the city's 105 existing stations.

(a) Estimate how many different plans for closing 10 stations exist.

(b) Would you want to close all stations in a given neighborhood? Would this be equitable?

(c) Can you think of one or more metrics that can be used to measure how good one plan is, compared to another?

1.8. In making your decision in problem 1.6:

(a) Did you assume that there were no competitors?

(b) Did you assume that they could serve only those inhabitants within a neighborhood?

(c) Did you consider locating on a boundary between two or three neighborhoods?

CHAPTER 2

GIS

2.0 INTRODUCTION

A geographical information system (GIS) is a particular form of information system that combines geographically (spatially) referenced data, as well as nonspatial attribute data. Information systems, such as Access, FoxPro, Paradox, and Oracle generally process and manage only attribute data that are not explicitly located in space. As an example, suppose we had a spreadsheet of data associated with each of the U.S. states. Aspatial information might include state name, total population, number of households, number of businesses, and so on. However, what about where each state is or which states neighbor (or border) other states? This is a role for GIS, as it is capable of storing and managing the political boundaries of each state, in addition to the attribute information. This enables one to identify, and view, each state on the surface of the earth. In addition, GIS analysis functionality allows for neighboring states to be identified through boundary evaluation. This is the major contrasting feature of GIS, because geographic extent is an explicit and important component of all information being stored, managed, and processed. Thus, GIS may be considered a hybrid information system that structures data and summarizes features based on the inherent characteristic of the data being managed—geographic extent.

Here is a formal definition of a geographic information system (GIS):

> GIS is hardware, software and procedures that support decision making through the acquisition, management, manipulation, analysis, and display of spatially referenced information.

This definition implicitly, if not explicitly, assumes that the real world is being represented in a digital environment. Given this, the earth, out of necessity, is approximated in a number of ways. First, there is the actual shape and form of the earth and how this is represented digitally. Second, Earth is approximated in how objects and themes are represented digitally. Finally, there are selective inclusion, or sampling, issues. We now discuss each approximation issue in turn, but driving representational simplification is the fact that functional concerns for data storage and computational processing are paramount for a successful and responsive GIS operating environment.

Earth is actually an irregularly shaped, three-dimensional object. A practical requirement in a digital environment has been to use a reasonable "regular" representation of Earth's surface in order to support an easy-to-use location referencing system.[1] Perhaps the most prominent assumption is that Earth is a perfect sphere. Of course, knowing that there is much topographical variability on the surface of the earth, it clearly is not a perfect **sphere**. In fact, a better approximation of the shape of Earth is as an oblate ellipsoid or **spheroid**. Better still is the **geoid**. These approximations are illustrated in Figure 2.1, and reinforce the notion that all of them only approximate the actual shape and size of Earth. As a result, there is undoubtedly representational error of some sort. Fortunately, such representational error has proven to be manageable, enabling significant data storage and computational efficiencies to be realized.

The second digital approximation issue raised is how objects and themes are represented on the earth's surface. This is also referred to as *data modeling*. Formally, data modeling has to do with a field versus object perspective. In practical terms, there are basically two spatial representations relied on in commercial GIS: raster and vector. A **raster** representation delineates space as a collection of grid cells and fills the entire space. On a more technical level, a raster layer is defined by first specifying the coordinates on the earth's surface, (x, y), where the initial raster cell is located, as well as its orientation and size. In addition, the number of cells in both the x and y direction must be given. Each cell in a simple raster has one attribute value. As an example, Figure 2.2 indicates ozone (O_3) readings for each 3×3 km grid cell of this layer. If there are multiple attributes, then additional layers would be included for each attribute. Such additional layers for Figure 2.2 could indicate other air pollutants, such as carbon monoxide, hydrocarbons, particulates, and so on. Further, additional layers could contain information on soil types, vegetation content, land use, and so on.

An alternative to raster is the **vector** representation of geographic space. Features in a *vector* representation are described by boundaries and do not

---

[1] A global referencing approach relies on latitude and longitude measures in degrees from the equator and prime meridian, respectively, to identify any location.

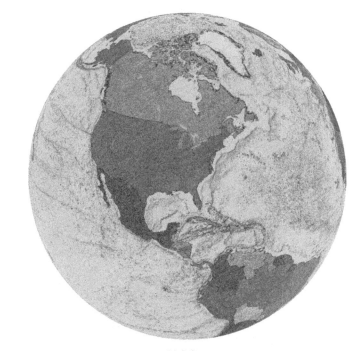

(a) Sphere

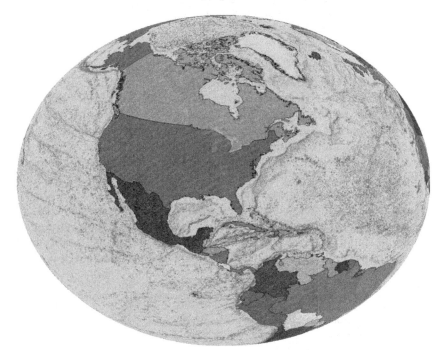

(b) Ellipsoid

Figure 2.1   Popular approximations of Earth.

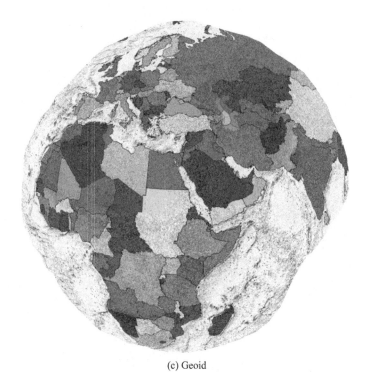

(c) Geoid

Figure 2.1   (*Continued*)

necessarily fill the entire space. Thus, features in a vector representation may be thought of as objects. As an example, Figure 2.3 shows cities, freeways, and parks. Nothing else is defined or identified in areas not corresponding to these features. The vector representation is characterized by three different objects: **point, line** and **area**.[2] Attached to each of these objects could be a range of attribute information. Formally, a point is defined as a coordinate pair, (x, y). Each point in the vector representation is unique and independent of other points. The line object builds on the point because it is mathematically defined using a beginning point and an ending point, as follows: $\{(x_1, y_1), (x_2, y_2)\}$. Of course, there is a functional form describing the shape of the line connecting these two points. Often, points are assumed to be connected by a straight line; a polyline approximates a line that is not straight.[3] The final vector object is an area (or **polygon**). An area may be thought of as a collection of points and

---

[2] Object orientation has begun to change this characterization somewhat as systems like ArcGIS can handle other features like circles, arcs, etc.

[3] A polyline may be mathematically defined as a series of points, $\{(x_1, y_1), (x_2, y_2), (x_3, y_3), \ldots, (x_n, y_n)\}$, where each consecutive point is connected by a straight line to the previous point.

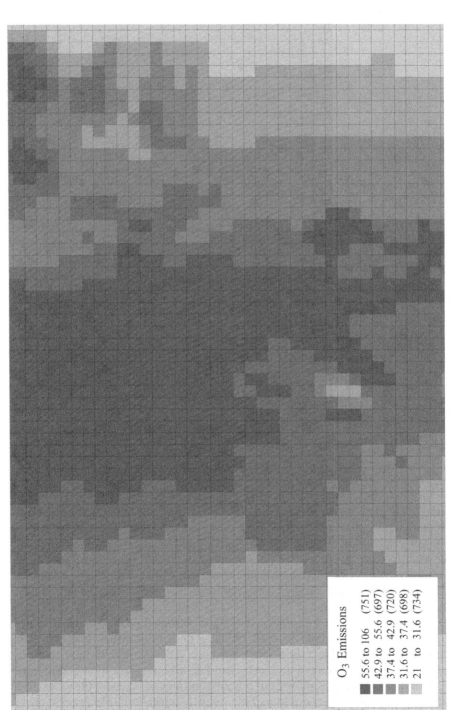

Figure 2.2 Raster representation of space.

O₃ Emissions

55.6 to 106   (751)
42.9 to 55.6   (697)
37.4 to 42.9   (720)
31.6 to 37.4   (698)
21 to 31.6 (734)

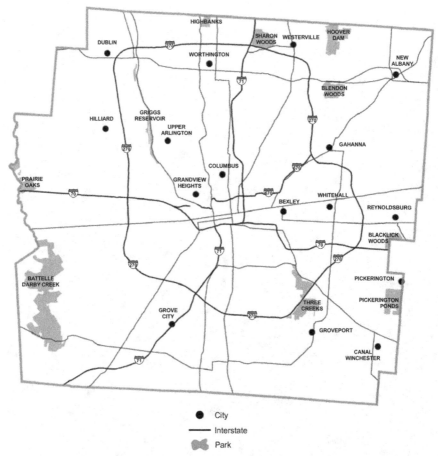

Figure 2.3 Vector representation of space.

lines corresponding to its boundary. In GIS, a polygon is defined by a series of points, $\{(x_1, y_1), (x_2, y_2), (x_3, y_3), \ldots, (x_m, y_m)\}$, where consecutive points are connected by a straight line and (x_1, y_1) and (x_m, y_m) are the same point in order to close the polygon. The boundary of an area object corresponds to some observed or defined feature on the surface of the earth. As an example, areas could delineate suburbs, congressional districts, lakes, forests, states, countries, and so on.

The point, line, and area objects consist of both spatial and aspatial attribute information. An example of each of these objects is given in Figure 2.3. Attached to each object is a label attribute. There could be any number of other attributes. The point objects could detail information on population, economic performance, number of schools, and annual taxes for the cities they identify. The line object could include freeway attribute information such as the number of lanes, speed limit, year constructed, and so on. The area object could identify quantities of fauna and flora, recreational amenities, hours of operation, and so on for each park. Thus, a range of attribute information may be attached to each vector object.

There are advantages to be gained from both the raster and vector representations, depending on the context of the analysis being conducted. The raster representation is a simple data structure with many organizational benefits. It is easy to understand and is useful for summarizing environmental characteristics of geographic space. On the technical side, the raster representation does not allow for point and line objects to be incorporated efficiently or accurately. Although data volume may be high due to its space filling property, it is efficiently stored because positions are relative (e.g., represented by row and column indices). For multiple raster layers, certain computational processing can be very efficient. Alternatively, the vector representation is a complex data structure, but it is extremely well suited for handling spatial objects (points, lines, polygons). The data volume can be relatively low for the vector representation, although positional data are required for every object. Computational processing for a vector layer(s) can be cumbersome.

The final digital representation approximation issue was **selective inclusion**. GIS was defined as a system that could be applied to analyze a specific region or subregion in almost any context. Of course, this can only happen if needed data are acquired or created. Selective inclusion has to do with the fact that information in a digital environment is the result of someone making a decision about what to include in a database, or study, relative to what actually exists on or near the surface of the earth. That is, spatial sampling is taking place. Although we commonly conceive of geographic information in terms of layers, not unlike the layers depicted in Figure 2.4, an important question

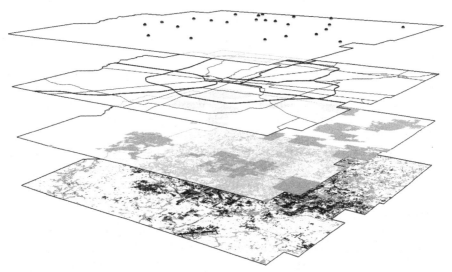

Figure 2.4 Layers of geographic information.

is whether all possible layers of information about Earth are represented. What about within a given layer: Have we omitted any objects or features? Also relevant to the issue of selective inclusion is the temporal dimension of geographic information. Do layers reflect changes across time, or are they simply cross-sectional? Given time constraints, fixed or limited budgets, and knowledge/understanding limitations, selective inclusion is a reality in any application of GIS. However, best-practice use of GIS would suggest that any project would ensure that relevant objects were included and appropriate layers considered.

This section has provided an introductory perspective of GIS. In the sections that follow, we return to the defining components of GIS: acquisition, management, manipulation, analysis, and display. Each component is discussed in detail, establishing a basis for the location analysis and modeling that follows in subsequent chapters of the text.

2.1 DATA ACQUISITION

If not apparent to begin with, a potential GIS user quickly finds out that needed spatial information in a digital form is a critical issue. It is virtually impossible to do any meaningful analysis without supporting spatial information. Possibilities for getting the spatial information needed for any project or study include public data repository (or government agencies), private vendors, collecting and organizing it yourself, or paying (or hire) someone to collect and organize it. In the remainder of this section we review data acquisition sources and/or approaches, enabling the use of GIS.

2.1.1 Existing Sources

There are actually many existing sources of digital spatial information that can be used in a GIS. Some are free or readily available to the public, while others can be purchased from a private vendor. Perhaps the most common source in the United States is Census data (www.census.gov), summarizing at varying scales population characteristics of the nation, states, counties, cities, and towns. Other data produced by government agencies include 100-year floodplains, vegetation classifications, and transportation. It is often the case that GIS vendors include some basic data with their system, such as political boundaries of nations and states. There continue to be efforts to bring together, free of charge, readily available spatial information sources in digital libraries, such as Project Alexandria (www.alexandria.ucsb.edu) and Geospatial One-Stop (geodata.gov).

Alternatively, there are many commercial spatial data providers. Some specialize in transportation data, such as TeleAtlas (www.teleatlas.com) and NAVTEQ (www.navteq.com), while others focus on geodemographics and market research, such as, Claritas (www.claritas.com). Given the importance and significance of digital spatial information in the use of GIS, it is not surprising to see the data provider and service industry emerge and thrive, currently exceeding $5 billion in annual sales and expected to grow substantially in the coming years. Thus, commercial data providers are making profits through the sale and distribution of digital spatial information to users. The point is that while spatial information exists, it may be expensive to acquire.

2.1.2 Semiexisting Sources

By semiexisting sources we mean that the spatial information is not necessarily in a GIS-compatible digital format. As an example, one might have a map from the mid-1800s showing locations where gold has been found in California. Technically, the information about where gold was found exists, but it is contained in a paper map, not as digital information. Another example is a spreadsheet of addresses indicating the residential locations of consumers who have purchased a particular product. Again, the information exists, and in this case it is in a digital format, but it is not amenable for use per se in GIS in order to be evaluated geographically. In both cases, however, it is possible to process this information in order to produce a digital form that can be used in a GIS. We now discuss three basic approaches for processing semiexisting sources of information: scanning, digitizing, and geocoding.

Scanning is the process of converting a hardcopy map into a digital image. Most people are likely aware of scanners for converting text on a page into a digital form. A similar type of process is done for maps, where the scanner is used to detect the presence of information on the map pixel by pixel (or raster cell by raster cell). The resulting scanned image is a digital version of the map, and can be accessed in some way by most GIS.

Digitizing is the process of capturing, or creating, vector objects from hardcopy maps or other geographic information source (e.g., photographs and images). Manual digitizing relies upon a piece of equipment called a digitizing table, where a cursor or puck is used to trace points, lines, or polygons of interest on the map when it is attached to the table. Another approach is heads-up (or on screen) digitizing, when the geographic information source is in some digital form like an image or photograph. Given a scanned map image, as an example, one could import the image into GIS and then manually digitize vector objects in the image.

Geocoding is the process of converting a street address to a latitude and longitude measure on the surface of the earth. A requirement is a database containing records of street segments, the geometry of each street segment, and the address ranges on each side of the street segment. This is often called a *street centerline database*, because the centerline of streets represents the street segment geometry. If a street and address are not found in the database, then there is no way to identify the associated latitude and longitude of the address. An address is successfully geocoded when the street is found in the database and the address location is estimated, thereby identifying the latitude and longitude of that address. With the latitude and longitude, a point on the earth's surface can be found, and it corresponds to the street address. Most commercial GIS packages offer functionality to geocode addresses, and there are commercial vendors specializing in geocoding services. However, successful geocoding is a function of the street centerline database relied on, so difficulties can arise if this database is out of date, inaccurate, or of poor quality.

2.1.3   Surveying and Airborne Approaches

A final data acquisition approach to be discussed is through surveying and airborne approaches. These are included together because they are increasingly interrelated and/or interdependent. We now discuss the following basic approaches for generating spatial information: surveying, GPS, areal photography and remote sensing.

Surveying is an approach for creating vector-based spatial information (points, lines, polygons) by measuring angles and distances from known positional locations. Key here is *known* positional locations, or reference points. The traditional approach to surveying relies on transits and theodolites to measure angles and on measuring tapes to obtain distance. It requires two people to do this. With changing technology, total stations are now more likely to be used to measure angles and distances in surveying. In general, surveying ensures high positional accuracy—down to the millimeter level in some cases. However, it is a time-consuming approach.

GPS (global positioning system) is a satellite navigation system operated by the U.S. Department of Defense, originally designed for military use. It is a constellation of satellites orbiting Earth at about 20,000 km. The satellites have atomic clocks that transmit highly accurate radio signals that can be read by handheld or mounted receivers. This enables position on the earth's surface to be determined, as well as velocity and time, assuming that the receiver is in view of a sufficient number of satellites. Thus, vector information can be created. For example, a receiver could be used to identify the location of a bus stop (point), record the delivery route of a FedEx vehicle (line), or demarcate the catchment area of a watershed (polygon). With differential GPS, signal errors can be corrected, and positional accuracy to the centimeter level is possible. This is done through the use of ground reference stations to adjust GPS readings.

Areal photography is taken from above the surface of the earth, possibly in an air balloon, plane, or helicopter. This produces a digital image (or possibly a photograph that is subsequently scanned into a digital image). A digital image can be georeferenced and then used to derive features or attributes on the earth's surface. For example, heads-up digitizing could be used to create vector objects, such as roads, lakes, rivers, buildings, fields, or forests. Often, high positional accuracy can be achieved, down to the fraction of a meter.

Remote sensing is generally used to create raster-based spatial information. Specifically, sensors mounted on a satellite are used to measure solar energy (electromagnetic radiation), though sensors can also be mounted on planes or helicopters as well. This enables physical, chemical, and biological properties to be derived on or near earth's surface, but requires processing and interpretation of the sensor readings. Spatial and temporal resolution can vary substantially, with some platforms capable of producing measurements for a raster cell a few meters or less in size and other platforms giving a raster resolution of up to 10 km or more in size for an individual cell.

2.2 DATA MANAGEMENT

An important issue for GIS is the capability of efficient storage and quick access to both spatial and attribute information. Storage and access issues have long been the concern of database management systems (DBMS) more generally, but the added complication of managing information in terms of spatial location and proximity has been challenging. As has been said previously, there are effectively two basic data models relied on in GIS, raster and vector. They are, in fact, fundamentally different conceptual and organizational approaches to spatial information management. Thus, we discuss each in turn below.

2.2.1 Raster

As defined earlier in the chapter, the raster data model organizes space through the use of a tessellation, often a regular square cell (or pixel), though others are possible (e.g., triangle, parallelogram and hexagon). For illustrative purposes, Figure 2.5 shows a raster with rows and columns labeled. The raster

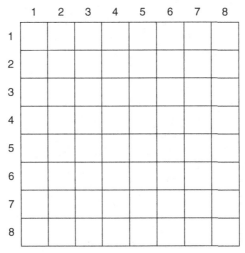

Figure 2.5   Basic raster boundary structure.

layer is positioned through the placement of the cell in row 1, column 1. Thus, we need basic information about cell size (e.g., 30 × 30 m), orientation (e.g., north), and coordinates of this cell. Beyond this, the layer is based on some number of rows and columns of cells, so this must be given as well. With this information, a raster representation for an area of interest is defined. Referring back to Figure 2.5, there are eight rows of cells extending out to eight columns. Given the geographic location on the earth's surface of the initial cell, as well as orientation and cell size, it is simple to determine the geographic location of any of these 64 cells. What is noteworthy about the raster structure is that there is no need to store each cell boundary individually, because there is spatial regularity. Knowing the location of the initial cell, and other supporting details like cell size and number of rows and columns, it is possible to easily construct the spatial geometry of the raster model. This enables considerable storage efficiencies to be achieved.

Of significance with the raster representation is that we know not only where each cell is located, but also the attribute value associated with each cell. Attribute values could be categorical, binary, integer, or real. The attribute values shown in Figure 2.2 correspond to ozone levels in each raster cell, and are reported as real valued. The values of each raster cell must obviously be managed by the GIS, and this is where coordinated linkage with cell boundaries is important. It turns out there are a number of alternatives for an attribute data structure to store and manage raster information. Some are more economical in terms of storage space, while others are more efficient in terms of access and processing speed.

Storing attribute data for a raster model is based on a **scan order** through the raster cells. Four common scan orders are shown in Figure 2.6. A simple scan order is row by row, illustrated in Figure 2.6a. Beginning in the upper-left-hand corner, or row 1, column 1, attribute data would be stored according to the order of the scan. Thus, for row by row, the attribute for the row 1, column 1 cell, would be listed, followed by the attribute for the row 1, column 2 cell, then the row 1, column 3 cell, and so on. If the raster attribute is soil type (see Figure 2.7), then the data would be stored as follows for the row by row order:

1 1 3 3 2 2 2 2 1 1 2 2 2 2 2 2 . . .

The Morton order (see Figure 2.6c) differs in the scan of the cells, beginning with row 1, column 1, then row 1, column 2, next to row 2, column 1, followed by row 2, column 2, etc. For the soil type example in Figure 2.7, this would result in the following attribute data storage:

1 1 1 1 3 3 2 2 3 1 3 1 1 1 1 2 2 . . .

The reason that alternative scan orders can be important is that some offer greater data compression potential than others, reducing storage needs. This is

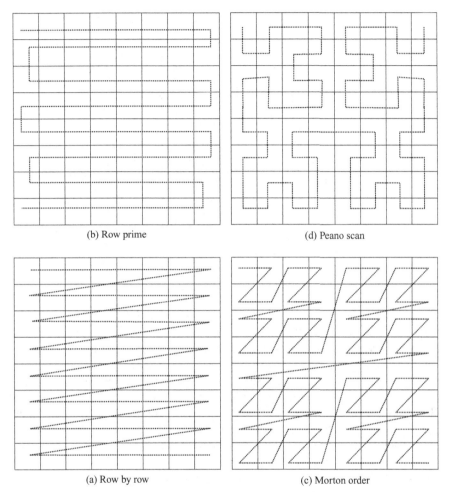

Figure 2.6 Alternative scan orders (beginning at row 1, column 1).

achieved through an encoding scheme, such as run-length, block, or wavelet. As an example, run-length encoding replaces the same consecutive attribute value with a count of that attribute. Thus, 1 1 3 3 2 2 2 2 1 1 2 2 2 2 2 2 ... for the row by row order becomes:

2 1, 2 3, 4 2, 2 1, 6 2, ...

Attributes, then, are stored in a pairing format, where the first piece of information is an integer count and the second is the actual attribute value for those cells. The run-length encoded row by row scan order, as an example, is interpreted as follows: 2 1 specifies that the first two cells have an attribute value of 1; 2 3 indicates that the next two cells have an attribute value of

1	1	3	3	2	2	2	2
1	1	2	2	2	2	2	2
3	1	1	1	2	2	2	2
3	1	2	2	3	3	2	2
3	3	1	2	3	3	3	3
3	1	1	2	1	3	3	3
3	1	1	2	1	1	3	3
1	3	2	1	1	1	3	1

Figure 2.7 Soil type (1 = clay, 2 = sand, 3 = rock).

3; 4 2 identifies the next four cells as having an attribute value of 2; etc. This is how data compression is achieved, by reducing the actual number of attribute values stored. It is not uncommon to see high compression rates (up to or exceeding a factor of 40) for a raster layer, depending on the scan order and encoding scheme.

The raster data model is useful and important because it can represent a study region in a complete way, as an attribute value is given for every location. Further, it can do this in an efficient manner by handling the spatial location and geometry of cells with minimal storage requirements. Though not discussed here, other data management approaches are possible for a raster layer, such as quadtrees and other hierarchical data structures, offering potential storage and access efficiencies as well.

2.2.2 Vector

In general terms, there are a number of DBMS approaches, including relational, network, hierarchical, object and object-relational. The prominent data management approach in vector-based GIS has been **relational DBMS**, though this has arguably evolved to more of a hybrid object-relational DBMS. Again, issues of efficient storage and quick access to information are critical for the success of any developed system. In fact, such issues have been responsible for the evolution of DBMS in GIS. In the remainder of this section, we review object-relational DBMS to support the spatial representation of vector features.

To begin, a relational DBMS structures information using linked tables. As an example, one table could provide information on the attributes of bus stops, another table could track bus stop maintenance information, and a final table would give the positional coordinates (latitude and longitude) of the stops themselves. The object-relational DBMS differs because of the need to track vector objects. On the one hand, the database generally has considerable attribute information, and it makes sense to manage this using well developed relational DBMS functionality. On the other hand, dealing with geographic space and spatial objects complicates things. One of the reasons for this is that the geometry of vector features varies. For example, a point is always referenced by two pieces of information, a latitude and longitude. However, a polyline may be defined by as few a two points or as many as hundreds, or even thousands of points. It depends on the line feature. A similar situation exists for polygons. The object-relational DBMS approach has evolved to handle attribute data and feature geometry in an integrated way. Though discussed in the next section, the object-relational DBMS approach goes beyond storage considerations as a primary consideration is access to data and operations that may be applied.

For the management and storage of data in a vector GIS, consider the U.S. Census tracts shown in Figure 2.8. These are polygons, and each contains attribute information about the area it represents. Figure 2.9 provides a logical view of the object-relational DBMS approach for managing and storing the aspatial and spatial information in this case. In Figure 2.9a, the attribute table is shown, indicating the various attribute values reported for each Census tract. Figure 2.9b also reports information about each Census tract, but in this case it is the polygon geometry. The linkage of the two files is possible through the use of the feature ID, which is given in each table.

As mentioned previously, the relational DBMS and object-relational DBMS approaches are not the only possible ways to approach the management and storage of information in GIS. However, these have been the prominent approaches to date. Given this, we have limited the focus here to the basic relational/object-relational approaches.

2.3 DATA MANIPULATION

The previous discussion of data management could have included issues of data manipulation, as this is generally considered part of DBMS. We have opted to separate management (storage and access) from manipulation in our overview of GIS because of the unique needs that exist in dealing with spatial information, and the implications for data manipulation. In particular, there are some basic data manipulation approaches for dealing with spatial data. In this section we focus on conversion, aggregation, overlay, and interpolation.

2.3.1 Conversion

A primary feature of GIS is its ability to integrate layers of spatial information. This is only possible by first identifying a common coordinate system. Thus,

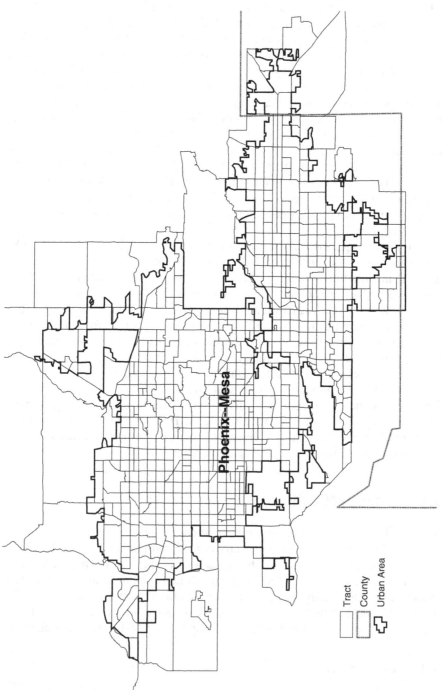

Figure 2.8 Census tracts (polygons) in Phoenix, Arizona.

ID	Shape	Point Data
106200	Polygon	-112.05243 33.59837, -112.03894 33.59571, -112.048 33.58829, -112.06182 33.581, -112.03786 33.59694, ...
106100	Polygon	-112.08128 33.59253, -112.06412 33.58784, -112.09963 33.5821, -112.09573 33.60035, -112.06523 33.60709, ...
106300	Polygon	-112.02458 33.5893, -112.03786 33.59694, -112.01325 33.59692, -112.01309 33.58246, -112.03894 33.59571, ...
105400	Polygon	-112.03465 33.57871, -112.04998 33.585, -112.03894 33.59571, -112.03268 33.58814, -112.0484 33.58224, ...
105300	Polygon	-112.07382 33.57509, -112.06493 33.5826, -112.06509 33.58039, -112.08246 33.57296, -112.08254 33.5822, ...
105200	Polygon	-112.05665 33.57476, -112.0484 33.58224, -112.05003 33.5677, -112.0651 33.58176, -112.06182 33.581 , ...
105102	Polygon	-112.09072 33.57801, -112.08254 33.5822, -112.09964 33.57485, -112.0996 33.58079, -112.09963 33.5821, ...
104501	Polygon	-112.09146 33.57076, -112.08246 33.57296, -112.09961 33.5676, -112.09962 33.57248, -112.09964 33.57485, ...
104502	Polygon	-112.01485 33.55113, -112.02335 33.57219, -112.01599 33.56722, -112.00322 33.56831, -112.03605 33.56369, ...
104700	Polygon	-112.05224 33.5613, -112.04714 33.57112, -112.04329 33.55568, -112.044 33.55529, -112.04805 33.57124, ...
104600	Polygon	-112.07382 33.56028, -112.0652 33.56799, -112.07385 33.55282, -112.08259 33.55291, -112.08254 33.56753, ...
104801	Polygon	-112.09109 33.56028, -112.08254 33.56753, -112.08259 33.55291, -112.09967 33.55309, -112.09961 33.5676, ...
104802	Polygon	-112.05642 33.54579, -112.04864 33.55418, -112.04746 33.53825, -112.06504 33.53828, -112.06521 33.55273, ...
103615	Polygon	-112.09107 33.54574, -112.08259 33.55291, -112.09489 33.53856, -112.09549 33.53857, -112.09967 33.55309, ...
103700	Polygon	-112.07384 33.54557, -112.07385 33.55282, -112.06504 33.53828, -112.08245 33.53836, -112.08259 33.5529, ...
...		

(b) Object definition table

ID	WHITE	BLACK	AMERI_ES	ASIAN	HAWN_PI	OTHER	MULT_RACE	HISPANIC	...
106200	3295	16	11	53	2	37	39	136	
106100	4499	162	99	47	2	225	138	564	
106300	4468	190	110	74	1	310	158	823	
105400	3423	60	37	34	0	106	69	275	
105300	4643	90	63	64	3	619	162	1402	
105200	5243	184	183	124	3	662	216	1569	
105102	4032	33	20	134	4	44	66	216	
104501	2853	134	145	353	10	938	170	2429	
104502	3027	126	218	262	22	1628	291	3144	
104700	6258	226	147	66	3	812	211	2608	
104600	3101	146	107	32	3	588	192	1432	
104801	3574	28	26	62	4	118	87	383	
104802	5817	96	41	124	8	106	120	409	
103615	3572	265	166	126	1	1018	225	2505	
103700	6656	185	84	224	6	367	143	880	
...									

(a) Attribute table

Figure 2.9   Logical view of information management and storage.

a major need in GIS is the capability to carry out **coordinate transformation** tasks, or *conversion*, such as translation, scaling, rotation, and reflection. This means that one or more of the information layers (e.g., Figure 2.4) may not correspond exactly to the common coordinate system being used, and as a result would need to be converted/transformed in some way. That is, the spatial coordinates of features represented would need to be altered through a common translation, rotation, etc. to be consistent with the other data layers.

A second category of data conversion in GIS is *rubber-sheeting*, where a data layer component would need to be stretched and/or pulled in various ways to correspond to or spatially match up with other data. Consider, for example, the integration of the roadway networks in two adjacent counties, where each county is responsible for the creation and management of its network. If our study spans the two counties, then we need to integrate both networks into the same road layer. Rubber-sheeting would be the process of matching up the intersection of streets along the common or shared edge(s), assuming they do not match exactly.

A third major category of data conversion in GIS is *projection*. This is the process of taking the three-dimensional Earth and projecting it into a two-dimension coordinate system—flattening it. There are many possible approaches for projection, but all result in some distortion or error. The reason for this is that it is impossible to represent a three-dimensional object in two dimensions without distortion/error of some sort. More discussion on this topic is left for Chapter 6.

Other data conversion approaches in GIS worth mentioning include clipping, raster/vector conversion, and line thinning and smoothing.

2.3.2 Aggregation

An important feature of GIS is the ability to spatially aggregate information, sometimes referred to as reclassification. In a raster layer this could be accomplished by increasing underlying raster cell size. An example of such **aggregation** is shown in Figure 2.10. The original data for land use type is given in Figure 2.10a, where the cell size is 25 m. The cells are aggregated using GIS, and the result is shown in Figure 2.10b, where cell size is now 125 m. A similar process exists for a vector layer, although it depends on the type of objects represented. For point objects, scale often dictates that some level of aggregation is important. For example, consider the various cities in the Columbus, Ohio, region shown in Figure 2.11a. This view of the different incorporated entities of Columbus makes sense at this scale, but in the context of cities across the eastern United States, as shown in Figure 2.11b, an aggregate representation of the city is more meaningful. Thus, aggregation in this case is the combination of neighboring points. If the data layer were polygon based, aggregation likely would take the form of merging neighboring polygons, or rather dissolving interior boundaries of aggregated polygons. In all cases, however, aggregation involves taking input objects and creating one new output object, combining in some way the associated attribute information.

2.3.3 Overlay

A third major feature of data manipulation in GIS is **overlay**. For convenience, it is assumed that the scale of the spatial layers is the same. Overlay is interpreted a little differently in raster and vector GIS. In a raster system, overlay takes a number of raster layers, each representing a different attribute, and applies logical or arithmetic operations (e.g., and, or, xor, addition, subtraction, multiplication, division, assignment) to produce an output layer. Thus,

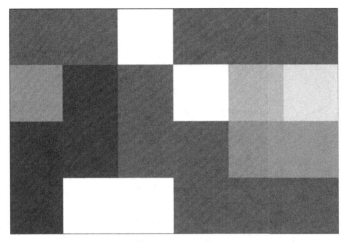

(b) Aggregate cells

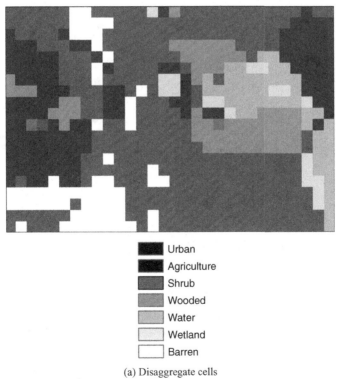

■ Urban
■ Agriculture
■ Shrub
■ Wooded
□ Water
□ Wetland
□ Barren

(a) Disaggregate cells

Figure 2.10   Raster cell aggregation.

(b) aggregate Columbus area information

(a) disaggregate local area information (Columbus)

Figure 2.11 Point aggregation.

overlay in a raster system is conditioned upon having the same underlying raster grid cell structure for all input layers. Overlay in raster is equivalent to *map algebra*. We will return to this topic in Chapter 5.

For vector GIS, overlay is more general, often call topological overlay. The objects of input vector layers are considered to not coincide, thereby raising a need to define new objects in a new layer representing the lowest common denominator of the two inputs. An example of this process is depicted in Figure 2.12, where there are two input layers containing different, noncoincidental polygons. The resulting overlay layer will consist of each unique polygon shown in Figure 2.12.

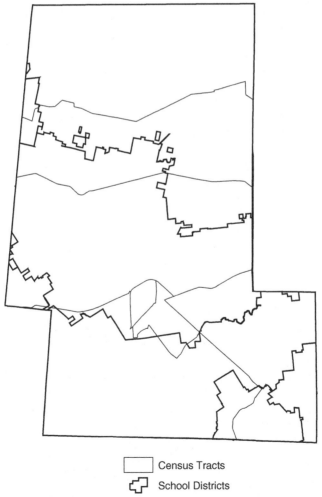

☐ Census Tracts

⊏⊐ School Districts

Figure 2.12 Topological overlay.

2.3.4   Interpolation

The final major data manipulation feature of GIS to be discussed is **interpolation**. The definition of interpolation is *a process of estimating attribute values in areas where information cannot be directly acquired*. One classification of interpolation differentiates point and areal. Another classification makes a distinction between exact and approximate interpolation.

A *point interpolation* method estimates the attribute value at specific locations using observed values at other points. As an example, Figure 2.13 gives two layers of information. One is a raster layer for which we wish to know the air quality across space. The second layer is the point-based air-quality monitoring stations. The challenge is to use the sample information (monitoring station readings) for interpolating what the air quality is for each raster cell.

Areal interpolation is different from point interpolation because it basically estimates polygon attributes values (e.g., total population) for a set of spatial units (e.g., school districts) using as input another set of spatial units (e.g., Census tracts). An example is the school districts layer shown in Figure 2.12, where the total population by district is not known and must be determined. Population is, however, known for the Census units layer shown in Figure 2.12. Thus, *areal interpolation* is the process of estimating the attribute value for each polygon in the school district layer using the known attribute values for the polygons in Census unit layer.

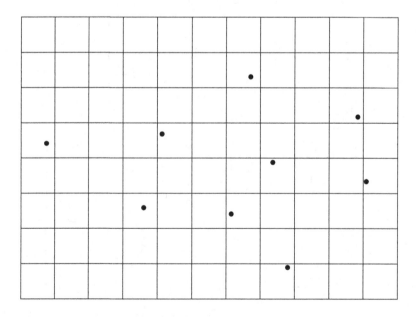

●   Monitoring station

▢   Raster cell

Figure 2.13   Interpolation from known sample points.

A second classification is an exact versus approximate interpolation method. An *exact method* always returns observed values at sample locations (point interpolation) or maintains total polygon attribute values (areal interpolation). *Approximate interpolation* methods, by contrast, may not return or maintain the same observed values. There are many relied upon exact and approximate interpolation approaches, including proximal, inverse distance weighting, kriging, trend surfaces, dasymetric mapping, and pycnophylactic methods.

2.4   DATA ANALYSIS

A perception about GIS is that data analysis capabilities are rather simple and limited, because the visual analysis possible in presenting and mapping spatial information is often very powerful in and of itself. The reality is that GIS actually supports many forms of analysis in addition to visual or cartographic output. In this section, we review the range of data analysis capabilities using GIS, including query, proximity, centrality, and service zone. We leave for the next section an overview of visual analysis.

2.4.1   Query

A prominent DBMS analytical technique applied to attribute data has been query, and is well developed in terms of its use. Specifically, *query* in a DBMS is accomplished using **SQL** (structured query language). In GIS, SQL has evolved to deal with both aspatial and spatial queries. The syntactic structure of SQL is as follows:

SELECT <columns>
FROM <tables>
WHERE <conditions>

Of course, access to and operational syntax depends on the system being used. There are many operators possible in such queries: AND, OR, EQUALS, INTERSECTS, TOUCHES, WITHIN and CONTAIN, to name a few.

Suppose we were interested in identifying those households with particular attributes, perhaps reflecting potential consumers of a new product. In particular, assume that we want to identify all homes with at least three bathrooms and four bedrooms. This would be an aspatial query because only attributes of residential parcels are of interest. The result of this query would be those residential parcels that meet all imposed conditions, and they are shown in Figure 2.14 for these indicated conditions (parcels with three or more bathrooms and four or more bedrooms).

A spatial query, by contrast, accounts for some spatial relationship. Such a query could be to identify all commercial properties near a freeway onramp,

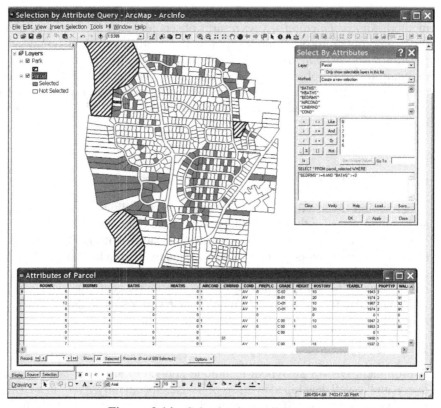

Figure 2.14 Selection by attribute query.

finding all residential properties close to a lake or river, or highlighting in the database all objects in a specified geographic area. An example of a user-defined spatial query is shown in Figure 2.15, indicating those parcels within 700 feet of parks.

2.4.2 Proximity

Given that GIS is specifically designed to manage information corresponding to something on the surface of the earth, it seems intuitive that an analytical capability in GIS would be to determine the proximity between locations. This includes distance but also topological relationships, such as adjacency, contiguity, intersection and connectivity, and object buffers.

Distance is a measure of proximity between two given locations, and can be defined mathematically. In GIS, we can conceive of two fundamental types of distance: global and planar. A global distance measure takes into account the curvature of the earth (three-dimensional), whereas a planar measure is limited to two-dimensional space.

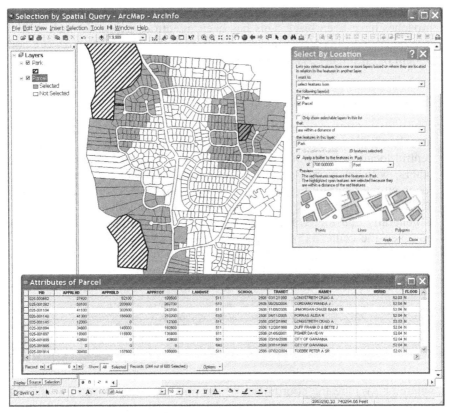

Figure 2.15   Selection by spatial query.

Important topological relationships are adjacency, contiguity, intersection, and connectivity. Two objects are adjacent if they are next to each other. For example, if two polygons share a common boundary, they are said to be adjacent. An area is contiguous if it is possible to travel/move between all parts of the area without leaving the area. Such an area can comprise a number of polygons, so the question in this case is whether the polygons are mutually adjacent to each other. Intersection is whether two objects meet or overlap in some way, and where this occurs. As an example, do two roads (or line segments) intersect? Connectivity is somewhat related to contiguity in the sense that it reflects movement between two locations. Often, connectivity is considered in networks, and whether a path exists from one node to another node. Finally, a buffer is a topological transformation of an input object (point, line, polygon, or raster cell) using a specified width or travel time, and can be regular or irregular in shape. As an example, a regular width buffer for a point is a circle having a radius equal to the width of the buffer. Similar conceptual extensions result when buffering lines, polygons, or raster cells.

Admittedly, the formal definitions of proximity-based data analysis approaches have been brief. This has been intentional, because each of these individual topics is elaborated on in different chapters of the text as a component of GIScience issues in location modeling.

2.4.3   Centrality

Centrality is often associated with statistics and the notion of central tendency in a distribution. Spatial information necessarily gives rise to an interest in central location, not unlike its use in statistics. Although Chapter 6, among others, will get more to the heart of central locations, in this section we focus on the centrality of an object. For a point object, centrality is readily defined. It is simply the point itself. For a line (or polyline), the midpoint is generally considered the center, and is easy to compute. For a polygon, however, the center is not so straightforward. One view of the center of a polygon is its *centroid*, or, rather, the average of all the polygon vertices. This is fairly easy to compute and intuitive in many ways. Mathematically, the centroid is

$$(\bar{x}, \bar{y}) = \left(\frac{\sum_i x_i}{n}, \frac{\sum_i y_i}{n} \right) \tag{2.1}$$

where (x_i, y_i) are the coordinates of the polygon vertices and n is the total number of vertices. Often, a centroid is inside the polygon, but this need not be the case in general. Furthermore, the density of vertices defining the polygon greatly influences the location of the centroid. For these reasons, other views of centrality for a polygon are needed. One alternative is the **skeleton**, or **medial axis**. Formally, the skeleton of a polygon is the locus of the centers of circles that are tangent to the polygon at two or more points, with all such circles being contained in the polygon. For the polygon shown in Figure 2.16a, the associated skeleton is given in Figure 2.16b. It is worth noting that the skeleton has proven useful in location analysis, with important spatial properties.

2.4.4   Service Zone

A *service zone* is an identified, or identifiable, area that has some significance to a location-specific entity. Here we review three types of service zones: proximal area, catchment area, trade area, and viewshed.

A *proximal area* refers to the geographic space served by its closest facility. GIS supports the identification of catchment or trade areas through creation of **Thiessen polygons**, also referred to as a **Voronoi diagram** (as well as Dirichlet and proximal polygons). Formally, Thiessen polygons, given a set

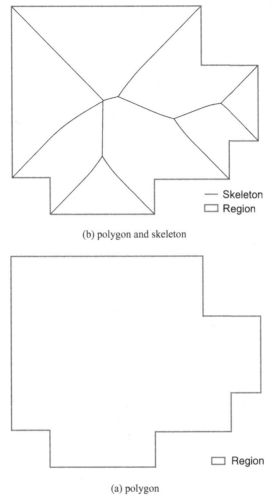

(b) polygon and skeleton

(a) polygon

Figure 2.16   Skeleton of a polygon.

of generator points, are those polygons defined such that any location (x, y) is associated with its closest generator point. Polygon boundaries are defined by the half-plane of neighboring generator points. As an example, Figure 2.17 shows the Thiessen polygons for the indicated set of generator points.

A *catchment area* is the area serviced by a facility (e.g., school), but could also be the area inhabited by some species (e.g., spotted owl, kit fox, goshawk, etc.). In the context of facility service, it could be equivalent to the proximal area, but might differ as well. A common interpretation of a catchment area in physical geography is spatial extent associated with natural boundaries such as a watershed.

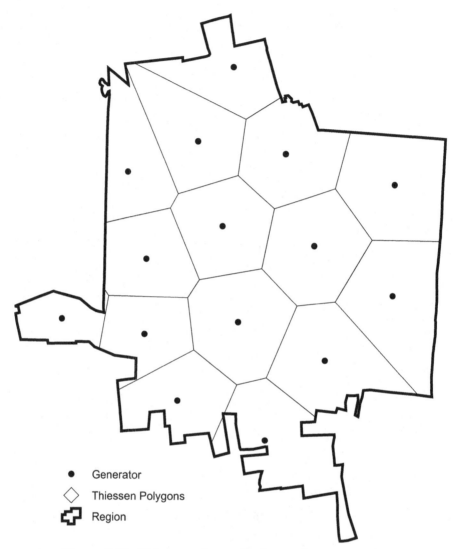

Figure 2.17 Thiessen polygons for the set of generator points.

A related service zone is the *trade area*. Commonly referred to in business and retail geography, a trade area is the geographical area containing customers (or potential customers) served by a business, firm, retailer, or shopping center. There are many methods proposed for identifying and/or delineating trade areas, including radial rings, drive time, Thiessen polygons, and gravity-based models. Further discussion is left for Chapter 4.

Another type of service zone is the *viewshed*. A viewshed is the surface area visible from one or more observation points. As a service zone, the

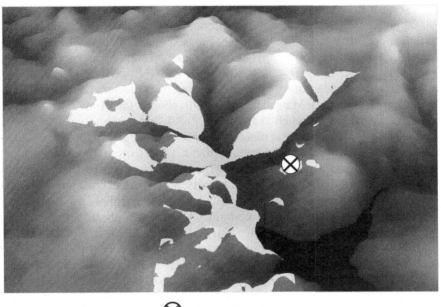

⊗ Observation point

∽ Visible area

DEM

High: 609 ft

Low: 433 ft

Figure 2.18   Viewshed from an observation point.

viewshed could represent the area capable of observation from a lookout tower, or watchtower, or even surveillance equipment. If the lookout tower is used for forest-fire spotting, as an example, then the viewshed is the area capable of being monitored. Figure 2.18 shows the viewshed associated with the indicated observation point.

The service zone is a particularly important GIS analysis capability that supports location analysis and modeling. As we will see throughout the text, many models require potential service zones as input.

2.5 DATA DISPLAY

As mentioned previously in this chapter, data display has been a defining characteristic of GIS. In particular, GIS has come to be synonymous with the visualization and output of spatially referenced information. Part of the reason for this is that visual display of geographical data is very powerful, enabling a user to observe and infer trends, relationships, and so on based on human cognitive capabilities. Another reason is simply that GIS technology and digital spatial information has facilitated map creation and output by even the most novice of users.

Arguably, the biggest data display asset of GIS is the integrated presentation of information layers. Many examples in this chapter have illustrated this layer integration capability, such as Figures 2.3, 2.4, and 2.11b.

Of course, data display is much more than just integration of spatial layers, because effective communication is critical. Thus, cartography is particularly important in data display, which is why it is its own subfield in geography. Cartography in data display relies heavily on artistic expression. Considerations such as visual representation, color choice, symbols used, and so on are important factors in good communication. Such considerations impact the display of points, lines, polygons, and raster cells. It is, in fact, possible to depict point-based information in various ways. For example, Figure 2.19 shows symbols varying in size, corresponding to their relative total population. This can be contrasted to their presentation in Figure 2.11b. It is also possible to show variation relative to attributes of line objects, such as flow,

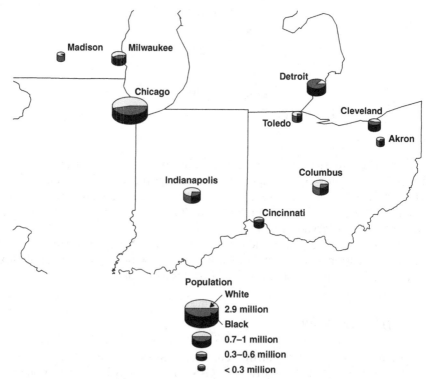

Figure 2.19 Visual display of point attributes.

direction, and congestion. As an example, Figure 2.20 illustrates the amount of flow along transportation segments of an interstate system.

Not surprisingly, polygon objects, or areas, can also communicate associated attribute information in various ways. As with points and lines, visual display can show how an attribute varies in space. Perhaps the most prominent area based display of spatial variation is through the use of a **choropleth map** or output. A choropleth map attempts to classify attribute values of polygons into a specified number of simplifying classes. Often, 4 to 7 classes are recommended for effective comprehension by a user. An example of a choropleth display is given in Figure 2.21. In this case, five classes are shown for total population (2000) in each Census tract. The classes, then, are meant to summarize variation and facilitate understanding. There are, in fact, a number of standard choropleth classification approaches, including natural breaks, quantile, equal area, equal interval, and standard deviation.

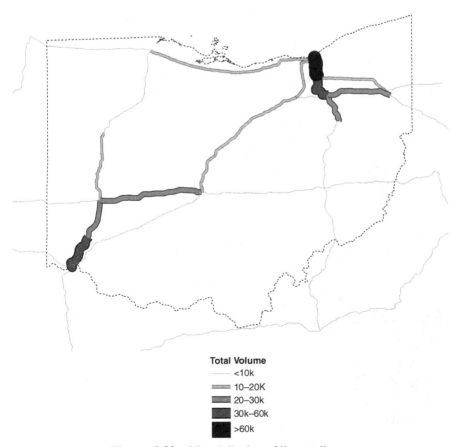

Total Volume
<10k
10–20K
20–30k
30k–60k
>60k

Figure 2.20   Visual display of line attributes.

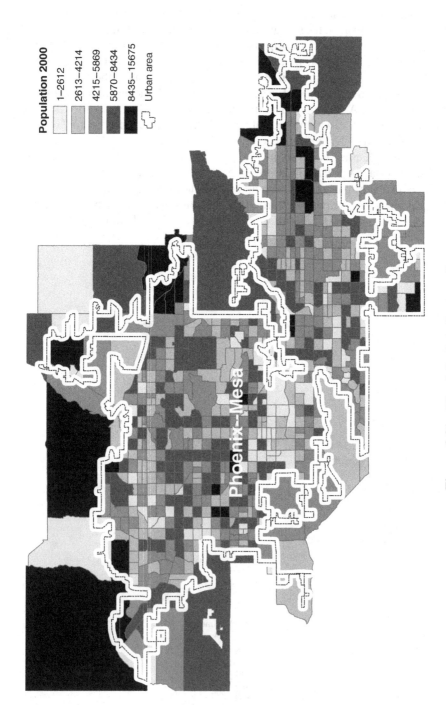

Figure 2.21 Visual display of area attributes.

Population 2000

- 1–2612
- 2613–4214
- 4215–5869
- 5870–8434
- 8435–15675
- Urban area

Phoenix–Mesa

All are based on taking the attribute range and dividing it up in some way, where each class is then defined by so-called break points along the attribute range. The natural breaks approach defines a prespecified number of classes based on minimizing within group variance. The quantile approach creates a predetermined number of classes such that each contains an equal number of observations. The equal area approach defines classes so that each class contains approximately the same total area. The equal interval approach divides the attribute range into so that each class has an equal width. Finally, the standard deviation approach defines classes by standard deviation from the mean attribute value.

Our discussion of data display would not be complete without giving some attention to current trends, and many have potential implications for location analysis and modeling. Perhaps the more general trend is the notion of **GeoVisualization**, where the idea is to expand on how human and physical information is communicated by enabling exploration, synthesis, presentation, and analysis. This can involve effective 3-D representation, the ability to examine space–time relationships, animation of change, and the use of multimedia.

2.6 SUMMARY

In this chapter we have attempted to provide an overview of GIS based on definitional characteristics. In doing this, the intent was to establish a basis for working with spatial information, recognizing geographical abstraction issues, appreciating data reliability and quality considerations, understanding how spatial data is managed and manipulated, and having knowledge about the analytical capabilities of GIS. Thus, while GIS offers much potential to support location analysis and modeling through the use of the data it manages and its ability to display and visualize modeling results, GIS represents so much more. It is only through the understanding of this technology and its theoretical underpinnings that business site selection and location analysis will continue to mature and advance. In fact, much of current research in location science explores the changing theoretical structure of certain models, relaxes operational assumptions, addresses issues of data uncertainty, and uses GIS analytical capabilities to aid in the solution of some location models. Yet, this is only possible through the integration of location science and GIS, and it is only just the beginning. Of course, GIS too has implications for location analysis and modeling. One issue is that GIS gives rise to greater detail in modeled processes because of the availability of a finer level of spatial information. This increases user and decision maker expectations, so models must be less abstract. Such increased detail comes at a cost, however, because there are computational impacts and they are significant. Greater detail and specificity means larger planning optimization problems and the need for more advanced and sophisticated solution techniques.

As an overview chapter on GIS, we have necessarily omitted many important topics. Given space limitations, this is a reality, so issues such as data updating, metadata, and data reliability, among others, are not included, but the interested reader can find excellent coverage of this material in the referenced texts. However, some topics not included in this chapter, or only given cursory treatment, are actually discussed in detail in the GIScience sections of the chapters that follow. Examples include trade areas, the modifiable areal unit problem, overlay, map algebra, coordinate systems and projections, distance, scale, topological relationships (adjacency, contiguity, intersection, connectivity, etc.), buffering, and error and uncertainty.

Finally, one might conclude from this overview that GIS is a black-box product. This is not at all the case. Many commercial systems provide functionality that can be accessed in different ways, and extended, in common programming environments and/or scripting languages. Further, there is an Open Source GIS movement that continues to make common GIS functionality available as source code.

2.7   TERMS

raster
vector
point
line
polygon (or Area)
selective inclusion
sphere
geoid
spheroid
interpolation
overlay
aggregation
coordinate transformation
scan order
relational DBMS
GeoVisualization
Choropleth map
Thiessen polygons (Voronoi diagram)
Skeleton (medial axis)
SQL

2.8 REFERENCES

Church, R. L. 1999. Location modelling and GIS. In *Geographical information systems*, 2nd ed., ed. P. A. Longley, M. F. Goodchild, D. J. Maguire and D. W. Rhind, 293–303, New York: Wiley & Sons.

Church, R. L. 2002. Geographical information systems and location science. *Computers and Operations Research* 29:541–562.

DeMers, M. N. 2005. *Fundamentals of geographic information systems*, 3rd ed. New York: John Wiley & Sons.

Longley, P. A., M. F. Goodchild, D. J. Maguire, and D. W. Rhind. 2005. *Geographic information systems and science*, 2nd ed. New York: John Wiley & Sons.

2.9 EXERCISES

2.1. Describe the levels of the U.S. Census data hierarchy. Identify attributes found in Census information. What is the lowest spatial level of this hierarchy, and how is it defined?

2.2. Differentiate GIS from a database management system.

2.3. What are the major analytic capabilities of GIS, and how can you imagine it supporting location modeling?

2.4. The convex hull is the smallest convex polygon containing all points, where some subset of the points defines the vertices of the convex hull. The minimum enclosing rectangle is the smallest rectangle containing all points. Identify the convex hull and minimum enclosing rectangle for the following points. Show each graphically, and formally specify the polygons they define.

Point	x-coordinate	y-coordinate
1	32	31
2	29	32
3	27	36
4	29	29
5	32	29
6	26	25
7	24	33
8	30	35

CHAPTER 3

MODEL-BUILDING FUNDAMENTALS

3.0 INTRODUCTION

Many corporations and governmental agencies use models, including simulation and optimization, to derive solutions to complex location problems, ranging from site selection to land allocation to supply chain management. Models can aid in decision making for design, operation and management. In this chapter, model-building fundamentals are described. Ideally, building models is a subject that everybody should be interested in. But practically speaking, many are confused by both the mathematical notation that is often used as well as the specific jargon that seems to accompany any subject in science and mathematics. The purpose of this chapter is to demonstrate how we can build models that are useful in location planning. This is attempted while keeping the jargon to a minimum. A general discussion of mathematical notation is first provided. Once basic concepts are introduced, models are built for three problems. The first involves allocating resources to different places. The second problem entails locating a factory. The third problem requires decisions to be made regarding which schools to close in a school district. These examples span different issues, from nonlinear to integer optimization models, from finding a "new" location, to deciding which locations to close in order to reduce costs.

3.1 REVIEW OF MATHEMATICAL NOTATION

Many find mathematical notation difficult at first, but over time realize that it becomes easier to use with practice. Think of it as a language that is used to convey a quantitative view of a model or problem. Learning to converse in mathematical expressions is somewhat like learning a foreign language. You no doubt had to translate "word" problems into mathematical formulas in high school. You may want to forget about problems like these:

"Tommy had 5 times as many apples as Helen, and Stuart had one third as many apples as Helen. If Stuart had exactly 56 apples less than Tommy, then how many apples did each of them have?"

Actually, solving such a problem becomes simpler once it has been translated into quantitative expressions. We begin this review with a description of variables and expressions.

3.1.1 Variables

All models have variables. In statistics, such variables are called independent and dependent variables. In this review, such a distinction can be made as well, but for the time being we will just refer to a *variable* of the model. Worth noting is that in this chapter we refer to decision variables using UPPERCASE letters, whereas known constants are given in lowercase. To the extent possible, this notational convention is followed throughout the book.

We represent variables with a character, for example X or Y. Sometimes subscripts are used, (e.g., X_1, X_2, and X_3). Think of it as a method of saying there are several different variables represented by the same letter, but fully distinguishable by the subscripted number.

Variables may take on a range of values. The basic idea is that the value of each variable will be determined based on relationships specified in equations. For example, consider the following equations:

$$X + Y = 4 \qquad (3.1)$$

$$X = 1 \qquad (3.2)$$

Since $X = 1$ in equation (3.2), then substituting 1 for X in equation (3.1) yields $1 + Y = 4$. Subtracting 1 from each side of this equation gives $Y = 3$. For this example, we say that there is a unique solution, derived directly from the equations. Other equations are not as easily solved, may yield alternate solutions, or could require an iterative solution process.

3.1.2 Mathematical Expressions

A **mathematical expression** is one or more terms combined to represent some relationship. For example, the two mathematical statements, (3.1) and (3.2), are expressions that are written as equalities. Expressions may be equalities

TABLE 3.1   **Mathematical expressions**

Linear	Nonlinear
$3X_1 + 5X_2 + 4$	$7X_1X_2 + 8X_2$
$4Y_1 - 6Y_2$	$2X_1^2 + 9X_2^{-3} + 2.8$
$5X + 7Y$	$\sin Y + 3X$

or inequalities. For example, $X^2 + Y^2 = r^2$ is the equation or mathematical expression defining a circle centered at the origin with radius r. Expressions can represent forms that are linear, nonlinear, or trigonometric, for example. Quantitative models are typically described as a set of one or more mathematical expressions, involving variables. **Linear functions** are comprised of linear terms; that is, a scalar or constant times a variable. **Nonlinear functions** in contrast, contain products of variables, variables raised to a power or exponent, or trigonometric functions of variables. Examples of expressions are given in Table 3.1.

All models involve one or more mathematical expressions, or equations, usually written as equalities or inequalities. For example, let us return to the word problem involving Tommy, Helen, and Stuart and how many apples they have. First, we need to define a variable for each unknown. Define the unknown quantity for each person as follows:

$T =$ number of apples Tommy has
$H =$ number of apples Helen has
$S =$ number of apples Stuart has

Next, the relationships between them must be expressed. Since Tommy has five times more apples than Helen, we have $T = 5H$ as one condition. As Stuart has only one-third the number of apples as Helen, then $S = H/3$ is another condition. And the last relationship is that Stuart has exactly 56 apples less than Tommy, so $S = T - 56$. Thus, we have a set of mathematical expressions that relates the number of apples these individuals have as follows:

$$T = 5H \tag{3.3}$$

$$S = \frac{1}{3}H \tag{3.4}$$

$$S = T - 56 \tag{3.5}$$

These equations are linear because each expression is linear (i.e., made up of scalars multiplied by variables and constant terms). The simplest way to solve this set of equations is by using linear algebra. Doing so yields the solution that $H = 12$, $T = 60$ and $S = 4$. Returning to the original problem, this means that Helen has 12 apples, Tommy has 60 apples, and Stuart has 4 apples.

3.1.3   Inequalities

Some **models** may actually have expressions where the relationships are in the form of inequalities. As an example, consider the following inequalities:

$$X + Y \leq 10 \tag{3.6}$$

$$X \geq 3 \tag{3.7}$$

$$Y \geq 0 \tag{3.8}$$

Is there a unique solution to these simple equations? The answer is no. Notice that $X = 3$ and $Y = 0$ maintain all three conditions and is therefore a feasible solution, as is $X = 4$ and $Y = 5$. In fact, there are many combinations of values for X and Y satisfying the previous equations. Thus, a model may not have just one feasible solution, but many such solutions. For two variables X and Y, we can plot the region of feasibility for inequalities as shown in Figure 3.1. All points in the shaded region of Figure 3.1 satisfy the three conditions. This region is bounded by three lines: $X + Y = 10$, $X = 3$ and $Y = 0$ (the x-axis).

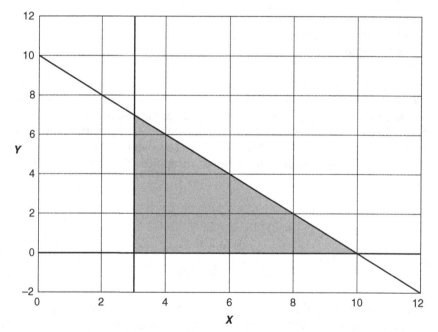

Figure 3.1   Feasibility region for values of X and Y.

Given that a model might have many solutions, it is reasonable to want to distinguish between such solutions. For example, why not select the feasible solution that has the highest profit or the feasible solution that has the lowest cost? This is the goal of an optimization model, to select the best solution from among all feasible solutions. Of course, our criteria for best must be defined as well in order to accomplish this.

It is worth mentioning that it is possible for a model to have no feasible solution. For example, what if a model included two inequalities, $X < 10$ and $X > 12$? In this case, no variable X could simultaneously meet both conditions. Therefore, these two inequalities together dictate that no solution is capable of satisfying all requirements. Models are built to represent problems. If associated constraints have no feasible solution, then the problem itself has no feasible solution, without changing one or more of the restrictions that are used to define the problem. Knowing that a problem has no feasible solution can be very informative when it comes to making a decision.

3.2 FORMULATING AN OPTIMIZATION MODEL

Conceptually, an optimization model is quite simple. There are decisions to be made, and there are constraints on what can feasibly be done. Given this, an optimization model represents a formalization of a process for finding the best solution associated with the decisions to be made. An optimization model, therefore, has three basic components:

1. Decision variables
2. Objective(s) to optimize
3. Constraining conditions

The **objective** and **constraint set** are expressed in terms of one or many mathematical expressions involving the decision variables. The goal is to take any problem of interest and then define and structure it mathematically.

Some contend that formulating a model is often more art than science, particularly when one is interested in actually solving the optimization model to support planning and decision making. In fact, there is much to learn about formulating optimization models. With variables and mathematical expressions in mind, we now move on to how they can be used to specify and formalize optimization models.

3.2.1 Apple Shipment

The first optimization model to be described returns to the plight of Tommy, Helen, and Stuart, but now focuses on a supplier of apples for these three entrepreneurs. Let's suppose that the GoldenD apple orchard is located in Wenatchee, Washington. Tommy, Helen, and Stuart are valued customers of GoldenD, as it grows high-quality apples. Tommy owns a business in Santa Maria, California, specializing in baked apple pies, a major ingredient being apples. Helen owns a juice drink business in Boise, Idaho, and apples are a significant ingredient. Finally, Stuart owns a restaurant in Chicago, Illinois, that offers many dishes requiring apples. The savvy owner of GoldenD wants to make a profit and maintain good customer relations. Further, there is only a limited supply of apples, so the owner must decide how many apples can be supplied to Tommy, Helen, and/or Stuart.

The GoldenD has 12 tons of apples to sell. Tommy requires 3 tons of apples, but could use as much as 12 tons if it is available. Helen needs as many tons of apples as she can acquire from GoldenD. Finally, Stuart must have at least 1 ton of apples to sustain his business, but could make use of as much as 2 tons if possible. Based on past commitments to Tommy, Helen, and Stuart, the owner of GoldenD will supply Helen with two times that given to Tommy, but will ship Stuart only one third that of Tommy. Of importance as well is that GoldenD must absorb the transportation cost to ship apples, so is naturally looking to minimize these costs. GoldenD has estimated shipping costs as follows (in thousands of dollars per ton): 11 (Santa Maria), 4 (Boise), and 20 (Chicago).

Obviously the first step here is to define, or rather redefine, our decision variables for this problem. Thus, we have the following variables:

T = tons of apples supplied to Tommy
H = tons of apples supplied to Helen
S = tons of apples supplied to Stuart

Interpreting these variables in the context of our apple supply problem must now be done. With the associated transportation costs being important here to GoldenD, the mathematical function corresponding to total costs is $11T + 4H + 20S$. Further, as already stipulated, only 12 tons of apples can be allocated. Thus, we cannot supply more than 12 tons, or, more precisely, $T + H + S \leq 12$. We know that Tommy must have at least 3 tons of apples, so $T \geq 3$, but no more than 12 tons, meaning $T \leq 12$. Similarly for Stuart, $S \geq 1$ and $S \leq 2$ are conditions to maintain. Finally, GoldenD has established a relationship between allocations for Tommy and Helen, $2T = H$, and Stuart and Tommy, $S = T/3$. With this formalization of the problem, the following optimization model is of interest, containing decision variables, an objective, and constraints:

$$Minimize \quad 11T + 4H + 20S \tag{3.9}$$

Subject to:

$$T + H + S \leq 12 \tag{3.10}$$

$$T \geq 3 \tag{3.11}$$

$$T \leq 12 \tag{3.12}$$

$$S \geq 1 \tag{3.13}$$

$$S \leq 2 \tag{3.14}$$

$$2T - H = 0 \tag{3.15}$$

$$3S - T = 0 \tag{3.16}$$

$$S, T, H \geq 0 \tag{3.17}$$

It is worth noting that we have included **nonnegativity conditions** in (3.17) for completeness, because it would make no sense to ship a negative amount of apples. With the problem now formally defined, GoldenD would no doubt be most interested in the best solution for this planning problem. While we leave details about how to solve this problem for later in the chapter, suffice it to say that the best solution is $T = 3, H = 6$, and $S = 1$.

3.2.2 Manufacturing Plant Location

The second planning problem is to locate a manufacturing plant, or factory, in an urban area. The factory manufactures a product requiring two different raw materials. As an example, the product could be bicycle frames or steel vats for processing milk, requiring bolts, rivets, and other components from one supplier and sheet metal and tubular steel from another supplier. These are called raw materials, or input demand. The product from the factory is shipped to a single market. This market could be a store or retail outlet, for example. Thus, the problem is to find the best location for this plant, taking into account the costs associated with shipping materials to the plant, as well as the costs for shipping the finished product to the market.

The industrial area where this plant is to be sited is shown in Figure 3.2, indicating the street network, the places where raw materials are acquired and the location of the market. The plant can effectively be located anywhere. The expected transportation routes to the manufacturing plant, given the street network, correspond to rectilinear distance travel. That is, movement along a street is either east–west or north–south in direction.

The challenge is how to structure an optimization model for the problem of identifying the best location for the factory. The locations of the raw materials and the market are fixed. Thus, in the plane the coordinates (x, y)

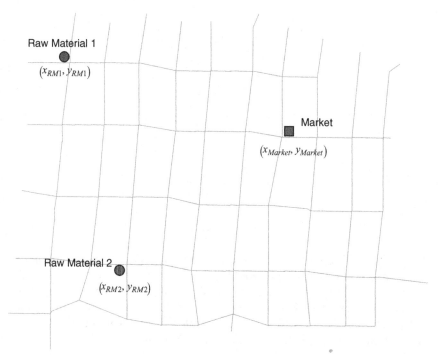

Figure 3.2 Plant manufacturing location.

refer to their location in geographic space. In general terms, this information is denoted:

(x_{Market}, y_{Market}) = coordinates of the market
(x_{RM1}, y_{RM1}) = coordinates of raw material 1 source
(x_{RM2}, y_{RM2}) = coordinates of raw material 2 source

Of course, raw materials must be transported to the sited factory and the manufactured product must be transported to the market. The amount to be transported can also be represented in general terms:

w_{RM1} = quantity of raw material 1 needed to manufacture product
w_{RM2} = quantity of raw material 2 needed to manufacture product
w_{Market} = quantity of product shipped to market

The quantities here are total weight, or tons. What remains is to determine the best location for the factory, taking into account the location of the raw materials and the market, as well as costs to transport to/from the selected factory site. The decision variables, therefore, are

(X_{fac}, Y_{fac}) = coordinates of the factory/manufacturing plant

If we assume that the cost of shipping is directly proportional to the tonnage and the distance shipped, then the cost to ship raw material 1 to the factory is

$$w_{RM1} \left(|X_{fac} - x_{RM1}| + |Y_{fac} - y_{RM1}| \right) \tag{3.17}$$

This expression is often referred to as weighted distance, as it is the product of a weight and a distance of transport. Of course this is a rectilinear distance measure given the orientation of travel depicted in Figure 3.2, and it is a nonlinear function of the decision variables due to the absolute value operator.

This problem involves finding the location for the plant, (X_{fac}, Y_{fac}), that minimizes the sum of weighted distances for acquiring raw materials and transporting product to market. Our optimization model is therefore

$$Minimize \quad \begin{array}{l} w_{RM1} \left(|X_{fac} - x_{RM1}| + |Y_{fac} - y_{RM1}| \right) + \\ w_{RM2} \left(|X_{fac} - x_{RM2}| + |Y_{fac} - y_{RM2}| \right) + \\ w_{Market} \left(|X_{fac} - x_{Market}| + |Y_{fac} - y_{Market}| \right) \end{array} \tag{3.18}$$

There are no explicit constraints for this model, except that the plant location is in our region. Further, in order to solve this model we would need to know the specific values of the input data for this application: (x_{Market}, y_{Market}), (x_{RM1}, y_{RM1}), (x_{RM2}, y_{RM2}), w_{RM1}, w_{RM2}, and w_{Market}. This leaves only (X_{fac}, Y_{fac}) as our unknowns, for which we seek a solution.

Although the mathematical notation for this problem is presented in general terms, it is possible to view this problem more generically. The language of mathematics is powerful, and we can use notational conveniences to our advantage in order to save time and effort in describing a model. To do this, let us number each of the three locations in the problem from 1 to 3, where point 1 is the location of raw material 1, point 2 represents the location of raw material 2, and point 3 represents the location of the market. We will use the index i to represent the set of locations, where $i = 1$, 2, or 3 depending on which location we are referring to. For example, if we refer to $i = 3$, we are talking about the market. The weighted distance from the factory to any one of the three locations can therefore be described as follows:

$$D_i = \left(|X_{fac} - x_i| + |Y_{fac} - y_i| \right) \tag{3.19}$$

where (X_{fac}, Y_{fac}) represents the location of the factory to be sited. Thus, weighted distance from the factory to any one of the three locations can be represented as follows:

$$w_i D_i = w_i \left(|X_{fac} - x_i| + |Y_{fac} - y_i| \right) \tag{3.20}$$

Since we want to minimize the sum of weighted distance to the three points representing raw materials and the market, the objective function in our optimization model becomes

$$Minimize \quad w_1 D_1 + w_2 D_2 + w_3 D_3 \tag{3.21}$$

We can represent this model even more efficiently by utilizing summation notation. This can be done as follows:

$$Minimize \quad \sum_{i=1}^{3} w_i D_i \tag{3.22}$$

Thus, in objective (3.22) the sum of terms operation is denoted by Σ with the following interpretation:

$$\sum_{i=1}^{3} w_i D_i = w_1 D_1 + w_2 D_2 + w_3 D_3 \tag{3.23}$$

This is a very succinct way to define this problem, and it is also very extensible. For example, say we had a third raw material that is needed to manufacture the product. Then, we can call this location 4 using our indexing scheme and rewrite the model as

$$Minimize \quad \sum_{i=1}^{4} w_i D_i \tag{3.24}$$

All that is needed to make this modification is to change the range of the summation to include a fourth value of index i. Thus, the use of subscripts and the summation notation allows us to write a model in a succinct, efficient, and extendable manner.

3.2.3 School Consolidation

Our final optimization model example stems from the need to identify schools in a district for closure. The provision of public education is a big enterprise in the United States, and abroad. States, counties, cities, and special districts provide services ranging from elementary to high school education, as well as college and vocational programs. As such, public education in the United States is one of the largest services provided by government. In California, public education is the largest single element of the state budget. School enrollment tends to fluctuate over time, where there are periods of growth and periods of decline. Additionally, some school systems face a continuing long-term struggle in controlling costs. Thus, if you observe school systems across the United States at any point in time, you might see some districts expanding rapidly to accommodate growth by building new schools and adding portable units to existing schools, while at the same time other districts must close schools in light of declining enrollment or to trim expenses. Suppose that a school district operates a number of schools and the combined capacity of the existing schools exceeds that of the student enrollment by a significant amount. Further, suppose that the attendance areas for the schools are not balanced, in that some schools operate at attendance levels that are at 50 % of school capacity and others operate at attendance levels that are 99 % of capacity, as an example. Such a situation is likely problematic in a number of ways. First, schools operating at 50 % of capacity are not efficient. The annual costs of the school principal, nurse, secretary, and so on still must be borne, even though fewer students attend the school. Second, schools that have low enrollment cannot offer certain classes, like Spanish or French, unless the demand is high enough. Third, the costs of heating and maintenance might be lower as some classrooms might not be used, but a sizable portion of the school needs to be heated or cooled, regardless of the enrollment (e.g., gymnasium, auditorium, band room, library, etc.). Thus, the average cost of operation per student is higher for underutilized schools than schools operating close to capacity. In contrast, if a school is operating at capacity, it might be efficient with respect to expenses, but there is little flexibility to handle new enrollment. What happens if a new family moves into a house across the street from a school that is full? Finally, beyond the issue of flexibility, it is hardly equitable to have some schools in a district required to teach classes of 50 students in size, in the case of schools at or near capacities, when underutilized schools may have classes with 20 or fewer students.

School districts cope with fluctuating enrollments by adding new schools during periods of growth and closing schools during periods of enrollment decline. As an example, Columbus Public Schools in Columbus, Ohio, is addressing changes in enrollment and must close 11 of 86 elementary schools, representing an anticipated savings of $11,000,000.

The problem to be addressed here is therefore deciding which schools to continue operating and which schools to close. Issues to take into account in this case are minimizing disruptions in current school assignment patterns and sending students to the nearest open school if at all possible. Further, recognizing the need for flexibility and equity, we would also like to ensure a fairly balanced utilization of schools that remain open. Achieving such goals is challenging, so the use of models to develop detailed plans is essential.

To structure an optimization model reflecting the identified planning goals, some notation is first needed:

i = index of student tracts, or demand areas $(i = 1, 2, \ldots, n)$
j = index of existing schools $(j = 1, 2, \ldots, m)$
d_{ij} = shortest distance from student tract i to school j
a_i = number of students in tract area i
c_j = enrollment capacity for school j
p = number of schools to remain open

The decisions to be made in this case are whether a school is to remain open or not and which schools students are to attend:

$$X_j = \begin{cases} 1 & \text{if school } j \text{ remains open} \\ 0 & \text{if school } j \text{ is closed} \end{cases}$$

Z_{ij} = the fraction of the total number students in tract i assigned to school j

With these variables, there are three major issues that need to be addressed: (1) keep p schools open and close the rest; (2) assign students to the schools that remain open; and, (3) balance utilization rates among the schools that remain open. The first issue can be structured using the following expression:

$$\sum_{j=1}^{m} X_j = p \qquad (3.25)$$

This constraint specifies that exactly p of the existing schools are to be kept open. The second issue is that all students be assigned to schools that remain open. This can be done as follows for tract i:

$$\sum_{j=1}^{m} Z_{ij} = 1 \qquad (3.26)$$

There would be one constraint for each tract. For a specific tract i, the left-hand side of the equation represents the sum of fractional assignments for tract i. This sum must equal 1, making sure that the entire tract is assigned to a school. Not only must students be assigned to schools, but they can only be assigned to those schools that remain open. Thus, we also need to ensure that students are not assigned to a school that is being closed. This can be done by the following constraint for a given school j:

$$\sum_{i=1}^{n} a_i Z_{ij} \leq c_j X_j \qquad (3.27)$$

There is one of these constraints for each school. For a specific school j, the right-hand side of the inequality is the product of the capacity of school j times the decision as to whether school j is to remain open. If school j is closed, $X_j = 0$ and the product on the right-hand side will be zero, thus constraining the number of students that assign to that school to be no greater than zero! If the school is kept open, then $X_j = 1$ and the right-hand side will equal c_j, allowing students to be assigned up to the capacity of the school. The final issue is that utilization levels among open schools should be balanced. To do this, the following decision variables are needed:

U_j = utilization of school j

B_{jk} = deviation between utilization levels of schools j and k

The utilization rate of school j is the ratio of the assigned students to its capacity, and can be calculated as follows:

$$U_j = \frac{\sum_{i=1}^{n} a_i Z_{ij}}{c_j} \qquad (3.28)$$

Note, the utilization rate of a closed school will be zero, as no students will be assigned to it. Constraint (3.27) ensures that each school will not have an assigned enrollment greater than the capacity of that school. Consequently, the utilization rate will always be less than or equal to 1. If the utilization rates among the schools are to be as equal as possible, the deviation between utilization rates for each pair of open schools must be determined and optimized. The deviation between utilization rates for any pair of open schools j and k can be derived using the following two inequalities:

$$-U_j + U_k - B_{jk} \leq 1 - X_j \qquad (3.29a)$$

$$U_j - U_k - B_{jk} \leq 1 - X_k \qquad (3.29b)$$

These inequalities allow utilization levels between open schools to be accounted for using the variable B_{jk}. To understand how these two constraints work, there are three cases to consider. The first case involves the situation where both schools j and k remain open. Let us assume for the moment that the utilization rate at school j is greater than at school k (i.e., $U_j \geq U_k$). The right-hand values of both constraints will be zero, as both $X_j = 1$ and $X_k = 1$. Since $U_j \geq U_k$, the difference between these two terms on the left-hand side of constraint (3.29a) will be negative, allowing the constraint to be maintained while $B_{jk} = 0$. However the difference $U_j - U_k$ will be positive in the second constraint (3.29b) and this will force $B_{jk} = U_j - U_k$. If we assume the reverse to be true, that is, $U_k \geq U_j$, the two constraints would force $B_{jk} = U_k - U_j$ using similar logic. Thus, if both schools are open, the value of B_{jk} will equal the difference in their utilization rates.

The second case involves opening one school, say j, and closing the other, say k. Observe that the right-hand side of (3.29a) will be zero in value, but the difference in $-U_j + U_k$ will be negative, allowing B_{jk} to be zero in value. The right-hand side of the second constraint (3.29b) will be 1, which allows B_{jk} to remain at zero even when there is a positive difference between $U_j - U_k$.

Finally, what if both schools are closed? Then, their utilization rates are both zero and their difference in rates $U_j - U_k = 0$, and the constraints will be maintained as $B_{jk} = 0$. The basic idea is that these two constraints, working in tandem, will force B_{jk} to be equal to the difference in utilization rates only when schools j and k both remain open, and in other cases will allow B_{jk} to remain at zero in value.

For the school closure problem, we can structure objectives that reflect: (1) minimizing the distances students must travel to their assigned schools; and, (2) minimizing the differences between utilization rates among schools that remain open. These two objectives are structured as follows in our developed optimization model:

$$Minimize \quad \sum_{i=1}^{n} \sum_{j=1}^{m} a_i d_{ij} Z_{ij} \tag{3.30}$$

$$Minimize \quad \sum_{j=1}^{m-1} \sum_{k=j+1}^{m} B_{jk} \tag{3.31}$$

Subject to:

$$\sum_{j=1}^{m} Z_{ij} = 1 \quad \text{for each tract } i = 1, 2, \ldots, n \tag{3.32}$$

$$\sum_{i=1}^{n} a_i Z_{ij} \leq c_j X_j \quad \text{for each school } j = 1, 2, \ldots, m \tag{3.33}$$

$$\sum_{j=1}^{m} X_j = p \tag{3.34}$$

$$c_j U_j = \sum_{i=1}^{n} a_i Z_{ij} \quad \text{for each school } j = 1, 2, 3, \ldots, m \tag{3.35}$$

$$-U_j + U_k - B_{jk} \leq 1 - X_j \quad \text{for each } j \text{ and } k, \text{ where } k > j \tag{3.36a}$$

$$U_j - U_k - B_{jk} \leq 1 - X_k \quad \text{for each } j \text{ and } k, \text{ where } k > j \tag{3.36b}$$

$$B_{jk} \geq 0 \quad \text{for each } j \text{ and } k, \text{ where } k > j \tag{3.37}$$

$$Z_{ij} \geq 0 \quad \text{for each } i = 1, 2, \ldots, n \text{ and } j = 1, 2, \ldots, m$$

$$X_j = \{0, 1\}, \quad U_j \geq 0 \quad \text{for each } j = 1, 2, \ldots, m$$

This is a mixed integer–linear optimization model, as all constraints as well as objectives are linear expressions. It is mixed linear–integer because some variables are restricted to be **integer variables** (zero or one) and others are **continuous variables** (greater than or equal to zero), as specified in constraints (3.37). Church and Murray (1993) originally formulated this school consolidation model in the case where balancing utilization rates is important. Lemberg and Church (2000) show how to modify attendance boundaries over time in order to handle fluctuating enrollments.

3.3 MODEL SOLUTION

In the previous section, three optimization models were structured to address some type of planning issue and/or problem. Nothing was said, however, about how such models are solved. For a given model applied to a particular planning application, one could identify solutions using two basic approaches: *exact* and *heuristic*. In either case, an important feature of any solution approach is maintaining feasibility. That is, one is interested in a solution that satisfies all imposed constraining conditions. An *algorithm* is generally recognized as an approach with a finite sequence of steps to solve a problem, so often a solution approach will be referred to as either an exact or heuristic algorithm. Beyond this, it is most desirable to identify the best solution possible—the optimal solution. An *exact method* or *algorithm* is an approach that guarantees an optimal solution to a problem, assuming the problem is bounded and that a feasible solution exists. An important distinction is that the solution identified by an exact method is provably optimal, and therefore better than any other feasible solution that could be found. Examples of some well-known exact methods include linear programming (simplex algorithm), linear programming with branch and bound, maximum flow algorithm, spanning tree algorithm, transportation simplex, and Dijkstra's shortest path algorithm, to name a few. It is always preferable to have an optimal solution to an optimization problem obtained using an exact method.

General purpose optimization software usually employs a modeling interface based upon a **modeling language**. The modeling language allows a user to specify a problem using a compact and easy-to-read format. In this text we present a number of models in the modeling language called LINGO.

An unfortunate reality is that sometimes it is not possible to use or apply an exact method. For a given model, an exact approach may not exist, or the problem application may be too large or too difficult to be solved by an exact method. In some cases, solution by an exact approach may take too long, or the cost to implement, develop, or purchase software that employs an exact method may be too expensive. Thus, if an exact method either does not exist or is not feasible, a *heuristic* solution approach is needed. A heuristic is a technique, or algorithm, that gives a solution to the model, but cannot prove or verify anything about the quality of the solution. Typically, heuristics are designed to produce feasible solutions and are finite in operation. An identified solution using a heuristic may be optimal, but this cannot generally be proven, or it may simply be of very poor quality. A common characteristic of a heuristic is that it is able to solve a problem quickly, and may be relatively easy to implement. Well-known heuristics for solving optimization problems include greedy, simulated annealing, genetic algorithms, and tabu search, to name a few.

It so happens that our three example problems in the previous section can be solved by an exact method. In particular, the approach used to solve these problems relies on linear programming or linear programming with branch and bound.

3.3.1 Apple Shipment Application

Returning to the apple shipment problem involving Tommy, Helen, and Stuart, recall that the formal optimization model is specified by equations (3.9) through (3.16). This model is interpreted in LINGO syntax in Figure 3.3, where the objective and each of the constraints are written in virtually the same manner as formulated in (3.9) through (3.16). The only exception is that LINGO requires a multiplication sign (*) between a constant and a variable. This is so LINGO can decipher what is intended by the modeler. Note that $\leq$ can be set up in LINGO by stating either $<$ or $<=$, and $\geq$ can be specified by either $>$ or $>=$. Observe also that LINGO needs a sense of the form of optimization (here, it is *Min =*) and the *END* statement, which specifies the end of the model specification. In solving the model interpreted in Figure 3.3, LINGO produces the output given in Figure 3.4. This indicates that the solution is optimal, and is split into three elements: the objective value, values of the variables, and constraint activities. The optimal solution is $T = 3, H = 6$ and $S = 1$, resulting in an objective function value, (3.9), of 77. Thus, the minimum total cost to supply apples to Tommy, Helen, and Stuart in order to satisfy the stipulated conditions is $77.

```
MODEL:

Min = 11*T + 4*H + 20*S;

T + H + S <= 12;
T > 3;
T <= 12;
S > 1;
S <= 2;
2*T - H = 0;
3*S - T = 0;
T >= 0;
H >= 0;
S >= 0;

End
```

Figure 3.3 Apple shipment model in LINGO format.

```
Global optimal solution found.
   Objective value:                    77.00000
   Total solver iterations:                   0


          Variable           Value       Reduced Cost
                 T        3.000000           0.000000
                 H        6.000000           0.000000
                 S        1.000000           0.000000

               Row   Slack or Surplus       Dual Price
                 1        77.00000          -1.000000
                 2         2.000000           0.000000
                 3         0.000000           0.000000
                 4         9.000000           0.000000
                 5         0.000000         -77.00000
                 6         1.000000           0.000000
                 7         0.000000           4.000000
                 8         0.000000          19.00000
                 9         3.000000           0.000000
                10         6.000000           0.000000
                11         1.000000           0.000000
```

Figure 3.4   LINGO solution output.

The LINGO output not only reports the optimal solution value, 77, and the values of each of the decision variables, $T = 3$, $H = 6$, and $S = 1$, but also provides information on solution quality and the effort to solve the model. The LINGO report shown in Figure 3.4 indicates that a "global optimal" was found, meaning that the solver was able find and verify the optimal solution. Also, the "Total solver iterations" is reported as well, but is zero in this case. This simply means that LINGO could easily solve this model, and required zero iterations in its solution process to do so. The LINGO output also includes information on "reduced cost," "slack or surplus" and "dual price." Understanding these terms requires first that you know that the constraints in the model are referred to as *rows*. LINGO numbers constraint rows in the order that they are given, starting with the objective function. For each constraint row, there is a difference between the right-hand side value and the left-hand side value, given variable values, and suggests a slack or surplus relative to the inequality. For example, the first constraint, listed as row 2, was formulated as follows:

$$T + H + S \leq 12 \tag{3.38}$$

Since the values of the decision variables equal $T = 3$, $H = 6$ and $S = 1$, then 10 tons of apples will be shipped from Wenachee to the three customers. Thus, the sum of the activities on the left side of the constraint equals 10, which is less than the allowed maximum amount of 12. This leaves a slack of

2, so the slack activity for this constraint (row 2) is 2 in the solution report (see Figure 3.4). If a constraint is defined as a less than or equal to ($\leq$) constraint, then row activity values given in the report are called *slack*. For a greater than or equal to ($\geq$) constraint (e.g., row 3 corresponding to $T \geq 3$), the row activity is a surplus. Since $T = 3$ in the optimal solution, this constraint is binding as the surplus value is zero in the report. If a surplus value is positive, it means that a constraint is not only met, but exceeds the minimally required value. By observing slack and surplus values, we can understand more about the solution relative to the constraints.

The *reduced cost* and *dual price* tell us even more about the optimal solution. The *dual price* represents the rate of change in the objective value, should an extra unit of resource be made available, or should a requirement be lowered by a unit. Such changes represent modifying values on the right-hand side of the model constraints. For example, the dual price for row 2 is zero. This indicates that, should the limit on apples be raised from 12 to 13 tons, as an example, the optimal objective would not change. This makes sense, of course, as less than 12 tons of apples are being shipped to the customers, so it does not make any difference if more apples are available for shipment. *Reduced cost* refers to specific variables and the optimal solution. The value of the reduced cost represents the rate of change in the value of the objective per-unit increase of a decision variable (for those variables that are at zero in value). For this problem, note that the reduced costs are zero for T, H, and S. This is due to the fact that these decision variables are already part of the solution. Reduced-cost values tell us about possible interplay/interchangeability between variables that are active (i.e., positive in value) and variables that are inactive (i.e., zero value) in an optimal solution.

3.3.2 Manufacturing Plant Location Application

The second model was to site a factory, taking into account input of raw materials and output destined for the market. The optimization model for this problem is summarized in (3.22), or (3.18) or (3.21). Although absolute value functions are nonlinear, this model can also be structured using linear expression, or, more specifically, as a linear programming problem. To do this requires decomposing the distance into two components, the X direction and the Y direction. This means we need to specify distance to the factory as follows:

$$D_i = DX_i + DY_i \tag{3.39}$$

where

$$DX_i = |X_{\text{fac}} - x_i|$$
$$DY_i = |Y_{\text{fac}} - y_i|$$

If distances are sought as being as small as possible, then we can define each component using two lower-bound constraints. In the case of the X direction we have

$$DX_i \geq X_{\text{fac}} - x_i \tag{3.40a}$$

$$DX_i \geq x_i - X_{\text{fac}} \tag{3.40b}$$

This ensures that we get the actual positive difference. The distance in the Y direction is defined in a similar manner. Using both of these constructs together allows us to define the following linear equivalent for (3.22):

$$Minimize \quad \sum_{i=1}^{3} w_i DX_i + w_i DY_i \tag{3.41}$$

Subject to:

$$DX_i \geq X_{\text{fac}} - x_i \quad \text{for each } i = 1, 2, 3 \tag{3.42}$$

$$DX_i \geq x_i - X_{\text{fac}} \quad \text{for each } i = 1, 2, 3 \tag{3.43}$$

$$DY_i \geq Y_{\text{fac}} - y_i \quad \text{for each } i = 1, 2, 3 \tag{3.44}$$

$$DY_i \geq y_i - Y_{\text{fac}} \quad \text{for each } i = 1, 2, 3 \tag{3.45}$$

$$X_{\text{fac}}, Y_{\text{fac}} \geq 0 \tag{3.46}$$

$$DX_i, DY_i \geq 0 \quad \text{for each } i = 1, 2, 3$$

This model represents the one-facility location model using rectilinear distance measure (or Manhattan metric), where all terms are linear. Thus, it is a linear programming problem and can be solved using LINGO.

In order to apply this model to solve a problem, all associated input information is first needed, such as the location of the raw materials, the location of the market, and the shipments quantities. This information is as follows: $(x_{\text{RM1}}, y_{\text{RM1}}) = (10, 42)$, $(x_{\text{RM2}}, y_{\text{RM2}}) = (20, 19)$, $(x_{\text{Market}}, y_{\text{Market}}) = (45, 33)$, $w_{\text{RM1}} = 15$, $w_{\text{RM2}} = 17$, and $w_{\text{Market}} = 18$. The interpretation of this model in LINGO syntax is shown in Figure 3.5.

Using LINGO to solve this problem yields the optimal location of $(X_{\text{fac}}, Y_{\text{fac}}) = (20, 33)$, giving a total weighted distance for shipments of 973 (the solution report is not given here in order to conserve space). LINGO confirms that a global optima is found, requiring six iterations to solve. In comparative terms, the manufacturing plant location model was more difficult to solve than the apple distribution problem, as zero iterations were required in that case.

```
MODEL:

Min = 15*DX1 + 15*DY1 + 17*DX2 + 17*DY2 + 18*DX3 + 18*DY3;

DX1 - Xfac >= -10;
DX1 + Xfac >= 10;
DY1 - Yfac >= -42;
DY1 + Yfac >= 42;
DX2 - Xfac >= -20;
DX2 + Xfac >= 20;
DY2 - Yfac >= -19;
DY2 + Yfac >= 19;
DX3 - Xfac >= -45;
DX3 + Xfac >= 45;
DY3 - Yfac >= -33;
DY3 + Yfac >= 33;

Xfac >= 0; Yfac >= 0;
DX1 >= 0; DY1 >= 0; DX2 >= 0; DY2>= 0; DX3 >= 0; DY3 >= 0;

End
```

Figure 3.5 Manufacturing plant location model in LINGO format.

3.3.3 School Consolidation Application

The final model detailed in this chapter is associated with school consolidation. To illustrate this model, there are 10 Census tracts containing elementary school students and three existing schools. There are 717 total students, yet each school has a capacity of 375 students. Thus, the three schools combined offer too much system capacity, suggesting in this case that one school could be closed in order to decrease overall costs of providing educational services.

Necessary inputs for the model specified in (3.30) through (3.37) include distances from tracts to each school, the number of students in each tract, and school capacities. The distances are given in Table 3.2. The number of

TABLE 3.2 Distances (miles) between student tracts and schools

Tract	School A	School B	School C
1	0.61	0.54	1.34
2	0.86	0.29	1.61
3	1.22	0.17	2.03
4	0.76	1.70	0.16
5	0.50	1.15	0.76
6	0.76	1.79	0.25
7	0.35	1.39	0.57
8	0.33	0.78	1.09
9	0.11	1.17	0.8
10	0.3	0.82	1.19

students in each tract are identified in Table 3.3. Finally, capacities for each school were already noted, so $c_A = c_B = c_C = 375$.

Given the necessary inputs, the model can be specified in LINGO format, and is shown in Figure 3.6. Recall that this model has two objectives, so they are included in the LINGO as one objective by adding the individual objectives as weighted linear functions using a weight w as follows:

$$Minimize \quad w \sum_{i=1}^{n} \sum_{j=1}^{m} a_i d_{ij} Z_{ij} + (1 - w) \sum_{j=1}^{m-1} \sum_{k=j+1}^{m} B_{jk} \qquad (3.47)$$

Examining a range of weights, w, enables one to identify plans where average student assignment distance is traded off with balanced utilization between schools that remain open. In this case, student assignment distance is multiplied by the value of w and school utilization balance is multiplied by the value of $(1 - w)$. Differing from the previous examples is that the necessary input data for this model are included as sets in the LINGO file, with associated data given at the end of the file. These input data correspond to those summarized in Tables 3.2 and 3.3. Given the general LINGO model, it is possible to view the actual detailed specification of the problem by using menu pull downs (LINGO→Generate→Display model), not unlike the problem statements thus far (Figures 3.3 and 3.5). This algebraic statement of the problem with inputs as coefficients is given in Figure 3.7.

Solving this model indicates that schools A and B are to remain open, with the student assignments shown in Figure 3.8. Thus, school C is to be closed. In this case, the average distance a student is from his or her school is 0.45 miles, and school A has 359 assigned students and school B has 358 assigned students. Thus, school utilization is effectively balanced. In terms of model solution, LINGO confirms that a global optima was found, requiring 74 iterations to solve in this case (the actual model report is not given here, but is left to the reader to recreate).

TABLE 3.3 **Students attending school**

Tract	Students (a_i)
1	0.61
2	0.86
3	1.22
4	0.76
5	0.50
6	0.76
7	0.35
8	0.33
9	0.11
10	0.3

```
MODEL:

SETS:
   STUDENTS /1..10/: a;
   SCHOOLS /A,B,C/: X, U, c;
   UTIL (SCHOOLS, SCHOOLS): B;
   ALLOC (STUDENTS, SCHOOLS): d, Z;
ENDSETS

! Objective;
MIN = w * @SUM( ALLOC(I, J): a(I) * d(I, J) * Z(I, J)) +
(1 - w) * @SUM( UTIL(J, K) | K #GT# J: B(J, K));

! Assignment constraints;
@FOR( STUDENTS(I):
 @SUM( SCHOOLS(J): Z(I, J)) = 1);

! School capacity constraints;
@FOR( SCHOOLS(J):
 @SUM( STUDENTS(I): a(I) * Z(I, J)) <=
  c(J) * X (J));

! Number of schools to remain open constraint;
@SUM( SCHOOLS(J): X(J)) = p;

! Defining utilization at open schools constraints;
@FOR( SCHOOLS(J):
 @SUM( STUDENTS(I): a(I) * Z(I, J)) = c(J) * U(J));

! Deriving utilization differences between open schools constraints;
@FOR( UTIL(J, K)| K #GT# J: - U(J) + U(K) - B(J, K) <= 1 - X(J));
@FOR( UTIL(J, K)| K #GT# J: U(J) - U(K) - B(J, K) <= 1 - X(K));

! Variable definitions constraints;
@FOR( UTIL(J, K)| K #GT# J: B(J, K) >= 0);
@FOR( ALLOC(I, J): Z(I, J) >= 0);
@FOR( SCHOOLS(J):
 @BIN( X(J)));

DATA:
   p = 2;
   w = 0.01;
   a = 74, 81, 104, 56, 73, 65, 37, 99, 63, 65;
   c = 375, 375, 375;

   d = 0.61, 0.54, 1.34,
       0.86, 0.29, 1.61,
       1.22, 0.17, 2.03,
       0.76, 1.70, 0.16,
       0.50, 1.15, 0.76,
       0.76, 1.79, 0.25,
       0.35, 1.39, 0.57,
       0.33, 0.78, 1.09,
       0.11, 1.17, 0.8,
       0.3,  0.82, 1.19;
ENDDATA

END
```

Figure 3.6 School consolidation model in LINGO format.

```
[_1] MIN= 0.99 * B_A_B + 0.99 * B_A_C + 0.99 * B_B_C + 0.4514 * Z_1_A +
0.3996 * Z_1_B + 0.9916000000000002 * Z_1_C + 0.6966 * Z_2_A + 0.2349 *
Z_2_B + 1.3041 * Z_2_C + 1.2688 * Z_3_A + 0.1768 * Z_3_B + 2.1112 *
Z_3_C + 0.4256 * Z_4_A + 0.9520000000000001 * Z_4_B +
0.08960000000000001 * Z_4_C + 0.365 * Z_5_A + 0.8394999999999999 * Z_5_B
+ 0.5548000000000001 * Z_5_C + 0.494 * Z_6_A + 1.1635 * Z_6_B + 0.1625 *
Z_6_C + 0.1295 * Z_7_A + 0.5143 * Z_7_B + 0.2109 * Z_7_C +
0.3267000000000001 * Z_8_A + 0.7722 * Z_8_B + 1.0791 * Z_8_C + 0.0693 *
Z_9_A + 0.7371 * Z_9_B + 0.5040000000000001 * Z_9_C + 0.195 * Z_10_A +
0.533 * Z_10_B + 0.7735 * Z_10_C ;
[_2] Z_1_A + Z_1_B + Z_1_C = 1 ;
[_3] Z_2_A + Z_2_B + Z_2_C = 1 ;
[_4] Z_3_A + Z_3_B + Z_3_C = 1 ;
[_5] Z_4_A + Z_4_B + Z_4_C = 1 ;
[_6] Z_5_A + Z_5_B + Z_5_C = 1 ;
[_7] Z_6_A + Z_6_B + Z_6_C = 1 ;
[_8] Z_7_A + Z_7_B + Z_7_C = 1 ;
[_9] Z_8_A + Z_8_B + Z_8_C = 1 ;
[_10] Z_9_A + Z_9_B + Z_9_C = 1 ;
[_11] Z_10_A + Z_10_B + Z_10_C = 1 ;
[_12] 74 * Z_1_A + 81 * Z_2_A + 104 * Z_3_A + 56 * Z_4_A + 73 * Z_5_A +
65 * Z_6_A + 37 * Z_7_A + 99 * Z_8_A + 63 * Z_9_A + 65 * Z_10_A - 375 *
X_A <= 0 ;
[_13] 74 * Z_1_B + 81 * Z_2_B + 104 * Z_3_B + 56 * Z_4_B + 73 * Z_5_B +
65 * Z_6_B + 37 * Z_7_B + 99 * Z_8_B + 63 * Z_9_B + 65 * Z_10_B - 375 *
X_B <= 0 ;
[_14] 74 * Z_1_C + 81 * Z_2_C + 104 * Z_3_C + 56 * Z_4_C + 73 * Z_5_C +
65 * Z_6_C + 37 * Z_7_C + 99 * Z_8_C + 63 * Z_9_C + 65 * Z_10_C - 375 *
X_C <= 0 ;
[_15] X_A + X_B + X_C = 2 ;
[_16] 74 * Z_1_A + 81 * Z_2_A + 104 * Z_3_A + 56 * Z_4_A + 73 * Z_5_A +
65 * Z_6_A + 37 * Z_7_A + 99 * Z_8_A + 63 * Z_9_A + 65 * Z_10_A - 375 *
U_A = 0 ;
[_17] 74 * Z_1_B + 81 * Z_2_B + 104 * Z_3_B + 56 * Z_4_B + 73 * Z_5_B +
65 * Z_6_B + 37 * Z_7_B + 99 * Z_8_B + 63 * Z_9_B + 65 * Z_10_B - 375 *
U_B = 0 ;
[_18] 74 * Z_1_C + 81 * Z_2_C + 104 * Z_3_C + 56 * Z_4_C + 73 * Z_5_C +
65 * Z_6_C + 37 * Z_7_C + 99 * Z_8_C + 63 * Z_9_C + 65 * Z_10_C - 375 *
U_C = 0 ;
[_19] - B_A_B + X_A - U_A + U_B <= 1 ;
[_20] - B_A_C + X_A - U_A + U_C <= 1 ;
[_21] - B_B_C + X_B - U_B + U_C <= 1 ;
[_22] - B_A_B + U_A + X_B - U_B <= 1 ;
[_23] - B_A_C + U_A + X_C - U_C <= 1 ;
[_24] - B_B_C + U_B + X_C - U_C <= 1 ;
[_25] B_A_B >= 0 ;
[_26] B_A_C >= 0 ;
[_27] B_B_C >= 0 ;
[_28] Z_1_A >= 0 ;
[_29] Z_1_B >= 0 ;
[_30] Z_1_C >= 0 ;
[_31] Z_2_A >= 0 ;
[_32] Z_2_B >= 0 ;
[_33] Z_2_C >= 0 ;
[_34] Z_3_A >= 0 ;
[_35] Z_3_B >= 0 ;
[_36] Z_3_C >= 0 ;
[_37] Z_4_A >= 0 ;
[_38] Z_4_B >= 0 ;
[_39] Z_4_C >= 0 ;
[_40] Z_5_A >= 0 ;
[_41] Z_5_B >= 0 ;
[_42] Z_5_C >= 0 ;
[_43] Z_6_A >= 0 ;
[_44] Z_6_B >= 0 ;
[_45] Z_6_C >= 0 ;
[_46] Z_7_A >= 0 ;
[_47] Z_7_B >= 0 ;
[_48] Z_7_C >= 0 ;
[_49] Z_8_A >= 0 ;
[_50] Z_8_B >= 0 ;
[_51] Z_8_C >= 0 ;
[_52] Z_9_A >= 0 ;
[_53] Z_9_B >= 0 ;
[_54] Z_9_C >= 0 ;
[_55] Z_10_A >= 0 ;
[_56] Z_10_B >= 0 ;
[_57] Z_10_C >= 0 ;
@BIN( X_A); @BIN( X_B); @BIN( X_C);
END
```

Figure 3.7 LINGO formulation with inputs interpreted in the model.

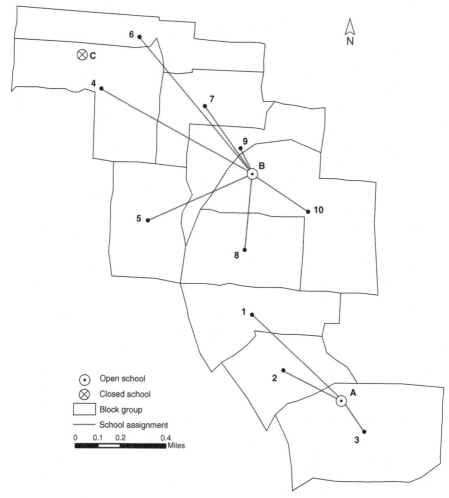

Figure 3.8 Selected schools and associated student assignments.

3.4 SUMMARY

In this chapter we have presented an introduction to model building. We have presented three different optimization models. The models ranged from a nonlinear unconstrained model to a somewhat complex mixed integer–linear optimization model. This chapter has concentrated on what might be termed the first two steps of location modeling. The first step is to define a problem, within the context of a verbal statement covering major conditions, as well as the intended objectives. The second step involves translating the problem statement into a model formulation. Although most of our interest here has been on the development of a model formulation, we have also demonstrated the use of a software package, called LINGO, in solving such models. In general, there are many approaches that can be taken to solve a model. Here, we have concentrated on the use of an off-the-shelf software package that can be used to set up a model using a modeling language. Modeling languages mimic the algebraic format needed in developing a model and are used to convert a model and input data into a form that a software package can apply a solution process.

3.5 TERMS

mathematical expression
linear function
nonlinear function
model
objective
constraint set
nonnegativity conditions
integer variable
continuous variable
exact
heuristic
modeling language

3.6 REFERENCES

Church, R. L., and A. T. Murray. 1993. Modeling school utilization and consolidation. *Journal of Urban Planning and Development ASCE* 119:23–38.
Lemberg, D. S., and R. L. Church. 2000. The school boundary stability problem over time. *Socio-Economic Planning Sciences* 34:159–176.

3.7 EXERCISES

3.1. Graph the following functions for X values between 0 and 100: $Y = X$ and $Y = X^2$. Compare and contrast the relationships you observe.

3.2. Below depicts sites A and B, separated by 10 miles (a straight road with no stops or turns. A vender is looking to locate at or between these two locations and has estimated potential demand for its product to be 100 at site A and 75 at site B. Assuming that X is the distance the vendor should locate from site A, produce a graph plotting total weighted assignment distance versus the value of X (distance from A). From this, suggest where the optimal (or best) location is for the vendor in order to minimize total weighted distance. If a requirement is added that A and B be no further than 7 miles to the vendor, where is the optimal location?

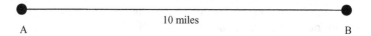

A   10 miles   B

3.3. Mathematically formulate the two problems described in exercise 3.2.

3.4. 3.4. For the school consolidation problem specified in section 3.2.3 and shown in Figure 3.7, what happens when the weight w is altered? How does total weighted student assignment and school utilization balance change when $w = 0.5$ and $w = 0.001$?

CHAPTER 4

TRADE AND SERVICE AREAS

4.0 INTRODUCTION

In business, there is an old question that goes something like, "What are the three most important factors in retail?" The answer is, "Location, location, location!" Although there are many factors that contribute to the success of a retail venture, location is undeniably one of the dominant considerations. Retailers also want to know about their customers—where they come from, how often they shop, what they buy, how much they spend, and so on. The more they know about and understand their customer's preferences, the better they can select and market their goods. This can also help them make good store location decisions. A good location can help to ensure success and a poor location usually dooms a store to failure. In fact, a primary need in retail location is the capability to estimate in advance the functional market area of a potential outlet before committing to a lease, investing in site improvements, or actually building a new facility.

In this chapter, we describe how to estimate the market area or trade area of a business. We also describe how service areas can be determined for the supply and distribution of product from manufacturers/distributors to retail sites. Modeling trade and service areas is an important task in making location decisions and is key to the success of any business. The GIScience section discusses the modifiable areal unit problem (MAUP), highlighting its implications for trade and service area delineation, and location analysis more broadly. As advanced topics in this chapter we review specification issues associated with the spatial interaction model, a variation of the transportation problem, and the use of trade and service area models in supporting site selection decision making.

4.1 PROBLEM DEFINITION AND MOTIVATION

You will recall from Chapter 2 the discussion of a service zone as an identifiable area that has some significance to a location specific entity, with examples being the proximal area, a catchment area, a trade area, and a viewshed. Thus, a service zone has a geographic footprint based on a spatial origin. A **trade** or **market area** and a **service area** are therefore types of service zones. They are related notions by definition. A trade (or market) area is the geographical area containing customers (or potential customers) served by a business, firm, retailer, shopping center, and so on. A characteristic feature of the trade area is that customers generally travel to the business/store. A service area can be defined much the same way as a trade area, but typically differs in that products and goods are delivered to customers. Given this, a trade area may be viewed as **descriptive**, where customers of a business are described in spatial and aspatial ways. Alternatively, a service area is **prescriptive** in that a company must prescribe how products are to be delivered to customers. We rely on this distinction of descriptive and prescriptive context in this chapter in detailing trade and service areas.

4.1.1 Descriptive Trade Area

When people travel to a grocery or department store, they make a choice. If there is only one store that is relatively convenient, then the choice is limited. But if there are several from which to choose, then there is a range of potential choices. An individual's decision to shop at a store, say Grog4Less, represents a small increment in sales to that store. However, the sum of all the choices made by consumers to shop at Grog4Less represents the revenue of the store. Suppose that the owner of Grog4Less has a preferred customer program, called the GrogCard. People with GrogCards get discounts on weekly specials, as well as receive cash back at the end of the year. The store also sends out a mailer to its customers with special coupons every few months.

So, what does Grog4Less get in return? Well, the store gets a wealth of information about its customers. First, it knows who its customers are. Second, it knows where customers live, allowing the manager of Grog4Less to generate a map of the store's trade area. Over time, the manager can see the changes in the customer base. For example, maybe there appears to be a growing number of customers in some areas around the store, or maybe there is a decline in customers to the north where a competitor, MoSuds, has recently opened a store. The size and extent of the market area for Grog4Less depends on the location of the store, the location of its competitors, the spatial distribution of potential customers, and the products and services it sells.

Identifying and delineating the trade or market area for a store, outlet, or business can be important in a number of ways. Urban areas grow, decline, and change in various ways over time. Companies must be sensitive to these changes if they wish to stay in business. Although the example of Grog4Less discusses potential for tracking and monitoring customers, not all customers participate in such programs and not all businesses can afford to undertake and maintain this type of monitoring effort. Further, if a store does not yet exist at a location, then the trade area cannot possibly be known. However, no one would even consider locating a store at a particular site without an estimate of the potential market. A general problem is determining a trade area, and this can be stated as follows:

> Given the spatial distribution of potential customers and competitors, estimate the market or trade area for a store at a specific location.

This problem is called the *trade* or *market area estimation problem*. We might base such an estimate on collected information, such as the frequent shopper program, credit card purchases, detailed survey information, or a model of some sort. In many cases, it may actually be some combination of these approaches. This problem is covered in greater detail in this chapter.

4.1.2 Prescriptive Service Area

Manufacturers also need to get products to the market. For example, Procter & Gamble makes a variety of household products at a number of factories. Much of its product is first transported to regional warehouses; from there, the products are transported to individual stores. When Wal-Mart places an order for detergent, as an example, Procter & Gamble must supply detergent in specific quantities to Wal-Mart's regional warehouses. After Wal-Mart takes delivery of the detergent from P&G, it is shipped directly to a store for sale. To make sure that the system is efficient, it is important for P&G to decide which factories will supply specific distribution centers and warehouses. The area or region served by a given factory or distribution center is the service area of that facility.

This example highlights the fact that a company must make prescriptive decisions about the shipment of products to customers (or warehouses or distribution centers). This must be done efficiently if a business is going to be competitive and make a profit. Given this, the prescriptive service area problem can be defined as follows:

> Given a set of product sources and a set of destinations, identify the most efficient way to allocate supply at sources to satisfy demand at destinations.

This generic problem definition can be made a little more specific by recognizing that sources are typically factories where products are made and destinations are those locations to which the product is to be shipped, such as customers, outlets, and warehouses. If this is to be accomplished efficiently, a modeling approach is obviously needed. **Allocation** of production capacity at a factory to supply specific demand locations essentially delineates a service area for each factory. This makes the task of specifying service areas somewhat analogous to problem of estimating the trade area for a store.

4.2 MATHEMATICAL REPRESENTATION

Depending on the descriptive trade (or market) area or prescriptive service area context, different supporting models are possible. Thus, the focus of this section is on modeling-based approaches for estimating the trade/market area for a business and prescribing a service area for a warehouse or manufacturing facility.

4.2.1 Descriptive Trade Area

There are effectively two approaches for delineating a trade area. One is to use assumed or ad hoc boundaries and the other is to use a model to derive a trade area. Approaches where an assumed or ad hoc boundary is created include the *customer-spotting method* and the *analog approach*. The customer spotting method, as the name implies, generates boundaries based on observed customer locations. Examples of this, both regular and irregular in shape, will be discussed later in the chapter. The analog approach relies on comparative data from existing stores to derive a trade area. Such comparative data include store similarity, competition, expected market share, size/density of potential customers near a store, and so on. Regression models are then used to estimate expected sales, or other performance metrics, for a defined trade area. The second approach for deriving a trade area is to use a model that explicitly accounts for geography. A *spatial interaction model* is generally used for this, though kernel functions and other geostatistical approaches are possible as well. We focus primarily on the spatial interaction approach in the remainder of this subsection because of its geographic specificity, general applicability, and its modest input requirements, something typically encountered in practice.

It turns out that there are many different spatial interaction models, but the underlying feature is that proximity or distance is a fundamental determinant of whether an individual (or area) will be a customer of a particular store. The most basic spatial interaction approach is the **gravity model**, which focuses on areas (or neighborhoods). Consider the following notation:

i = index of areas (j an index as well)
p_i = population of area i
d_{ij} = distance between areas i and j
k = proportionality constant
λ = distance decay factor
I_{ij} = interaction between areas i and j

The gravity model formalizes interaction between two areas as a function of distance and expected propensity to interact:

$$I_{ij} = k \frac{p_i p_j}{d_{ij}^\lambda} \qquad (4.1)$$

Equation (4.1) represents an estimate of the interaction between areas i and j as a proportion of the product of their populations, $p_i p_j$, divided by the distance separating them raised to the power of λ. This is called a gravity model because it attempts to mimic the equation of gravitational attraction, and was formalized in Carey (1858). Equation (4.1) suggests that interaction between two areas decreases as the distance separating them increases, and increases with increases in their populations. This model does not explain why interaction occurs, but estimates the general propensity for such interaction.

Reilly (1929) was the first to propose using the gravity model for dividing up the market area between two competing towns. Assume that there is a village at i situated between two towns, A and B. This arrangement is depicted in Figure 4.1. Of course, the two towns could just as equally be two stores offering the same goods and services. This village is small and does not have any grocery stores, so the people of the village must travel to either town A or B to shop for their groceries. Reilly effectively structured the following relationships:

$$I_{Ai} = k \frac{p_A p_i}{d_{Ai}^2} \qquad (4.2a)$$

$$I_{Bi} = k \frac{p_B p_i}{d_{Bi}^2} \qquad (4.2b)$$

I_{Ai} is the amount of grocery sales at town A from the intermediate village and I_{Bi} is the amount of grocery sales generated at town B from the intermediate village. These two equations estimate the split of grocery purchases by the people in village i between the two towns and are based on the gravity equation. Reilly then suggested that the ratio of the interaction of the

Figure 4.1 Determining the market area of a village between two towns.

village with towns A and B could be used to examine the market. Thus, the ratio is

$$\frac{I_{Ai}}{I_{Bi}} = \frac{k\dfrac{p_A p_i}{d_{Ai}^2}}{k\dfrac{p_B p_i}{d_{Bi}^2}} = \frac{p_A d_{Bi}^2}{p_B d_{Ai}^2} \tag{4.3}$$

Further simplification gives

$$\frac{I_{Ai}}{I_{Bi}} = \frac{p_A}{p_B}\left(\frac{d_{Bi}}{d_{Ai}}\right)^2 \tag{4.4}$$

Equation (4.4) is called **Reilly's law**. Note this equation does not require an estimate of the proportionality constant k and assumes a distance decay effect of $\lambda = 2$. The value of this ratio estimates how sales are split between the two nearby towns, based on their respective sizes and distances of the towns. For example, if town A is twice the size of town B but is equally close, you would expect twice as many people to purchase their groceries at town A.

It is also possible to use equation (4.4) to identify the point at which the trade influence between the two towns is equal. This point would demark the boundary between the trade areas of the two towns, as depicted in Figure 4.2. This point j is defined by setting the ratio in (4.4) equal to 1:

$$\frac{I_{Aj}}{I_{Bj}} = \frac{p_A}{p_B}\left(\frac{d_{Bj}}{d_{Aj}}\right)^2 = 1 \tag{4.5}$$

If $d_{AB} = d_{Aj} + d_{Bj}$ is the distance between the two towns, we can solve equation (4.5) for distance d_{Bj}. Of course, if we know the distance from B

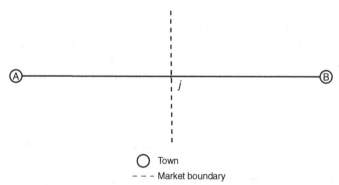

Figure 4.2   Market boundary between towns A and B.

to j along the line, we therefore know its location. Substitution and algebraic manipulation gives the following:

$$d_{Bj} = \frac{d_{AB}}{1 + \sqrt{\frac{p_A}{p_B}}} \tag{4.6}$$

This equation, (4.6), is called the **breakpoint formula**, and defines the indifference location j. That is, location j represents the point where consumers would be indifferent to shopping in either town A or B. It is based on the assumption that $\lambda = 2$. However, empirically derived values of λ often differ from the value of 2. In addition, as should be apparent in the derivation, equation (4.6) does not handle the division of customers between more than two stores or towns.

What are we to do when we have more than two stores (or towns)? Such a situation is shown in Figure 4.3 for three stores. It turns out that we can also derive the trade areas for multiple stores simultaneously using another spatial interaction model, the **Huff model**.

The complicating feature of more than two stores (or towns) is the need to take into account potential interactions between all pairs of stores. Let's assume there are m such stores. Thus, our notation now is as follows:

$i =$ index of areas $(i = 1, 2, 3, \ldots, n)$
$j =$ index of stores $(j = 1, 2, 3, \ldots, m)$
$p_i =$ population in area i
$s_j =$ attractiveness of store j
$\alpha_{ij} =$ probability that a customer in area i will shop at store j

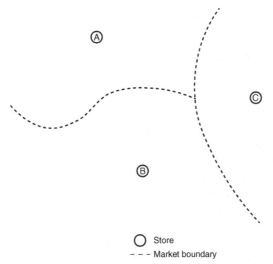

○ Store
– – – Market boundary

Figure 4.3 Market boundaries between competing stores.

Now we are able to account for store characteristics using an attractiveness measure, s_j, for each store j. Thus, a spatial interaction model for two or more stores is as follows:

$$\alpha_{ij} = \frac{\dfrac{p_i s_j}{d_{ij}^{\lambda}}}{\displaystyle\sum_{k=1}^{m} \dfrac{p_i s_k}{d_{ik}^{\lambda}}} \tag{4.7}$$

Equation (4.7) is also a ratio-based approach. The numerator accounts for the gravity-based interaction of area i and store j, and the denominator accounts for the interaction with all of the stores. Thus, equation (4.7) can be thought of as a multistore extension of the ratio given in (4.3). If (4.7) is simplified, we have

$$\alpha_{ij} = \frac{\dfrac{s_j}{d_{ij}^{\lambda}}}{\displaystyle\sum_{k=1}^{m} \dfrac{s_k}{d_{ik}^{\lambda}}} \tag{4.8}$$

Thus, population drops out and we have trade areas being a function of store attractiveness and distance. For any store j and area i combination, the expected probability of interaction of a customer can be determined. It is worth pointing out that the most commonly used measure of store attractiveness is store size (in square feet). The rationale is that the larger the store, the greater the selection and the greater the chance that an item is in stock and ready for purchase. Using store size as the measure of attractiveness in equation (4.8) was originally suggested by Huff (1964).

4.2.2 Prescriptive Service Area

The development of an allocation plan for a warehouse or manufacturing facility to deliver product to its customers has generally been approached using the *transportation problem*. This gives the prescriptive service area for each warehouse and is based on optimizing system efficiency. The transportation problem involves making efficient allocations between points of supply and points of demand.

Suppose a company has a system of several factories distributed across the country, each producing the same item. The factories already exist, and can vary their output somewhat, depending on the demand for product, but they do have an upper limit on the amount of product that can be produced in any interval of time. If the customers are distributors, who buy the product, store it in a warehouse and then deliver the product to retail customers upon need, then the company must ship their product to these warehouses. Based on this description, there is a product source (company's factories) and product demand (distributor's warehouses). In order to develop a prescriptive service area model, consider the following notation:

$i =$ index of demand (e.g., distribution warehouses) where $i = 1, 2, \ldots,$ n

$j =$ index of source/supply facilities (e.g., factories) where $j = 1, 2, \ldots,$ m

$c_{ij} =$ cost per unit to ship from source j to demand i

$e_j =$ cost of materials and production per unit at source j

$a_i =$ numbers of units of product required at demand i

$s_j =$ maximum supply available from source j

$X_{ij} =$ amount to be shipped from source j to demand i

Several conditions must be satisfied in allocating/transporting from source/supply facilities to demand. First, the amount shipped from a given source cannot exceed the capacity at that facility. For source facility j, this constraint can be written as

$$\sum_{i=1}^{n} X_{ij} \leq s_j \tag{4.9}$$

The left-hand side of equation (4.9) is the sum of product that is shipped from source j. The amount committed from this source is required to be less than its capacity, sj. A second condition that needs to be satisfied must be that all demand must be fulfilled. For demand i, this can be structured as

$$\sum_{j=1}^{m} X_{ij} \geq a_i \tag{4.10}$$

The sum represents the total amount that is shipped from all possible sources. This is the total amount committed by the company to demand i, and must equal or exceed a_i.

A final consideration is efficiency. Costs to the company are a function of production and transportation associated with the allocations from a product source to the point of demand. Mathematically, these costs are

$$\sum_{j=1}^{m} \sum_{i=1}^{n} (c_{ij} + e_j) X_{ij} \tag{4.11}$$

One cost is shipment, c_{ij}. In the case of production, another consideration is the production or expansion cost, e_j, for the factories in producing product. Equation (4.11) tracks the cost to produce and ship the product from each source to wherever the product has been allocated. Thus, the company would seek to optimize these costs.

The complete model can then be specified as follows:

$$Minimize \sum_{j=1}^{m} \sum_{i=1}^{n} (c_{ij} + e_j)X_{ij} \tag{4.12}$$

Subject to:

$$\sum_{j=1}^{m} X_{ij} \geq a_i \quad \text{for each } i = 1, 2, \ldots, n \tag{4.14}$$

$$\sum_{i=1}^{n} X_{ij} \leq s_j \quad \text{for each } j = 1, 2, \ldots, m \tag{4.15}$$

$$X_{ij} \geq 0 \quad \text{for each } i = 1, 2, \ldots, n \text{ and } j = 1, 2, \ldots, m \tag{4.16}$$

This model is known as the **transportation problem**, and was formalized in Hitchcock (1941). It is an allocation problem in that it prescribes what demand is served by which product sources. Further, it is a linear programming model and is easily solved by general purpose optimization software packages like LINGO. This model can also be cast as a special case of the generalized network flow problem, which can be solved by specially tailored linear programming algorithms; these specialized algorithms are very fast, and typically more computationally efficient than a general purpose linear programming solver.

4.3 GISCIENCE

An important topic associated with spatial information and the application of quantitative methods is something known as the **modifiable areal unit problem** (MAUP), but is also referred to as the *ecological fallacy* in some contexts. As we saw in Chapter 2, digital spatial information can be defined, created, and manipulated in a variety of ways. The MAUP is a recognition that spatial information for a given region can vary in scale and definition of the underlying reporting units. In terms of scale, it is possible to examine a region at different scales. The U.S. Census geography reflects such a variation in scale. For example, it is possible to look at the population distribution in a region by blocks, block groups, tracts, and so on (see Figure 4.4). In theory, we have the same information, just reported for a different-size spatial unit. Thus, a change in scale represents a spatial aggregation of underlying information.

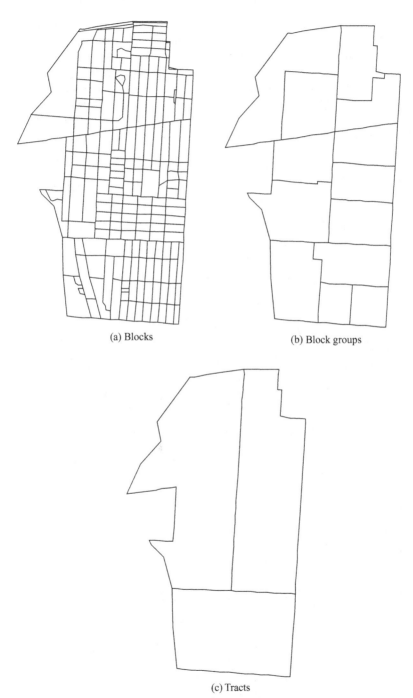

(a) Blocks

(b) Block groups

(c) Tracts

Figure 4.4   Different levels (scale) of the U.S. Census geography for a region.

Differing from the issue of scale is unit definition in the MAUP, sometimes referred to as *zonation*. Unit definition has to do with the fact that for a given region we can represent information using different reporting units, but at the same scale. For example, a region could have the same number of policing, school, and voting districts, yet none of the boundaries of any of the districts coincide. This difference is illustrated for the three layers shown in Figure 4.5, with school district boundaries that differ from the boundaries of Census tracts, and both differ from the city boundary.

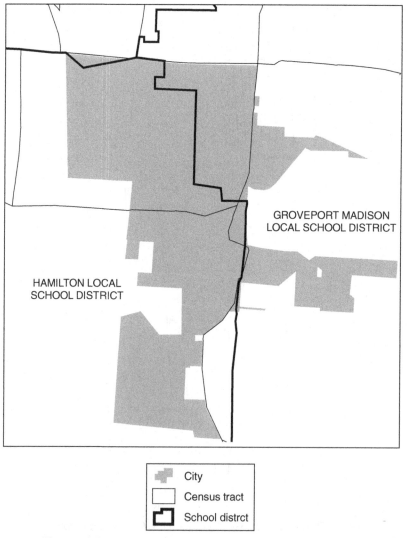

Figure 4.5   Differing unit definitions (zonation) in a region.

The implications of scale and unit definition for spatial analysis are that results might be different simply because of a change in scale or unit definition. Thus, the MAUP reflects the fact that a change or modification to spatial representation could alter findings in the application of a quantitative method. This no doubt is a potential problem because significance could change in a statistical test, a trade area could be altered, the importance of model parameters could change, and so on. As an example, it has been found in some cases that relationships in regression models were strengthened due to aggregation, or a change in scale. The reason for this was that aggregated areas represented by an average of values were more likely than not to be closer to the regression line than the individual area values. Hence, the coefficient of determination, R^2, was higher than it would otherwise be. What this ultimately implies is that one may find a significant relationship between two attributes at one level, but when examining these attributes at a different level the relationship is not observed. The statistical test and variables are the same. The only change is how space is represented. This is problematic, because validity can come into question as analysis can be subject to manipulation.

An important question in the context of this chapter is, what are the implications for retail analysis? Businesses need to be convenient to their customers. Companies, such as McDonald's, know that its patrons are likely to visit one of their restaurants only if it takes them no longer than X minutes to get there. Thus, a company needs to examine trade areas to better understand and plan its activities. Based on customer spotting, it is possible to simply draw rings of different sizes around a store. Most retailers, for example, divide the market area into three zones, as shown in Figure 4.6. The first zone is the area that is closest to the store and represents the area in which approximately 50 percent of the stores' customers live or work. This is called the *core* or *primary zone*. The *secondary zone* is the next ring drawn around the store and represents the source of approximately 25 percent of store customers. The *tertiary zone* represents another 15 to 25 percent of the customers. Customers outside the three zones usually account for less than 15 percent of the trade.

Trade zones can also be derived using travel times. Given average travel times along street segments, it is possible to identify all places that are within 5 minutes, 10 minutes, and so on, of travel of a possible store location. Then using demographic data, one can approximate the customer base within each travel time increment by adding up the customer base within each travel time ring, as depicted in Figure 4.7. Rings are distorted in certain directions, as travel speeds on some streets make areas more accessible to the store location than others. How do these areas change if the underlying spatial units are altered? Unless our information is reported for an individually identifiable customer, not a neighborhood or Census unit, this could influence the trade area obtained.

Beyond trade or service areas, the MAUP has many implications for location analysis more generally. The reason is that any method is potentially subject to MAUP effects. In fact, some location models have been found to be

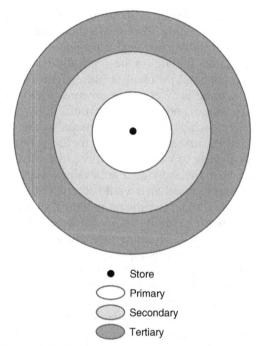

Figure 4.6 Regularly defined trade area segments.

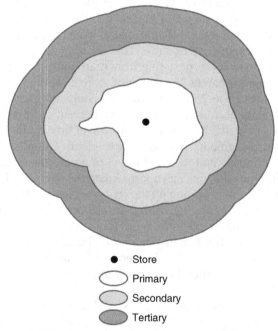

Figure 4.7 Irregular (travel time) trade area segments.

sensitive to an underlying spatial representation, and others have been shown to be relatively insensitive. This has meant that any method and associated analysis must somehow establish the contextual validity for what has been done with respect to scale/aggregation or unit definition (zonation). Some have approached this empirically, while others have sought out methods to address MAUP issues or have developed *frame-independent* methods.

4.4 MODELING APPLICATION

In this section we apply the models detailed in this chapter to determine a trade area and a service area.

4.4.1 Descriptive Trade Area

Our example involves a situation where there are three different stores (A, B, and C) essentially offering the same products. There are two residential areas (1 and 2) between these three stores. The stores and residential areas are shown in Figure 4.8. The question is, what is the expected number of customers from each of the residential areas that will shop at each store?

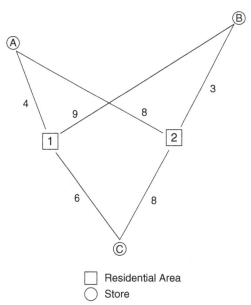

Figure 4.8 Stores and residential areas.

TABLE 4.1   Distance between stores and areas

Area	Store A	Store B	Store C
1	4	9	6
2	8	3	8

TABLE 4.2   Store attractiveness (square feet)

Store A	Store B	Store C
50,000	70,000	40,000

TABLE 4.3   Area population

Area	Population
1	1,000
2	3,000

To address this multiple store context, we need to apply the Huff model given in equation (4.8). Summarized in Table 4.1 are the distances between stores and residential areas. Further, the attractiveness measure is reported for each store in Table 4.2, and is given in terms of store size. Finally, the population of each residential area is given in Table 4.3. For this problem, it is assumed that λ equals 2 in equation (4.8). Therefore, we have all of the information needed to apply this model (the attractiveness measures, s_j, are given in Table 4.2 and the population values, p_i, are given in Table 4.3).

LINGO can be used to determine each α_{ik} value, although it is not an optimization problem per se. This model is structured in LINGO and is shown in Figure 4.9. This model specifies that there are sets of stores and areas, then specifies equation (4.8) using LINGO syntax. Solving this model gives the expected proportion of customers from a residential area likely to go to a specific store, and derived values are reported in Table 4.4. For example, the model finds that about 61 percent of the customers from area 1 will shop at store A. Note that the proportion of customers from each area across all stores sums to one.

4.4.2   Prescriptive Service Area

A company with three factories (A, B, and C) seeks to optimize its distribution of product from factories to warehouses (1, 2, 3, and 4). Thus, a

```
! Spatial interaction model (Huff);
Model:
Sets:
 stores /A,B,C/: s ;
 areas /1..2/: p ;
 links(areas,stores): ALPHA, d;
EndSets
Data:
 d = 4, 9, 6
     8, 3, 8;
 s = 50000, 70000, 40000;
 p = 1000, 3000;
 lambda = 2.0;
EndData

! Specify interaction terms;
@For(areas(i):
 @For(stores(j):
  ALPHA(i,j) = (s(j)/d(i,j)^lambda)/(@Sum(stores(k):
(s(k)/(d(i,k)^lambda))))
));

End
```

Figure 4.9 A spatial interaction model structured in LINGO for determining expected number of customers.

prescriptive service area for each factory must be determined. This problem is illustrated in Figure 4.10 as a transportation problem, with costs shown on each shipment link connecting a source (factory) to a demand (warehouse). These costs are summarized in Table 4.5 as well. Note that expansion costs for each source are the same in this case, so are not necessary to include in the model. Supply and demand information is given in Tables 4.6 and 4.7, respectively.

TABLE 4.4   Expected fraction of customers from each area shopping at each store

Area	Store A	Store B	Store C
1	0.612708	0.1694402	0.2178517
2	0.08506616	0.8468809	0.06805293

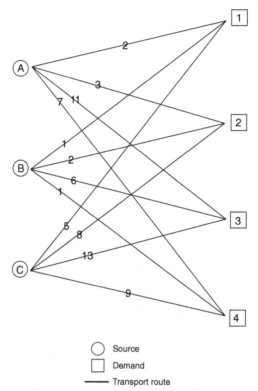

Figure 4.10   Sources providing product to demands.

TABLE 4.5   Costs to ship from factories to warehouses

Warehouse	Factory A	Factory B	Factory C
1	2	1	5
2	3	2	8
3	11	6	13
4	7	1	9

TABLE 4.6   Supply available at each source (factory)

Factory A	Factory B	Factory C
6	10	10

TABLE 4.7   Amount needed at each warehouse

Warehouse	Demand
1	7
2	5
3	3
4	8

The transportation problem, equations (4.12) through (4.15), can be stated algebraically given the cost, demand, and supply information summarized in Tables 4.5 to 4.7. This is as follows:

Minimize $2X_{1A} + X_{1B} + 5X_{1C} + 3X_{2A} + 2X_{2B} + 8X_{2C} + 11X_{3A} + 6X_{3B}$
$+ 13X_{3C} + 7X_{4A} + X_{4B} + 9X_{4C}$

Subject to:

$$X_{1A} + X_{2A} + X_{3A} + X_{4A} \leq 6$$
$$X_{1B} + X_{2B} + X_{3B} + X_{4B} \leq 10$$
$$X_{1C} + X_{2C} + X_{3C} + X_{4C} \leq 10$$
$$X_{1A} + X_{1B} + X_{1C} \geq 7$$
$$X_{2A} + X_{2B} + X_{2C} \geq 5$$
$$X_{3A} + X_{3B} + X_{3C} \geq 3$$
$$X_{4A} + X_{4B} + X_{4C} \geq 8$$
$$X_{ij} \geq 0 \quad \text{for} \quad i = 1, 2, 3, 4 \quad \text{and} \quad j = A, B, C$$

This model has 12 decision variables. There are two major constraints, three specify source capacities, and four indicate demand requirements. This problem can be specified using LINGO, as depicted in Figure 4.11. The form of the model is presented so that it follows the structure of the expressions (4.12) through (4.15). The data for this model are specified at the top of the LINGO file. Note that comparison of the LINGO structured model to the algebraic statement is possible using "LINGO → Generate → Display model" pull-down menus (or Ctrl+G) in LINGO.

The solution for this model is given in Figure 4.12. The total cost is 80, and seven iterations were required to identify the optimal solution. Demand 1 is supplied from source A (with 1 unit) and source C (with 6 units), giving a total amount supplied to demand 1 of 7. This is as stipulated in the model. Note

```
! Transportation problem;
Model:
Sets:
  sources /A,B,C/: s ;
  demands /1..4/: d ;
  links(demands,sources): X, c;
EndSets
Data:
  c =   2,   1,   5,
        3,   2,   8,
       11,   6,  13,
        7,   1,   9;
  s =   6,  10,  10;
  d =   7,   5,   3,   8;
EndData

! Objective;
Min = @Sum(links(i,j): c(i,j)*X(i,j) );

! Constraints on supply;
@For(sources(j): @Sum(demands(i): X(i,j)) <=  s(j) );

! Constraints on demand;
@For(demands(i): @Sum(sources(j): X(i,j)) >=  d(i) );

End
```

Figure 4.11 Transportation problem structured in LINGO.

that the supply allocated at a given source is not overcommitted. For example, source B allocates 10 units (2 units to demand 3 and 8 units to demand 4). This is a minimum cost solution of product allocation, from sources (factories) to demand (warehouses).

4.5 ADVANCED TOPICS

The review of trade and service areas thus far has been structured to illustrate that delineation can be approached from two perspectives, descriptive and prescriptive. In doing this, it has been necessary to limit the discussion of many important details about the models or potential extensions. In this section we return to spatial interaction modeling to discuss issues of parameter fitting and theoretical behavior. Also discussed in this section is a useful variant of the transportation problem. Finally, we discuss how trade areas are used in site selection, as well as issues that arise in doing this.

```
Global optimal solution found.
Objective value:                              80.00000
Total solver iterations:                              7


              Variable            Value       Reduced Cost
                 S( A)         6.000000          0.000000
                 S( B)        10.00000          0.000000
                 S( C)        10.00000          0.000000
                 D( 1)         7.000000          0.000000
                 D( 2)         5.000000          0.000000
                 D( 3)         3.000000          0.000000
                 D( 4)         8.000000          0.000000
              X( 1, A)         1.000000          0.000000
              X( 1, B)         0.000000          3.000000
              X( 1, C)         6.000000          0.000000
              X( 2, A)         5.000000          0.000000
              X( 2, B)         0.000000          3.000000
              X( 2, C)         0.000000          2.000000
              X( 3, A)         0.000000          1.000000
              X( 3, B)         2.000000          0.000000
              X( 3, C)         1.000000          0.000000
              X( 4, A)         0.000000          2.000000
              X( 4, B)         8.000000          0.000000
              X( 4, C)         0.000000          1.000000
              C( 1, A)         2.000000          0.000000
              C( 1, B)         1.000000          0.000000
              C( 1, C)         5.000000          0.000000
              C( 2, A)         3.000000          0.000000
              C( 2, B)         2.000000          0.000000
              C( 2, C)         8.000000          0.000000
              C( 3, A)        11.00000          0.000000
              C( 3, B)         6.000000          0.000000
              C( 3, C)        13.00000          0.000000
              C( 4, A)         7.000000          0.000000
              C( 4, B)         1.000000          0.000000
              C( 4, C)         9.000000          0.000000

                   Row  Slack or Surplus       Dual Price
                     1        80.00000         -1.000000
                     2         0.000000          3.000000
                     3         0.000000          7.000000
                     4         3.000000          0.000000
                     5         0.000000         -5.000000
                     6         0.000000         -6.000000
                     7         0.000000        -13.00000
                     8         0.000000         -8.000000
```

Figure 4.12   LINGO solution report.

4.5.1   Spatial Interaction Considerations

The gravity model specified in equation (4.1) includes two parameters, k and λ. Of course, the other spatial interaction approaches discussed include λ as well, though the work of Reilly, equations (4.4) and (4.6), assumed $\lambda = 2$.

In practice, if we are to apply either the gravity model or the Huff model, (4.8), we must assume or estimate interaction declines with distance, λ. Also, we could even consider a more generalized version of (4.6) where λ is not assumed to equal 2. In the modeling application, we also assumed $\lambda = 2$ in the use of (4.8). However, this may or may not be accurate in practice, because λ represents the distance decay behavior of people relative to the good or service being consumed.

Estimating parameters requires observed customer behavior. That is, we would need to know where a store's customers were coming from, thereby enabling us to derive a best-fit parameter. There are a number of potential approaches for doing this, depending on the information known and the particular analysis context, including regression, maximum likelihood, and so on.

What are the implications for incorrectly specifying the distance decay parameter? To answer this, recall that in equation (4.1) distance decay is represent as $d_{ij}^{-\lambda}$. Given this, as $\lambda \to 0$ (i.e., as λ approaches zero in value) then $d_{ij}^{-\lambda} \to 1$ (i.e., $d_{ij}^{-\lambda}$ approaches the value of one), which means distance is less of an obstacle for interaction between locations i and j. Alternatively, as $\lambda \to \infty$ (i.e., as λ approaches the value of infinity) then $d_{ij}^{-\lambda} \to 0$ (i.e., $d_{ij}^{-\lambda}$ tends toward zero). This means that distance becomes a greater deterrent to interaction between locations i and j. If a value of λ is assumed, then the implications are that we either place too much emphasis on distance decay or not enough.

Another complicating issue is that more parameters are possible with the gravity model. In some contexts, behavior might be influenced by population size. Thus, parameters are needed to better predict interaction, as follows:

$$I_{ij} = k\frac{p_i^\alpha p_j^\beta}{d_{ij}^\lambda} \tag{4.16}$$

This means that use of the gravity model, or any potential derivatives of it, must involve estimation of four parameters. Note that equation (4.1) is equivalent to (4.16) when $\alpha = \beta = 1$, which may or may not be appropriate, depending on the application.

4.5.2 Transportation Problem Considerations

Applying the transportation problem to determine prescriptive service areas is done with the goal of ensuring efficiency in operations. However, it is possible that some demand will be satisfied by more than one source. In fact, this was observed in the model application in the previous section (i.e., demand 1 was supplied by sources A and C). In some cases this might be undesirable or problematic. Customers might view this negatively, or it might be more costly to them to process more incoming shipments.

Therefore, it may be desirable to ensure that each demand is supplied by only one source. To add this type of restriction to the transportation model requires a change in allocation variables:

$$Y_{ij} = \begin{cases} 1 & \text{if demand } i \text{ supplied from source } j \\ 0 & \text{otherwise} \end{cases}$$

With this more restricted form of allocation, we can formulate the following model:

$$Minimize \quad \sum_{j=1}^{m} \sum_{i=1}^{n} a_i(c_{ij} + e_j)Y_{ij} \tag{4.17}$$

Subject to:

$$\sum_{j=1}^{m} Y_{ij} = 1 \quad \forall i \tag{4.18}$$

$$\sum_{i=1}^{n} a_i Y_{ij} \leq s_j \quad \forall j \tag{4.19}$$

$$Y_{ij} \in \{0, 1\} \quad \forall i, j \tag{4.20}$$

This is called the *single-source transportation problem*. What is different in this model is that when $Y_{ij} = 1$, the entire demand at i is supplied by shipments from source j. The objective, (4.17), is to minimize total costs. It is helpful to compare the objective of the transportation problem, (4.12), with objective (4.17). Notice that in (4.12), the decision variable, X_{ij}, will range from zero to a_i, while in (4.17) the decision variable, Y_{ij}, will either be zero or one. Essentially, Y_{ij} represents the portion of demand i that is supplied from source j, rather than the amount. This portion is then multiplied by a_i in the objective (4.17) to reflect the amount that is being shipped. Thus, both objectives calculate total cost as the amount shipped, times the cost per unit to supply and ship. Constraints (4.18) establish that each demand must be supplied from exactly one source. Constraints (4.19) keep the allocation of a given source to be less than or equal to its capacity. Integer restrictions are stipulated in (4.20).

This model is an integer linear programming problem. Solving this model requires software that can handle binary variables, such as linear programming with branch and bound, and is often more difficult to solve than the classical transportation problem.

4.5.3 Using Trade and Service Area Models in Site Selection

Trade and service area models can both play an important role in location analysis. For example, a company that is considering expanding production by locating another factory might well find that building costs are not very different among the many possibilities. What differs between locations is the cost of land, the cost of labor, the costs of raw materials, and the costs of distributing the product. The cost of the land and factory can be considered a sunk cost, but the costs of factory labor, raw materials, and product distribution will vary according to how much is to be manufactured at the new facility.

The amount to be manufactured at the new facility is a function of its placement within the context of other facilities. Optimally allocating capacity and transporting it to demand locationss forms the basis of the transportation problem, (4.12) to (4.15). Thus, given a set of existing factories and one new location, the transportation problem can be used to determine the allocation of the new factory and any reassignments that take place for the existing factories in order to estimate the costs of the new system in meeting demand. Other alternatives to factory placement can also be tested and the best alternative chosen. That is, if the number of alternatives for a new factory location is somewhat small, the transportation problem can be used to analyze the manufacturing and distribution costs of each configuration. Then the choice can be made among the configurations tested. The same can be said for closing a plant when too much capacity exists.

The same type of analysis is possible using an estimated trade area. Suppose a retailer is interested in siting a new store. By collecting information on sites of competitors, it is then possible to derive a trade area for a number of site alternatives and pick the site that yields the biggest potential market.

Even though the models described in this chapter are based on a fixed set of locations, such models can be quite useful in testing the impact of a new store or facility. That said, such an approach should be limited to the addition of only a single facility or perhaps the closing of a single facility. Unfortunately, this type of analysis and location decision making is frequently used in practice to make decisions for siting several new facilities. Doing this, however, violates the third law of location science (LLS3) detailed in Chapter 1 (*Sites of an optimal multisite pattern must be selected simultaneously rather than independently, one at a time*). If a change in more than one facility is desired, then the application of models designed for siting multiple facilities should be relied on, because it enables efficiencies to be achieved that myopic, one-at-a-time approaches cannot consider. Multiple facility models are detailed later in this text.

4.6 SUMMARY

This chapter has reviewed methods for identifying or delineating trade and service areas. Spatial interaction models are particularly important in the geographic specification of a trade area, and are typically based on the gravity model. The problem of delineating trade areas, like many geographic problems, is subject to the modifiable area unit problem (MAUP). With MAUP, changes in either scale or unit definition associated with spatial information have the potential to alter or impact modeling results.

This chapter also discussed the use of trade and service area models in making small incremental changes to a system, either by siting a new facility or closing an existing facility. This approach is not appropriate when multiple facilities are added, closed, or relocated. Finally, two forms of the transportation problem were introduced, in order to determine service area boundaries associated with existing supply facilities.

4.7 TERMS

trade or market area

service area

descriptive versus prescriptive

allocation

gravity model

Reilly's law

breakpoint formula

Huff model

transportation problem

modifiable areal unit problem

4.8 REFERENCES

Berman, B. and J. R. Evans. 2007. *Retail management: A strategic approach*, 10th ed. Upper Saddle River, NJ: Prentice Hall.

Carey, H. C. 1858. *Principles of social science*. Philadelphia: J.B. Lippincott.

Ghosh, A., and S. McLafferty. 1987. *Location strategies for retail and service firms*. Lexington, KY: Lexington Press.

Hitchcock, F. 1941. Distribution of product from several sources to numerous localities. *Journal of Mathematics and Physics* 20:224–230.

Huff, D. L. 1964. Defining and estimating a trade area. *Journal of Marketing* 28:34–38.

Reilly, W. J. 1929. Method for the study of retail trade relationships. *Research Monograph No. 4*. Austin, Texas: University of Texas Press.

4.9 EXERCISES

4.1. Given that $\frac{p_A}{p_B}\left(\frac{d_{Bj}}{d_{Aj}}\right)^2 = 1$ in equation (4.5) and $d_{AB} = d_{Aj} + d_{Bj}$, prove that $d_{Bj} = \frac{d_{AB}}{1+\sqrt{\frac{p_A}{p_B}}}$ in equation (4.6).

4.2. There are two cities connected by a residential corridor 20 miles long. City A has a population of 20,000 and city B has a population of 45,000. Where is the breakpoint or market boundary between the two cities? For the residents who are at the 10-mile mark (equally far from each of the cities), what portion of their shopping is expected to be directed to city A? to city B?

4.3. The transportation problem has been solved to determine an allocation plan to supply all demand locations from a set of sources. If costs increase by $5 per unit, regardless of the source, to a specific demand, will this have an impact on the allocations of the optimal allocation? Prove your result.

4.4. If the effect of distance decay is modified in the three-store, two-neighborhood area example discussed in section 4.4 (and detailed in LINGO in Figure 4.9), will this change the expected fraction of customers shopping at each store? Use LINGO to examine $\lambda = 0.5, 1, 1.5$, and 5.

4.5. It turns out the allocation derived using the transportation problem in section 4.4 should have actually taken into account expansion costs, e_j. These costs are 1.5, 0.5, and 2.2 for sources A, B, and C, respectively. Use LINGO to determine a new allocation plan. Does this change the solution in any way?

CHAPTER 5

SUITABILITY ANALYSIS

5.0 INTRODUCTION

Thus far in the text we have established the basic theory and background needed for the study of site selection and location analysis (Chapters 1–3), and in Chapter 4 (trade and service areas) we effectively began the process of evaluating specific configurations of facilities. In particular, we concluded the previous chapter by noting that site selection all too often relies on a trial-and-error process for identifying a location and then examining its derived trade/market/catchment area. Such trial-and-error searches are often confined to a small number of potential sites, which may not yield the best solution. For example, have desired system performance efficiencies and service capabilities been realized to their greatest potential? Additionally, have any good potential locations been missed that should/could have been considered? This chapter focuses on suitability analysis, which is the process of systematically identifying feasible potential site/facility locations, either in relative or absolute terms. With a set of feasible sites, it is then possible to explore issues of performance and service provision, topics covered in later chapters. The GIScience section reviews map algebra and data measurement types. An advanced topic in this chapter is the use of an approach for deriving consistent attribute weights for composite suitability.

5.1 PROBLEM DEFINITION AND MOTIVATION

As we will encounter throughout the remainder of this text, it is conceivable that we could be interested in siting a business, retail outlet(s), restaurant(s), fire station(s), power transmission corridor(s), park(s), landfill(s), nature reserve(s), and a host of other "facilities." Thus, a *facility* refers to any such possible endeavor that we wish to site, and could be representative of point, line, or polygon-based objects. In order to site the facility, however, a process of defining potential locations is typically required, as many types of facilities simply cannot be located just anywhere. There are many reasons why suitability analysis is important, as some locations are better than others for a given purpose (first law of location science, discussed in Chapter 1). For example, land may not be available in a region, available land may be unsuitable, suitable land may be available but the intended use is incompatible with neighboring land uses, and so on. Of course, what is ultimately considered suitable depends on the type of facility being located.

There are many different examples that illustrate the need for identifying suitable land in the context of siting a facility. One example is that state and federal natural resource departments are interested in those areas where habitat is threatened, with the intent of establishing a reserve of some sort. Where do the endangered species exist and what conditions will ensure their survival? Another example is a real estate investor wanting to identify areas for commercial development. What land is available for this activity, and are needed supporting services in place? A final example involves the location of a solid-waste landfill. Landfills must be sited away from residential areas, require open space and access to a road system, and cannot be placed above an aquifer, among other criteria. Suitability analysis is a process for identifying feasible, or superior, area(s) for some designated activity, such as a landfill or a commercial site.

A formal definition of **suitability analysis** is as follows:

Suitability analysis is a process of systematically identifying or rating potential locations with respect to a particular use.

In the context of this text, the use we refer to is associated with a good or service stemming from a facility to be located. The terms *identifying* and *rating* indicate that suitably could be measured in absolute or relative terms. These are, in fact, important distinctions within suitability analysis. **Relative suitability** suggests that possible locations vary in some relative sense, with some sites being more desirable for an intended use than others. Differing somewhat is **absolute suitability**, where a location is either classified as suitable or not suitable.

Thus, a parcel of land is suitable if it is considered appropriate for a given purpose. A place that is suitable for a factory site may be unsuitable for the location of a hospital, as an example. Thus, suitable hospital locations may be quite different from suitable industrial sites. This means that suitability cannot be assessed or measured without a defined purpose.

A final note about suitability analysis is that many often refer to suitability mapping, and this is mostly consistent with the notion of suitability analysis defined and discussed here. A distinction is the emphasis on a "map," or, more specifically, a suitability map. A *map* necessarily refers to a hardcopy output or digital display of derived suitability. The use of the term *map* or *mapping* is avoided in this chapter because of the intended use of suitability analysis to derive a digital, spatial information layer(s) for use in location analysis.

5.2   SUITABILITY ASSESSMENT PROCESS

McHarg (1969) helped to popularize the use of suitability mapping by describing a process to map land-use suitability.[1] The produced map was then used to assist in planning the most suitable route, or selecting the most suitable location, for a highway. At about the same time, the National Environmental Policy Act (P.L. 91–190) was passed, requiring the identification of alternatives, as well the review of those alternatives with respect to environmental impacts. McHarg's approach gained instant notoriety as an aid in planning with respect to minimizing environmental impact.

For the highway alignment problem that McHarg addressed, there were a number of major factors to be addressed: construction costs, project benefits, and project impacts. For each factor, one or more land elements (or attributes) were identified that could be used to account for variability. For example, construction costs were a function of difficult topography, soils type (and poor geologic foundation), poor drainage, absence of construction materials, and the number of structures required (e.g., bridges, drainage culverts, etc.). Project impacts accounted for community values lost, residential values lost, scenic values lost, historic values lost, recreational values lost, surface water resources impaired, wildlife resources impaired, and forest resources impaired. Finally, project benefits included reduced travel times, increased land value, increased convenience, increased safety, and maintaining environmental resources. A map was made for each factor–attribute combination, classifying areas into one of three zones: high impact (zone 1), medium impact (zone 2), and low impact (zone 3). For example, zone 1 for slope represented those areas with slopes in excess of 10 percent; zone 2 represented areas where slope was less than 10 percent and greater than 2 percent; and zone 3 represented areas where the slope was less than 2 percent. Each zone was assigned a specific color, where a dark hue was used to depict zone 1 (high impact/cost), a medium hue was used for zone 2, and no color for zone 3 (low impact, high benefit). Thus, in each produced map, the lighter the hue of the area, the lower the impact (or higher the benefit). Each map was drawn on a clear acetate sheet using the selected color for that theme. By overlaying all of the maps together and placing them on a light table, it was possible to obtain a composite view of all attributes simultaneously. Areas with a dark hue composite represent greater impact across attribute layers, while those appearing light have a lower impact (or high benefit). With this composite

---

[1] Although many credit Ian McHarg with the development of overlay mapping for suitability analysis, overlay techniques have been used since the early 1900s in planning.

map, highway alignments that tended to cross through lighter areas could be observed/identified.

McHarg's objective was to produce a composite map of suitability. He did this at a time when computer graphics and monitors did not exist. Today we can produce composite suitability layers and maps using GIS.

The basic *suitability assessment process* can be summarized as follows:

Step 1: Identify attribute layers that are important in determining the suitability of an activity, and collect (or acquire) this data for the planning region.

Step 2: Develop a methodology to assess suitability using the attribute layers.

Step 3: Apply the assessment methodology to generate a composite suitability score for each spatial unit.

This is essentially the process employed by McHarg (1969), except that it included a fourth step to produce a composite map. This overall process, and its use in McHarg (1969), appears to be deceptively simple, but it is patently not. Many, including McHarg, tend to misunderstand the importance of the details of step 2 and end up generating a suitability layer that is invalid. For this reason, much of the remaining discussion on suitability analysis will focus on the details of step 2.

In order to develop a suitability layer, we first need to list those attributes that are needed to appropriately "score" or derive suitability. A list of important attributes is usually identified by subject matter experts. For example, in a classic paper on identifying feasible sites for power-plant location, Dobson (1979) used a panel of experts to list those attributes that were considered important for locating a 1,000 megawatt fossil-fueled power plant and cooling tower. To develop the list of siting attributes/variables and importance weights, Dobson used a process called the nominal group technique, which is a process of conducting a meeting, identifying attributes, and voting to accept or reject them. The list of attributes developed by this expert panel is given in Table 5.1. Dobson chose to have the expert panel list important variables as well as suggest importance weights for three primary siting objectives. For example, proximity to stream flow is considered important in minimizing construction and minimizing adverse ecological impacts. The importance weights were developed on a scale of 0 to 10, with 10 being extremely important, and zero being of no importance.

Once the different data categories are determined and the data are collected for the region under study, then we can proceed to step 2 of the methodology for assessing/measuring suitability, which is the most important step, and is often the least understood.

Suitability analysis often involves the use of information in raster format, which is a field view of geographic space. Although suitability analysis can be, and is, applied using both raster- and vector-based information, we assume

TABLE 5.1   Factors and importance weights associated with power plant siting (after Dobson 1979)

| Variable | Siting Objective | | | |
	Minimize Construction and Operating Costs	Minimize Adverse Ecological Impact	Minimize Adverse Socioecologic Impact	Composite of all Objectives
Proximity to streamflow	10	2	0	10
Endangered species	0	10	0	10
Historic sites	0	0	8	8
Proximity to transmission lines	4	4	0	8
Proximity to fish spawning and nursing areas	0	8	0	8
Land use land cover	0	0	6	0
Land surface slope	4	2	0	6
Seismicity	6	0	0	6
Proximity to railroads	4	2	0	6
Surface water quality	0	4	0	4
State and federal lands	0	4	4	4
Planned land use land cover	0	0	4	4
Proximity to highways	2	2	0	4
Proximity to airports and airport property	0	0	4	4
Proximity to endangered species	0	4	0	4
Soil group	2	0	0	4
Excavation requirements	3	0	0	3
Overburden thickness	3	0	0	3
Mineral resources	0	0	2	2
Highways and proposed highways	0	0	2	2
Aquifer recharge zones	0	2	0	2
Thirty-mile site population factor	0	0	3	1
File-mile factor	0	0	4	1
Population density	0	0	3	1
Proximity to residential land use	0	0	4	1

for the moment that we are dealing with a raster data structure. As mentioned, the methodology for assessment of suitability is critical, and differs depending on relative or absolute context. Assessment involves rating, scoring, grading, and filtering attributes with respect to the proposed/intended land use. An example of absolute suitability, where an area is either suitable or it is not, is depicted in Figure 5.1. The composite suitability layer in this case, given in

0	0	0	0	0	0
1	1	1	1	1	0
1	0	1	1	1	1
1	1	0	0	0	0
1	1	0	0	0	0
1	1	0	0	0	0

(a) Suitability layer

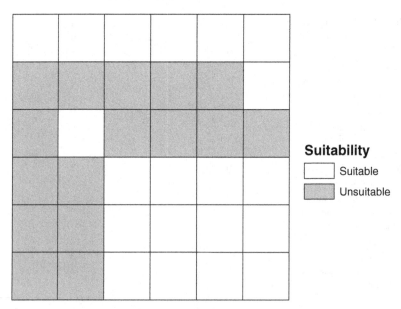

(b) Choropleth map

Figure 5.1 Absolute suitability example.

Figure 5.1a, reports cells values as either 0 or 1, with 0 being unsuitable and 1 being suitable for the proposed land use. Figure 5.1b shows this layer as a *choropleth map*.

The raster data is absolute from the perspective that a cell is either suitable or it is not. An example of relative suitability assessment is illustrated in Figure 5.2. The composite suitability layer is shown in Figure 5.2a, whereas a map produced using this layer is given in Figure 5.2b. The associated raster information is relative in the sense that each cell reports a value in some defined range. In this case, the range is from 1 to 10, with a value of 1 being most suitable and 10 least suitable. The associated choropleth map in Figure 5.2b displays the relative variation cartographically.

The remainder of this section provides details for suitability assessment in the two different contexts, absolute and relative.

5.2.1 Absolute Suitability

Suppose we are interested in siting a facility only in an area consisting of primarily open land (not developed), containing no wetlands, and close to a highway. This "shopping list" of conditions can be used to screen out those areas that do not match the desired characteristics. For example, we can integrate three associated information layers (e.g., land-use classification, wetlands, highways) for the region of interest, and then eliminate (filter out) all areas that are not classified as open land or that contain wetlands. We can also create a buffer along each of the highway segments, defining those areas that are within a certain distance of a highway. Finally, we can find the intersection of the highway buffers and open areas with no wetlands to identify those areas that meet all of our criteria, representing a composite layer. This is essentially data screening to identify the areas that are suitable (and those that are unsuitable). We may even further consider land cost, and then choose the least-cost feasible parcel for our facility location. What we have created is an absolute suitability layer. Screening allows us to filter out the "bad" and keep the "good."

Absolute suitability can be more formally stated using the following notation:

$$l = \text{index of attribute layers, where } l = 1, 2, \ldots, L$$
$$i = \text{index of areas, where } i = 1, 2, \ldots, n$$
$$r_{li} = \text{attribute value in layer } l \text{ of area } i$$
$$[d_l^{\min}, d_l^{\max}] = \text{range of acceptable values for attribute layer } l$$
$$S_i = \text{suitability value of area } i$$

The range of acceptable values for an attribute layer, $[d_l^{\min}, d_l^{\max}]$, can be established in a number of different ways. These may be the stipulated conditions of a business, known acceptable values from observation, or identified by a panel of experts, for example. For each area i, we can compare the raw data

4	4	3	2	1	2
5	5	6	6	5	3
5	4	5	7	6	5
6	5	3	4	3	3
8	7	4	4	2	1
10	7	4	2	1	3

(a) Suitability layer

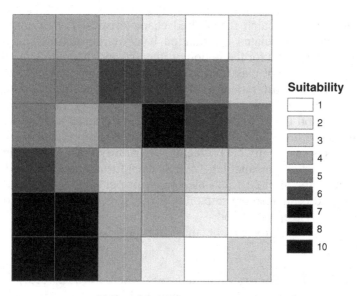

(b) Choropleth map

Figure 5.2 Relative suitability example.

attribute values, r_{li}, to the associated range $[d_l^{\min}, d_l^{\max}]$. Let F_{li} be a function that indicates whether $r_{li} \in [d_l^{\min}, d_l^{\max}]$. Thus, $F_{li} = 1$ if $r_{li} \in [d_l^{\min}, d_l^{\max}]$, and $F_{li} = 0$ if not.

If an area i maintains the range conditions for all layers, then it is suitable for the intended land use. Thus, absolute suitability can be defined mathematically using the indicator variable F_{li} as follows:

$$S_i = \prod_l F_{li} \tag{5.1}$$

This is interpreted as overall suitability of an area being a function of individual layer suitability, where the function in this case is the product (e.g., $S_i = \prod_l F_{li} = F_{1i} F_{2i} \ldots F_{Li}$). Thus, S_i will equal 1 in (5.1) only when it meets the desired range values for all attribute layers l. That is, it is suitable across all attributes being considered. If it is unsuitable for any layer, then S_i will equal 0, as any $F_{li} = 0$ will cause $S_i = 0$ in (5.1). The resulting suitability layer from this evaluation process is precisely what is shown in Figure 5.1a, as an example.

5.2.2 Relative Suitability

Absolute accessibility involves determining whether an area is suitable or not, whereas relative suitability involves calculating the degree of suitability for an intended purpose. Thus, areas are not merely binary, suitable or unsuitable, but rather have a graded variation of suitability. This means that we need a functional evaluation of attribute layers that takes into account land use in a relative way. To achieve this, assuming the attribute data are ratio scaled (see section 5.3 for more on this issue), we can introduce the following:

$$U_{li} = \text{utility value of area } i \text{ in attribute layer } l$$

This utility value is based on an evaluation of the underlying attribute layer data, r_{li}. The evaluation process then returns a value in a desired range. For example, it might be preferable to have utility values ranging from 0 to 100, where 0 is the most desirable (suitable) and 100 is the least desirable (unsuitable). Figure 5.3 illustrates this evaluation process for land acquisition costs. For example, a cost of \$50,000 in Figure 5.3 indicates that the associated utility value would be approximately 80.

Once utility values are derived for areas across attribute layers, the task of determining relative suitability must be undertaken. The most common technique used for suitability scoring is the **weighted linear combination**

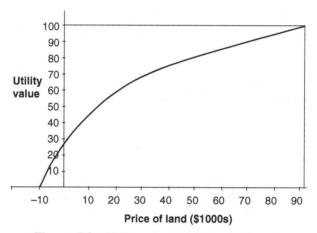

Figure 5.3   Utility value relative to land costs.

method. Given the previous notation, this is specified as follows:

$$S_i = \sum_l w_l U_{li} \tag{5.2}$$

where w_l is the importance weight for attribute layer l. Equation (5.2) represents a simple weighted combination of the utility values derived for each attribute. Often, **weights** are **normalized** for use in (5.2). That is, the weights sum to 1, or more formally $\sum_l w_l = 1$. If they are not normalized, it is fairly straightforward to do this.[2] Once the utility values are combined, the result is a suitability score, giving us a composite suitability layer.

The basic process to derive S_i is shown in Figure 5.4 for three attribute layers (A, B, and C). These layers are evaluated with respect to utility, from which a weighted utility layer is determined. Each layer is then combined to produce the composite suitability layer. Note that in Figure 5.4 the weights are $w_A = 0.2$, $w_B = 0.5$ and $w_C = 0.3$, so they are normalized and do sum to 1.

It is worth at least mentioning that many types of utility function specifications are possible, as are other suitability combination methods.

5.3 GISCIENCE

In this section we discuss two important topics, both of major significance to suitability analysis. One is map algebra, also referred to as cartographic

---

[2] Normalized weights can be obtained by introducing $\bar{w}_l$ in (5.2), where $\bar{w}_l = w_l / \sum_{l'} w_{l'}$.

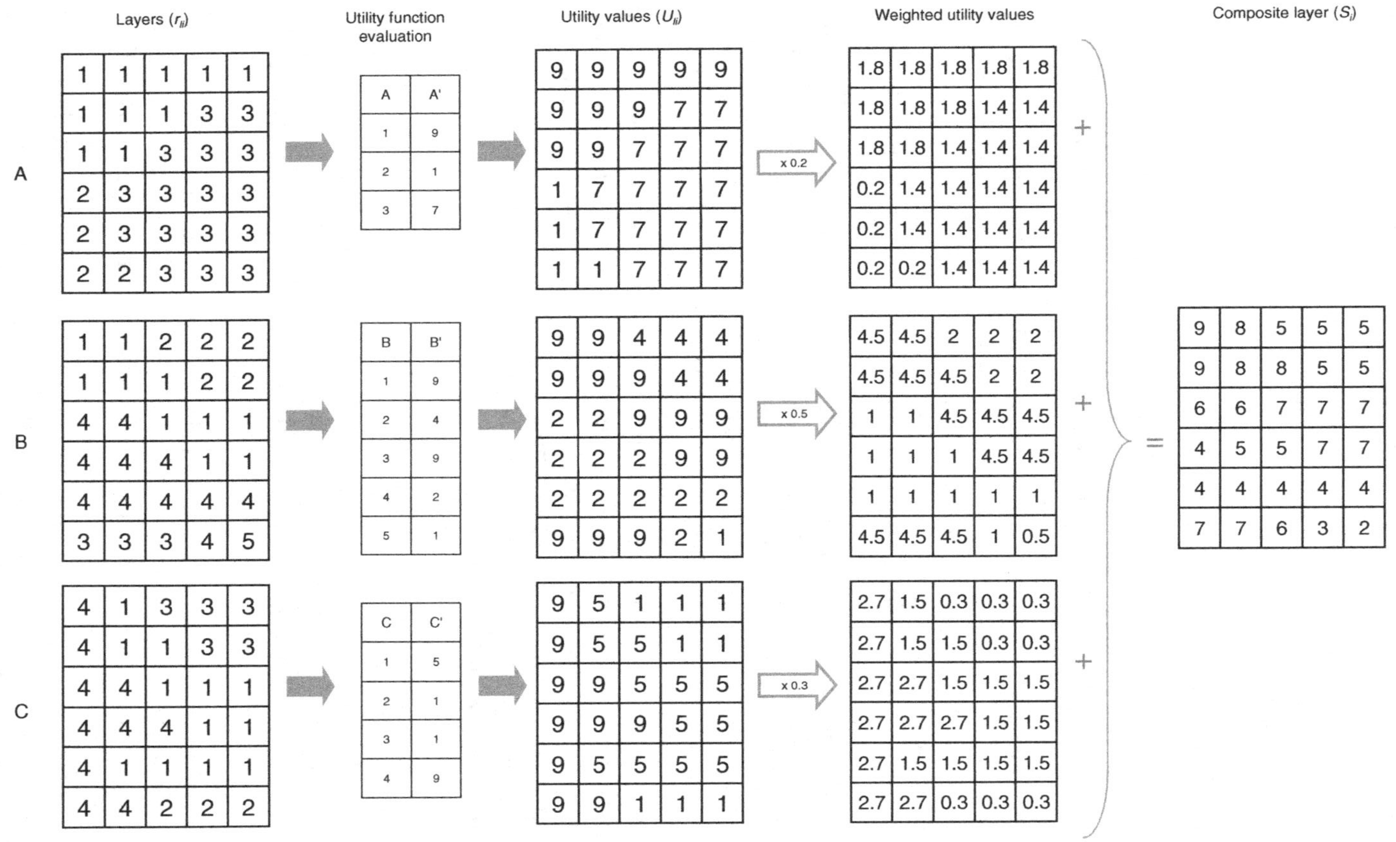

Figure 5.4 Relative suitability assessment example.

modeling. The second topic is data measurement types. As we will see, different measurement types are not appropriate for use in map algebra, but studies sometimes make the mistake of applying these methods anyway in suitability analysis. The problem is that ignoring such details can result in erroneous or invalid analysis.

5.3.1 Map Algebra

It is often necessary to process and/or manipulate data values in an attribute layer, thereby creating a new attribute layer. The assessment of suitability is in fact reliant on the ability to undertake evaluation involving input values in an attribute layer in order to produce an interpreted value in a new attribute layer. This was the essence of the suitability assessment process summarized in Figure 5.4. The indicator function, F_{li}, and utility function, U_{li}, are both examples of this, effectively representing new attribute layers.

Map algebra represents the rules and operational procedures applied to an attribute layer (input) to produce a new layer (output). While this basic idea is applicable for both a vector or raster data model, map algebra has generally referred to the processing of raster data. In many respects, map algebra is similar to matrix algebra, where different operations on a matrix are possible. When you apply a valid operation to a matrix, it is manipulated in some way, giving a new matrix. So too with an attribute layer, as there are many possible operators in map algebra, including arithmetic, relational, boolean, combinatorial, logical, accumulative, assignment, etc., and applying them in a valid way results in a new layer. Our discussion of suitability has, in fact, centered on the application of operators to an attribute layer(s) in order to derive a new layer. For this reason, the use of map algebra is generally seen as an important component of suitability analysis.

In map algebra, various functions are possible and can be classified as *local, focal* and *zonal*. Further elaboration on local and focal will help clarify this classification, and will utilize the following notation:

$$i = \text{index of cells, where } i = 1, 2, \ldots, n$$
$$l = \text{index of attribute layers, where } l = 1, 2, \ldots, L$$
$$r_{li} = \text{data value of cell } i \text{ in attribute layer } l$$
$$\Phi = \text{subset of layers considered}$$
$$V_i = \text{data value of cell } i \text{ in new attribute layer}$$

One point of clarification is that Φ enables the specification that only certain layers may be considered in an operation. Thus, $\Phi = \{1\}$, as an example, would indicate that only layer 1 is considered, whereas $\Phi = \{3, 8, L\}$ reflects layers 3, 8 and L being taken into account.

It is possible to apply specific operators to produce a new attribute layer. This new layer has an attribute value of V_i for each cell i. A local operator or function produces a new layer from one or more input layers, $l \in \Phi$.

The value of a cell i is defined by values from the same cell i in other layers:

$$V_i = f\left(r_{li}, l \in \Phi\right) \qquad (5.3)$$

where $f\ (\ )$ is some function. This is called a *local overlay operator* in map algebra. As an example, we could have the following for three layers as input: $V_i = \log r_{1i} + 2r_{2i} + \cos r_{3i}$. A reclassification local operator might involve assigning input layer data values in a certain range a particular value. For example, if $r_{li} \in [0, 49]$, then $V_i = 1$; if $r_{li} \in [50, 79]$, then $V_i = 2$; and so on. This is essentially what was discussed previously for absolute suitability.

The second class of functions noted was *focal*. In this case a new layer is produced using only one layer, but considering many cells in a prespecified neighborhood around cell i. For example, this could be all cells sharing a common edge or boundary with cell i, and would include cell i as well. Another example could be all cells within a certain distance of cell i. This neighborhood can be defined as

$\Omega_i =$ neighborhood of cell i

Thus, the map algebra operators would be applied to this set in one layer to derive the value of cell i in a new layer. In contrast to the multilayer case in (5.3), a generic functional specification of the new layer attribute value with respect to neighborhood cells in layer l is

$$V_i = f\left(r_{jl}, j \in \Omega_i\right) \qquad (5.4)$$

Of course any function is possible, like maximum or minimum. As an example, we might want the average value observed in the neighborhood set from a layer l:

$$V_i = \frac{\sum\limits_{j \in \Omega_j} r_{jl}}{|\Omega_i|} \qquad (5.5)$$

It is also possible to weight values as well.

5.3.2 Attribute Data Measurement

An issue raised early in the chapter was that methodological assessment in suitability analysis is done in a questionable manner in some cases. The primary reason for this is that people use underlying data inappropriately. All data can be classified into four different measurement types: **nominal, ordinal, interval**, and **ratio**. Each are defined in Table 5.2. A few important implications can be noted. First, the use of nominal data serves only to

TABLE 5.2   Data measurement types

Type	Definition	Example
Nominal	Data represent a name, class, or category (also referred to as categorical type)	Place names (e.g., Australia, New Zealand, United States, Mexico, Canada)
Ordinal	Data are nominal but ranked (also referred to as ranked type)	Assigned ranking of 1, 2, 3, . . . Also possible to assign nonnumeric rankings, like {best, next best, . . . , worst} or {most favorite, favorite, . . . , least favorite}.
Interval	Data are measured on a continuous scale, although the scale does not have a calibrated zero (i.e., an arbitrary zero)	Temperature readings
Ratio	Data are measured on a continuous scale with a calibrated zero	Chemical contaminants are often measured on a calibrated scale, where zero means no contaminants

identify. There is no basis for comparing nominal data values, because the name or label is arbitrary. Second, ordinal data add to the nominal type by implying a ranking, but it cannot convey any magnitude of difference in comparing observed data values. Third, with interval data there is an arbitrary zero point, so certain operations have no meaning or interpretation. The example given in Table 5.2 mentions temperature. In Fahrenheit, 32° represents the freezing point of water, but it is not absolute. In Celsius, the freezing point is zero. Finally, with ratio data operations such as addition, subtraction, multiplication, and division have a valid meaning, whereas with nominal, ordinal, and interval measures, this might not necessarily be the case.

Much raster data is, in fact, nominal, in that it serves to only describe the observed attribute. That is, it is not a measurement in the sense of ratio data. One must therefore take great care in the application of map algebra operators, as many/most operations assume the input values have a ranking, magnitudes of differences are significant, and zero has meaning.

Returning to McHarg (1969), he took each data category and divided it into three zones with a rank of low, medium and high. He colored the acetate sheet accordingly, and then overlaid this with other sheets of zoned data. Thus, he effectively added ordinal/ranked data with the use of the superimposed acetate sheets. This is problematic. Adding ranks does not necessarily convey any meaning, because there is no interpretation of magnitude. That is, is *low* twice as good/bad as *medium*? This clearly violates the constraints imposed on data manipulation given the data measurement type. Therefore, the maps produced by this approach are questionable at best, perhaps even quite misleading.

The bottom line is that there are restrictions on how a given data measurement type can be used. Our basic dilemma is that most of our data are usually nominal, so how can we calculate a suitability score when we cannot add such data together? There are essentially two methods that can be used to address this problem: screening/filtering (discussed previously in the chapter) and **data transformation**. In particular, utility theory provides a basis for moving from a nominal data measurement type, as an example, to ratio. Given space limitations, this will not be discussed further here, but the interested reader can consult Goodwin and Wright (1991) or Keeny and Raiffa (1976).

5.4   MODEL APPLICATION

In this section we present two cases where suitability analysis has been carried out for subsequent use in location site acquisition.

5.4.1   Absolute Suitability

The military is in need of a specialized operations area. The site cannot be located where there is sensitive habitat, near major streams and rivers, or too close to major roads. It cannot have general aircraft routes in the airspace above the site, cannot contain steep terrain, must be away from communities and historical landmarks, and cannot coincide with any special land-use management areas. This is an absolute suitability assessment problem.

The region shown in Figure 5.5 was found to meet terrain, habitat, airspace and historical landmarks criteria. Thus, what remains is identifying viable land with respect to proximity to road, streams/rivers and communities. Figure 5.5a depicts suitable land when roads are considered. Specifically, land within a quarter mile of a road is not suitable for the operations area. Thus, Figure 5.5a identifies suitable and unsuitable land with respect to road proximity. Figure 5.5b shows suitable land when streams/rivers are taken into account. Specifically, land within a quarter mile of a stream/river is not suitable for the operations area. Thus, Figure 5.5b identifies suitable and unsuitable land with respect to steam/river proximity. Figure 5.5c details the suitable land away from communities. Specifically, land within half a mile of a community is not suitable for the operations area. Thus, Figure 5.5c identifies suitable and unsuitable land with respect to community proximity.

Bringing each attribute layer together forms the composite suitability layer. For the operations area, feasible land is shown in Figure 5.6. The areas that are screened out, or unsuitable, are depicted in a dark shade, whereas the remaining land represents those areas where the operations area could be located. What would now be needed is a process or method for selecting where to site the operations area, given these feasible locations.

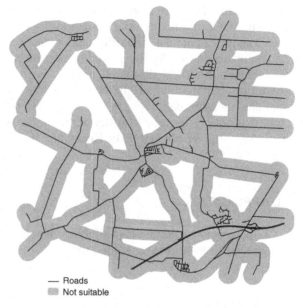

— Roads
▓ Not suitable

(a) Proximity to roads

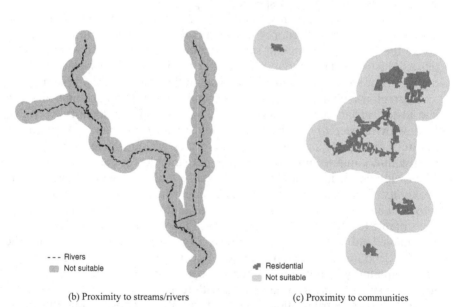

- - - Rivers
▓ Not suitable

(b) Proximity to streams/rivers

🔹 Residential
▓ Not suitable

(c) Proximity to communities

Figure 5.5   Absolute suitability assessment in locating an operations area.

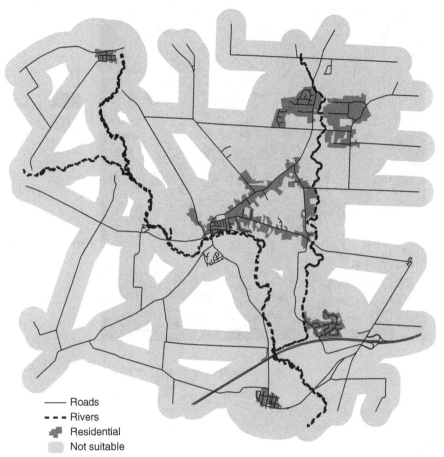

Roads
Rivers
Residential
Not suitable

Figure 5.6 Feasible composite layer for locating an operations area.

5.4.2 Relative Suitability

A home-building company is interested in constructing a new residential development in the region shown in Figure 5.7, which is approximately 400 square miles in size. Based on much preliminary analysis, this region is viable for such a development and costs will likely be more or less the same for acquiring the necessary land. This company typically builds homes on lots of three quarters of an acre, and prefers 200 homes in the development. Thus, the size of the development will be no more than 150 acres, so less than one square mile. One distinguishing factor in this region, however, is fire risk. Therefore, the builder would like to identify a development area with the least risk to fire.

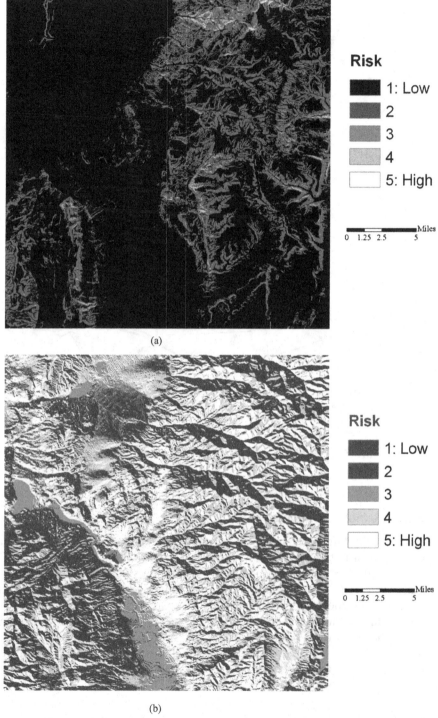

(a)

(b)

Figure 5.7 Relative suitability assessment in locating a residential development.

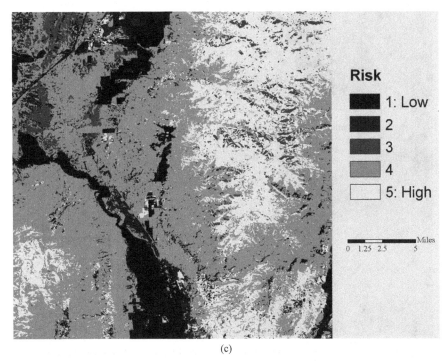

(c)

Figure 5.7   (*Continued*)

Fire risk is largely a function of spatial and environmental characteristics in this region. In particular, slope, aspect, and vegetation type are deemed important attributes associated with fire risk in this case. This is a relative suitability problem because all areas are viable, but some are less prone to fire risk than others.

The region in Figure 5.7 is represented as a series of raster layers, and each cell is 30 m × 30 m. Each attribute layer *l* is evaluated to determine a utility value, U_{li}, for each cell *i*. The utility value ranges from 1 to 5, with 1 being the least fire risk and 5 being the greatest fire risk. The utility values for each layer are shown in Figure 5.7, with Figure 5.7a showing slope, Figure 5.7b illustrating aspect, and Figure 5.7c indicating vegetation.

Map algebra was used to integrate the raster attribute layers given in Figure 5.7 in order to derive the composite suitability layer. Specifically, this was done as follows:

$$S_i = U_{1i} + U_{2i} + 2U_{3i} \tag{5.6}$$

where layer 1 is slope ($l = 1$), layer 2 is aspect ($l = 2$) and layer 3 is vegetation ($l = 3$). Figure 5.8 depicts relative suitability in terms of fire risk for a residential development. Suitability values range from 4 to 20. The areas

Figure 5.8 Composite layer of relative suitability for a residential development.

most suitable, or having the least fire risk, have values close to 1 and are darkly shaded, whereas the least suitable, or greatest fire risk, areas have values closer to 20 and are shown using lighter shades. Given the relative suitability assessment shown in Figure 5.8, there are clearly many feasible potential locations. As a result, there is now a need for a process or method to select a site for the residential development having the least risk of fire.

5.5 ADVANCED TOPICS

Up to this point, we have not been concerned with the specification of importance weights. Importance weights are primarily used in combining utility values into a composite score. Often, weights of importance are suggested by a decision maker or an expert panel. Technically speaking, such weights should be made so that they are sensitive to the magnitude of the individual objectives, as well as sensitive to the differences in magnitude used in other objectives. The ratio of weights between two competing objectives determines the relative importance of one to the other. Although, importance weights are

TABLE 5.3   Pairwise comparison matrix

	Wetlands	Species Richness	Road Density
Wetlands	1	1/5	1/2
Species richness	5	1	3
Road density	2	1/3	1

often determined by discussion and panel vote, the errors involved in this approach can be enough that a more formal approach should be taken. In this section, we describe a technique that has gained popularity in setting weights. This technique is called the **analytic hierarchy process** (AHP) and is described in Saaty (1980). This section is devoted to the description of AHP for establishing the importance weights.

AHP is composed of three main steps: (1) decomposing a problem into a hierarchy of elements, (2) making pairwise comparisons of elements on the same part of the hierarchy, and (3) developing the hierarchical score and applying it to the relevant data. In this section, we will show how AHP can be used to generate relative weights for a set of objectives. To do this, we do not need to discuss the development of a hierarchy or the application *per se*, but must describe the underpinnings of the second step of AHP. To show how to do this, suppose we wish to determine the relative importance of several factors involved in selecting land for habitat protection:[3]

1. Presence of wetlands
2. Species richness
3. Density of existing roads

Some of these indicators or metrics are self-explanatory; however, road density is probably not. We use road density as a surrogate measure for development. If roads are nonexistent, then the area contains little development and tends to be less disturbed. If the area has a high level of roads per square mile, then it is highly developed and fragmented. It would make sense to favor the selection of areas that have as few roads as possible for habitat protection. All of the factors are important, but how should we weight them? In AHP a pairwise comparison matrix, like that given in Table 5.3, is constructed for the set of objectives.

For each pair, the relative importance is taken from the comparisons listed in Table 5.4. The opposite comparison of two elements is always assigned the reciprocal value. For example, road density compared to wetlands is given a value of 2, representing a compromise between equally important and

---

[3] This example is kept simple for illustrative purposes.

TABLE 5.4 Ratio-scaled comparisons

Numerical value	Definition
1	Equally important or preferred
3	Slightly more important
5	Strongly more important
7	Very strongly more important
9	Extremely more important

slightly more important. The reciprocal of 2 (i.e., 1/2) is then specified for the comparison of wetlands to road density. Note that the diagonal is always set at 1.

Once we have made the comparisons using Table 5.4, we are ready to determine the importance weights for each factor. Importance weights can be generated from a pairwise comparison matrix by computing the principal right-hand eigenvector values, and can be approximated by computing:

$$
\begin{bmatrix} w_1 \\ w_2 \\ \vdots \\ w_n \end{bmatrix} = \lim_{k \to \infty} \frac{\begin{bmatrix} a_{ij} & \cdots & a_{nj} \\ \vdots & \ddots & \vdots \\ a_{nj} & \cdots & a_{nn} \end{bmatrix}^k \begin{bmatrix} 1 \\ \vdots \\ 1 \end{bmatrix}}{\begin{bmatrix} 1 & \cdots & 1 \end{bmatrix} \begin{bmatrix} a_{ij} & \cdots & a_{nj} \\ \vdots & \ddots & \vdots \\ a_{nj} & \cdots & a_{nn} \end{bmatrix}^k \begin{bmatrix} 1 \\ \vdots \\ 1 \end{bmatrix}}
\tag{5.7}
$$

where n is the number of objectives and a_{ij} the pairwise comparison values (e.g., Table 5.3). As an example for $k = 1$ and using the values from the comparison matrix of Table 5.3, we get:

$$
\begin{bmatrix} w_1 \\ w_2 \\ w_3 \end{bmatrix} = \frac{\begin{bmatrix} 1 & .2 & .5 \\ 5 & 1 & 3 \\ 2 & .333 & 1 \end{bmatrix} \begin{bmatrix} 1 \\ 1 \\ 1 \end{bmatrix}}{\begin{bmatrix} 1 & 1 & 1 \end{bmatrix} \begin{bmatrix} 1 & .2 & .5 \\ 5 & 1 & 3 \\ 2 & .333 & 1 \end{bmatrix} \begin{bmatrix} 1 \\ 1 \\ 1 \end{bmatrix}}
\tag{5.8}
$$

Solving this yields $w_1 = .121$, $w_2 = .641$, $w_3 = .237$. Figure 5.9 presents a model designed to solve for the principal right-hand eigenvector value when $k = 2$ in LINGO format. The solution to this model is given in Figure 5.10. Note the weights are slightly different than what was computed for the

```
! A special model for computing the
! principal right eigenvector value of matrix A;
MODEL:
SETS:
  factors / wetlands species roads / : w2, e, RowSum;
  Pairwise  (factors, factors): A, AK ;
ENDSETS

DATA:
  A = 1 .2 .5
      5  1  3
      2 .333  1;
  e = 1 1 1;
ENDDATA

!when k=2 we need to first calculate the product A*A;
!initialize values of RowSum and Rtotal;

 @for(factors(i):
  @for(factors(j):
     AK(i,j) = @sum(factors(k): A(i,k)*A(k,j) )
  ) );

! AK is the matrix A times the matrix A;
! Now calculate the weights w2(i);

 @for(factors(i):
  RowSum(i)= @sum(factors(j): AK(i,j)) );

  Rtotal = @sum(factors(i): RowSum(i));

 @for(factors(i):
  w2(i) = RowSum(i)/Rtotal );

!Now calculate the consistency ratio;

Lmax= (@sum(factors(j): A(1,j)*W2(j)))/w2(1);
CI = (Lmax-3.00)/(3.00);
CR= CI/(.58);

END
```

Figure 5.9 AHP importance weights model structured in LINGO.

case when $k = 1$. In general, the value of k is increased until the differences obtained from one solution to the next are negligible. The importance weights are summarized in Table 5.5 for this example.

It is possible that decision makers and expert panels are not consistent in specifying comparison values. It is common practice to compute a ratio as

TABLE 5.5 Derived importance weights

	Importance Weights
Wetlands	.121
Species richness	.648
Road density	.229

TABLE 5.6 Random inconsistency index

n	1	2	3	4	5	6	7	8	9	10
RI	0.00	0.00	0.58	0.90	1.12	1.24	1.32	1.41	1.45	1.49

a test to determine if the comparison matrix is consistent enough with the computed weights. For AHP, this consistency ratio (CR) can be specified as

$$CR = \frac{\left(\frac{\left(\sum_j a_{ij} w_j \Big/ w_1 \right) - n}{n - 1} \right)}{RI} \tag{5.9}$$

where RI is the random inconsistency index, and appropriate values can be found in a look-up table as a function of the number of factors, n. Table 5.6 shows these values. Note that the value of the consistency ratio is found to be 0.00353 using LINGO (see Figure 5.10). When the consistency ratio is less than 0.1, it is considered acceptable. It is this last property that makes AHP a very valuable technique. Not only is it designed to calculate a ratio measurement weight, but it tracks whether the matrix used to calculate the weights is itself consistent.

5.6 SUMMARY

Suitability analysis can be a significant and essential tool for location analysis. It has been used to support many different types of siting problems involving facilities such as power plants, landfills, industrial parks, highways, retail stores, warehouses, gas stations, and many others. There are two general approaches that can be used to assess suitability: absolute and relative. It cannot be overemphasized how important the absolute (or screening) suitability approach is. First, it does not violate issues of data measurement type. Second, it presents little difficulty in visual display, as an area is either feasible or it is

```
Feasible solution found.
   Total solver iterations:                          0

                               Variable           Value
                                 RTOTAL        42.39550
                                   LMAX        3.006155
                                     CI        0.2051679E-02
                                     CR        0.3537378E-02
                        W2( WETLANDS)        0.1218643
                        W2( SPECIES)         0.6486302
                        W2( ROADS)           0.2295055
                         E( WETLANDS)        1.000000
                         E( SPECIES)         1.000000
                         E( ROADS)           1.000000
                    ROWSUM( WETLANDS)        5.166500
                    ROWSUM( SPECIES)        27.49900
                    ROWSUM( ROADS)           9.730000
          A( WETLANDS, WETLANDS)             1.000000
          A( WETLANDS, SPECIES)             0.2000000
          A( WETLANDS, ROADS)               0.5000000
          A( SPECIES, WETLANDS)             5.000000
          A( SPECIES, SPECIES)              1.000000
          A( SPECIES, ROADS)                3.000000
          A( ROADS, WETLANDS)               2.000000
          A( ROADS, SPECIES)                0.3330000
          A( ROADS, ROADS)                  1.000000
         AK( WETLANDS, WETLANDS)            3.000000
         AK( WETLANDS, SPECIES)            0.5665000
         AK( WETLANDS, ROADS)              1.600000
         AK( SPECIES, WETLANDS)           16.00000
         AK( SPECIES, SPECIES)             2.999000
         AK( SPECIES, ROADS)               8.500000
         AK( ROADS, WETLANDS)              5.665000
         AK( ROADS, SPECIES)               1.066000
         AK( ROADS, ROADS)                 2.999000

                                    Row    Slack or Surplus
                                      1        0.000000
                                      2        0.000000
                                      3        0.000000
                                      4        0.000000
                                      5        0.000000
                                      6        0.000000
                                      7        0.000000
                                      8        0.000000
                                      9        0.000000
                                     10        0.000000
                                     11        0.000000
                                     12        0.000000
                                     13        0.000000
                                     14        0.000000
                                     15        0.000000
                                     16        0.000000
                                     17        0.000000
                                     18        0.000000
                                     19        0.000000
```

Figure 5.10   Importance weights solution.

not. Finally, getting consensus for a group of stakeholders can be difficult, and it is often easier to gain consensus for a standards-based absolute approach. The relative (or scoring) suitability approach raises issues, and significant care must be used in handling data of different measurement types. Many combine data of different types, like McHarg (1969), producing results that can be misleading or erroneous. Since most geographic attributes are nominal, they must first be transformed into a ratio measure before they can be combined into meaningful scores. This is the critical step in relative suitability analysis. Although GIS makes easy work of transforming and combining data, the main task is in developing the appropriate transformation functions and importance weights.

5.7   TERMS

suitability analysis
relative suitability (scoring)
absolute suitability (screening/filtering)
weighted linear combination
normalized weights
nominal, ordinal, interval, and ratio data measurement types
data transformation
map algebra
analytic hierarchy process

5.8   REFERENCES

Church, R. L., R. A. Gerrard, M. Gilpin, and P. Stine. 2003. Constructing cell-based habitat patches useful in conservation planning. *Annals of the Association of American Geographers* 93:814–827.

Dobson, J. E. 1979. A regional screening procedure for land use suitability analysis. *The Geographical Review* 69:224–234.

Goodwin, P., and G. Wright. 1991 *Decision analysis for management and judgment.* New York: Wiley.

Hopkins, L. 1977. Methods for generating land suitability maps: A comparative evaluation. *Journal for American Institute of Planners* 34:19–29.

Keeny, R. L., and H. Raiffa. 1976. *Decisions with multiple objective: Preferences and value tradeoffs.* New York: John Wiley.

McHarg, I. 1969. *Design with nature* Philadelphia: Natural History Press.

Saaty, T. L. 1980. *The analytic hierarchy process.* New York: McGraw Hill.

5.9   EXERCISES

5.1. Wal-Mart wants to locate a new store in the city of Winston. Describe how suitability analysis can be used to identify potential locations for this store. Also, suggest at least five desirable attributes that can be used in narrowing down the number of potential sites.

5.2. Consider the following table of information. There are 14 areas that have been evaluated in terms of six criteria. The values of these attributes for each site alternative are given in the table, along with standards that must be met. Use the absolute suitability approach to evaluate the 14 alternatives, where the indicated standard is the lowest acceptable value for that criterion.

Site alternative	Criterion 1	Criterion 2	Criterion 3	Criterion 4	Criterion 5	Criterion 6
1	59	56	48	57	54	60
2	51	50	61	52	51	60
3	48	50	60	55	51	55
4	49	45	27	62	59	49
5	53	53	39	54	57	37
6	59	55	31	61	51	58
7	41	59	56	62	59	55
8	48	50	44	50	53	42
9	41	46	57	55	53	50
10	10	53	66	60	54	56
11	46	20	54	50	49	58
12	70	33	51	35	46	62
13	57	46	54	57	20	65
14	55	35	55	100	30	90
Standard	40	30	50	40	50	50
Order of importance	**6**	**3**	**2**	**4**	**5**	**1**

5.3. Assume the values that are given in question 2 are ratio measurement values. Using weights of $w_1 = 10$, $w_2 = 40$, $w_3 = 50$, $w_4 = 30$, $w_5 = 20$ and $w_6 = 60$, determine which of the alternatives results in the highest normalized weighted sum score. If the same scoring procedure is applied for only those alternatives that meet the first five standards, which alternative gives the highest normalized weighted sum score? After the sixth? Compare all three results.

5.4. The leaders of Placer County, California, have been alarmed at sprawl and housing growth in the foothills of the Sierra Mountains. Ecologists have shown that this development will have a great impact on the natural environment of the county, stretching from the Central Valley to the shores of Lake Tahoe. To address the problem of degrading the natural environment, they have decided to draw urban limit lines for development, where development/sprawl outside of these lines will be strictly limited. They plan to compensate land owners outside of the growth lines by a special development tax. They have set a target to protect at least 50 percent of the area of the county from further development. Describe how suitability analysis could be used to assist county planners in drawing the lines. What issues do you consider important in selecting areas for development, or areas selected for protection?

CHAPTER 6

POINT-BASED LOCATION

6.0 INTRODUCTION

The two previous chapters have emphasized modeling of interactions between facilities and customers and suitability assessment for site location.
We now turn our attention to the problem of actually locating a single facility. This single facility could be a point, line, or area object. In this chapter,
we examine the siting of a point-based facility, but in subsequent chapters
we consider a line-based facility (e.g., utility corridor, bus route, delivery
route, etc.) and an area-based facility (e.g., landfill, nature reserve, recreation
area, etc.). There are many circumstances in which the problem is to locate a
point-based facility. Examples include locating an incinerator for solid-waste
reduction, identifying a headquarters for a large company, building a factory
for a new product line, establishing a break-of-bulk warehouse, and siting a
local switching center for a telephone company. Of course you will likely
recall that single-facility location was also discussed in Chapters 1 and 3, so
this chapter builds on this topic further.

There are effectively three general contexts under which we can consider
facility siting. One is in continuous space, as was considered in Chapters
1 and 3. Specifically, the facility can be sited anywhere, so there are an
infinite number of locations to consider. The second context is that there
exists a network, where locations are constrained to be at points on the
network. The third context is that there exist a finite set of discrete locations
for potentially siting a facility. The main emphasis of this chapter is on the
siting of a facility in continuous space. Following a general introduction, a
mathematical formulation is presented for the single-facility location problem
in continuous space, assuming Euclidean distance travel. We also describe an

iterative approach for solving this problem. The GIScience section reviews **map projections** and distance metrics, with an emphasis on the errors that can arise when the Euclidean distance measure is used in a continuous space location model. Advanced topics in this chapter include variants of the single-facility location problem as well as a discussion of the centroid as a locational construct.

6.1   PROBLEM DEFINITION AND MOTIVATION

There are many situations where a single facility is needed, and a variety of reasons for requiring just one. For example, it may be that a needed facility is so expensive to build and operate that only one can be afforded/justified, or it may be that demand for the product/service is small enough that it is not necessary to have more than one facility. As an example of a single facility, consider the handling of solid waste, where trash is picked up by collection vehicles and brought to a central facility. Recyclables are typically separated from the waste stream to the greatest extent possible at such a sorting facility. Then, the reduced amount of waste is transported in high volumes to a landfill. If there is no processing, then this is called a transfer facility. Many communities have sorting and transfer facilities, as they allow collection vehicles to dump their load and quickly return to the task of collection without having to make more lengthy and time-consuming trips to a landfill disposal site. A bulk-haul truck can carry the loads of many collection vehicles to the landfill from the transfer facility more efficiently than having collection vehicles haul waste directly to the landfill. First, it involves fewer hours of driver time (i.e., one bulk-haul truck driver vs. several collection truck drivers). Second, the bulk-haul truck is more efficient per ton mile in fuel consumption than collection vehicles. Finally, except for the driver, the collection crew members are idle while the collection vehicle is making the time-consuming trips to the landfill, which is not an efficient use of personnel. This is a classic location problem: where to place a facility between one transport protocol and another. In this case, we need a well-located facility between the collection areas and the landfill.

The *break-of-bulk* terminal is another related example of a single facility, where long-haul vehicles (e.g., trucks, trains, barges, aircraft, and ships) bring goods to a central facility in a region. Goods then are taken off bulk-haul carriers, sorted, then loaded onto smaller vehicles (e.g., trucks and vans) for final delivery to stores and outlets. This process is illustrated in Figure 6.1. Most medium to large companies rely on such terminal facilities for achieving distribution efficiencies. As an example, FedEx maintains a local package collection and distribution facility in virtually every city it serves, with the purpose of collecting packages, sorting, and consolidating them for long-distance transport (as well as receiving packages for local distribution). As a final example of locating a single facility, consider public services

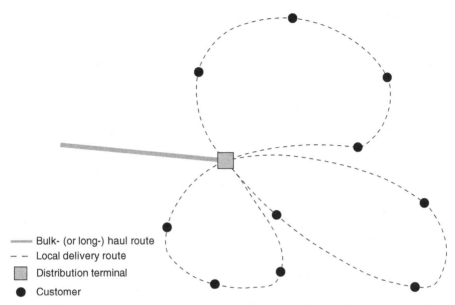

Figure 6.1   Distribution in a break-of-bulk terminal facility system.

such as post offices, municipal, courts, and clinics. Such facilities need to be placed so that they are as accessible as possible to everyone traveling to and from them. In this case, a desirable goal is to locate the facility so that it minimizes the average distance traveled by all users in getting to the facility.

The problem here, then, is to locate a single facility in order to be as efficient as possible in terms of travel and/or distribution. This problem can be formally stated as follows:

> Find the location for a facility that minimizes travel time and/or transportation costs in serving points of demand.

Depending on the planning context, the emphasis could be travel time or transportation costs, or both. The Weber problem, briefly introduced in Chapter 1, was described as locating a factory so that the transportation costs to get raw material to the factory and the distribution costs in shipping product to customers are both minimized, where costs are a function of Euclidean distance travel. This is precisely in line with the problem definition just given. Similarly, the single-facility problem presented in Chapter 3 was also to minimize transportation costs in material shipment and product distribution, but costs were a function of rectilinear distance travel. In the next section, we present a mathematical formulation of the Weber problem for locating a single point-based facility.

6.2 MATHEMATICAL REPRESENTATION

Although there are **continuous** and **discrete space** contexts we can consider, in this section we focus on continuous space siting of a single facility in a two-dimensional plane. Later in the chapter we will return to the discussion of discrete space location, as well as location in three-dimensional space. As just mentioned, the Weber problem is to locate a facility in order to minimize transportation costs, where these costs are interpreted as a function of Euclidean distance travel in two-dimensional space.

6.2.1 Formulating the Weber Problem

Planar models represent one of the simpler problem domains. As already noted, it is assumed that it is possible to place the facility virtually anywhere in the plane. Although this may not exactly be the case in many application instances, we can zero in on the essence of finding the most efficient location for serving a set of demand points. Demand often represents the number of service trips over some period of time (e.g., day, month, year). It may also be expressed as a weight or cost of transport for products or materials that need to be shipped to or from the facility. The following notation will be used in formalizing this planning problem:

$$i = \text{index of demand points } (1, 2, \ldots, n)$$
$$(x_i, y_i) = \text{coordinate location of demand point } i$$
$$a_i = \text{demand at point } i$$
$$(X, Y) = \text{location of facility}$$

Given this notation, Euclidean distance between demand point i and the located facility, (X,Y), is defined as follows:

$$\sqrt{(X - x_i)^2 + (Y - y_i)^2} = \left((X - x_i)^2 + (Y - y_i)^2\right)^{1/2} \qquad (6.1)$$

It is also possible to simply refer to this distance from demand i to the facility location as d_i, where $d_i = ((X - x_i)^2 + (Y - y_i)^2)^{1/2}$. Incorporating weighted demand and all demand areas, the single facility location problem assuming Euclidean distance travel is

$$Minimize \sum_{i=1}^{n} a_i \left((X - x_i)^2 + (Y - y_i)^2\right)^{1/2} \qquad (6.2)$$

This model, (6.2), defines the problem of finding the point location for a facility, (X, Y), that minimizes total weighted distance in serving all demand points. Each term represents a product of the demand weight times the distance to that demand from the located facility. Of course, (6.2) is a nonlinear function because of the decision variables in the square root operator.

As noted previously, Weber (1909) is credited for the formalization of the basic problem, where Euclidean distance travel is assumed. As a result, it is often simply called the **Weber problem**.[1] Solving this basic problem has been the topic of much research interest since at least the 1600s. It is possible to solve the Weber problem using some commercial software. LINGO, in fact, does have a nonlinear solver extension option, but this must be purchased in addition to the basic package. Thus, it may or may not be possible to solve (6.2) using commercial optimization software, depending on the limitations of the software utilized.

6.2.2 Iterative Solution Approach for the Weber Problem

Most optimization packages like LINGO are limited in their ability to optimize nonlinear functions or constrained nonlinear problems, and certainly in precomputer times commercial software was obviously not available. It so happens that the summation in (6.2) is a convex function. Since the sum of convex functions is itself a convex function, then (6.2) is also a convex function. Nonlinear problems are not easy to solve in general, but convexity often simplifies the search for an optima, since a local optima will be unique, and therefore will be the global optima.

Since the objection function (6.2) is convex, principles of calculus can be used to provide important insights. In fact, a relatively simple algorithm has been devised to optimally solve the Weber problem based on key insights through calculus. In particular, the derivative of function (6.2) with respect to X is informative, and is as follows:

$$\frac{d}{dX} = \sum_{i=1}^{n} -\frac{1}{2}a_i((X - x_i)^2 + (Y - y_i)^2)^{-\frac{1}{2}}(2)(X - x_i) \qquad (6.3)$$

Simplifying (6.3), substituting $d_i = ((X - x_i)^2 + (Y - y_i)^2)^{-\frac{1}{2}}$ and setting the equation to zero, we solve for the critical points on the function:

$$\sum_{i=1}^{n} \frac{a_i}{d_i}(X - x_i) = 0 \qquad (6.4)$$

----

[1] It should be mentioned that Fermet in 1640 suggested the following geometric problem: given three points, find a fourth point that minimizes the sums of the distances to the first three points. Thus, some prefer to name this problem in honor of Fermet. However, Weber suggested this problem as an economic reality, rather than a geometric puzzle.

This is equivalent to

$$X \sum_{i=1}^{n} \frac{a_i}{d_i} - \sum_{i=1}^{n} \frac{a_i x_i}{d_i} = 0 \qquad (6.5)$$

Solving (6.5) for X gives

$$X = \frac{\sum_{i=1}^{n} \frac{a_i x_i}{d_i}}{\sum_{i=1}^{n} \frac{a_i}{d_i}} \qquad (6.6)$$

A similar derivation process with respect to the variable Y results in the following:

$$Y = \frac{\sum_{i=1}^{n} \frac{a_i y_i}{d_i}}{\sum_{i=1}^{n} \frac{a_i}{d_i}} \qquad (6.7)$$

This is seemingly convenient, except that variables X and Y are not actually isolated on the left-hand side of these equations, because they are both in the function of distance d_i. Thus, (6.6) and (6.7) define the optimal facility location as:

$$(X, Y) = \left(\frac{\sum_{i=1}^{n} \frac{a_i x_i}{\left((X - x_i)^2 + (Y - y_i)^2\right)^{1/2}}}{\sum_{i=1}^{n} \frac{a_i}{\left((X - x_i)^2 + (Y - y_i)^2\right)^{1/2}}}, \frac{\sum_{i=1}^{n} \frac{a_i y_i}{\left((X - x_i)^2 + (Y - y_i)^2\right)^{1/2}}}{\sum_{i=1}^{n} \frac{a_i}{\left((X - x_i)^2 + (Y - y_i)^2\right)^{1/2}}} \right)$$

$$(6.8)$$

From a algebraic perspective, (6.8) is disappointing, as it is not possible to isolate the unknown variables X and Y. However, Weiszfeld (1937) demonstrated that (6.8) can be used in an iterative fashion to solve for the optimal facility location, or Weber point. Specifically, it was suggested that a successive approximation approach was possible, where an improved estimate can be derived from the previous estimate in identifying the optimal facility location. Define the following:

$$\left(X^k, Y^k\right) = \text{estimate of Weber point at iteration } k$$

Based on this, it is possible to determine distance values d_i^k as follows:

$$d_i^k = \left(\left(X^k - x_i\right)^2 + \left(Y^k - y_i\right)^2 \right)^{1/2} \tag{6.9}$$

This is merely the distance from estimate (X^k, Y^k) to demand point i. Using these distance estimates, one can then determine a better estimate of the optimal facility location as (X^{k+1}, Y^{k+1}). Specifically, this is the following:

$$\left(X^{k+1}, Y^{k+1}\right) = \left(\frac{\displaystyle\sum_{i=1}^{n} \frac{a_i x_i}{d_i^k}}{\displaystyle\sum_{i=1}^{n} \frac{a_i}{d_i^k}}, \frac{\displaystyle\sum_{i=1}^{n} \frac{a_i y_i}{d_i^k}}{\displaystyle\sum_{i=1}^{n} \frac{a_i}{d_i^k}} \right) \tag{6.10}$$

Weiszfeld suggested that at each iteration, one could use the current estimate for the optimal facility location to obtain a better estimate. So, the process begins with an initial guess, (X^0, Y^0), and is repeated until there is effectively no change between one estimate and the next.

There is one potential problem with this approach, however. If an estimate (X^k, Y^k) should coincide with a demand point i, then the distance, d_i^k, will equal zero for that demand point. This means that the denominator will be zero in (6.10) when computing the next estimate (X^{k+1}, Y^{k+1}). This results in an undefined value, and cannot be computed. It turns out that there are several methods that can be used to avoid this complication. The easiest approach is to use a distance approximation:

$$\left(\left(X^k - x_i\right)^2 + \left(Y^k - y_i\right)^2 + \varepsilon \right)^{1/2} \tag{6.11}$$

where ε is a small positive constant. Using equation (6.11) instead of (6.9) does not affect convergence to the optimal point, but does prevent the possibility of dividing by zero. This technique is called the *hyperboloid approximation procedure*.

This iterative procedure for solving the single facility location problem with Euclidean distances (Weber problem) is known as the **Weiszfeld algorithm**, and has proven to be very effective in practice and is most often the approach used to solve the Weber problem.

6.3 GISCIENCE

The Weber problem is conceptually quite simple. All that is needed to support analysis is a measure of demand and the coordinates of each demand point. What could be simpler than calculating the Euclidean distance from each demand point to a possible facility location? In fact, distance calculation is not so easy, and is an age-old problem of cartography and GIS. In this section, we discuss projections and coordinate systems, as well as distance metrics.

6.3.1 Projections and Coordinate Systems

You will recall from Chapter 2 that Earth is an irregularly shaped three-dimensional object, and representing it in a digital environment has necessarily required certain approximations to be made. Often, Earth is simply assumed to be a sphere. For our purposes here, we will assume that a sphere is a reasonable approximation. A referencing approach on a sphere relies on latitude and longitude measures, (ϕ, λ), in degrees from the equator and prime meridian, respectively, to identify any location. For a variety of reasons, many technologies for handling spatial information assume a two-dimensional space. That is, they assume a flat or projected Earth. Projection then is the process of taking the three-dimensional Earth and flattening it into two dimensions. Again, there are many valid reasons for doing this, including data input, analysis, and geovisualization, but it does create distortions of some sort in the process. Specifically, it is impossible to represent a three-dimensional object in two dimensions without introducing some type of error. All projections introduce distortion of some kind, either in shape or area, or some combination of the two. This distortion often translates to errors in distance measurement, so it is of great concern for spatial modeling, and location analysis in particular.

A Cartesian coordinate system, or simply **coordinate system**, is the representation of space in two dimensions, where an origin is established and relative position is measured in the x direction and y direction, (x, y), from the origin.

A projection can be viewed as a mathematical transformation between the three-dimensional Earth and the coordinate system (two-dimensional space):

$$x = f_1(\phi, \lambda) \tag{6.12}$$

$$y = f_2(\phi, \lambda) \tag{6.13}$$

where $f_1()$ and $f_2()$ are generic functions describing the transformation. For the Mercator projection, as an example, this transformation is

$$x = \lambda \tag{6.14}$$

$$y = \ln\left(\tan\left(\frac{\phi}{2} + \frac{\pi}{4}\right)\right) \tag{6.15}$$

Of course, one can readily transform back to latitude and longitude from a coordinate system as well.

The significance of projections and coordinate systems is that there are many options for transforming between the three-dimensional Earth and two dimensions, including cylindrical, azimuthal and conic. Each have different associated distortions. Some projections preserve shape, some preserve area and others preserve neither shape nor area. As a result, distance is distorted, and the level of distortion depends on location. This can be readily observed as well. Figure 6.2 depicts a large region of the world using the Mercator projection. Distance is depicted between Los Angeles, California, and London, England, and measures 8,346 miles. This measure is easily confirmed using (6.1), as the figure shows London at about (0, 4150) and Los Angeles at (−8182, 2504). Note that −8182 represents miles west of the prime meridian. This gives $\sqrt{(0 - (-8182))^2 + (4150 - 2504)^2}$, which is 8,346 miles. However, the distance between Los Angeles and London is actually only 5,434 miles. Even within the U.S. distance errors can be observed. Consider, for example, Nashville and Los Angeles as the Mercator projection suggests 2,177 miles between the two cities, yet the actual distance is 1,866 miles. Again, this error is due to the distortion introduced in the projection process as it is impossible to represent the three-dimensional earth in two dimensions without any error. On a more positive note, for a smaller area, like a city or town, distortion errors may not be significant, but this depends on the type of projection, position on the Earth, and application context.

6.3.2 Spherical Distance

As noted previously, Earth is a three-dimensional object, often represented as a sphere in a digital environment. Location on Earth is measured relative to the equator (north or south, in degrees) and in terms of its position relative to the prime meridian (east or west, in degrees). Measurements west of the prime meridian are also given as a negative angle, as are latitudes south of the equator. For example, Los Angeles is at (34.54, −118.64) (in decimal degrees).

Geographical distance must necessarily account for the curvature of the Earth when a three-dimensional representation is utilized. As an example, this curvature can be seen in Figure 6.3, where proximity between Los Angeles and London is being examined. On a sphere, the distance between two locations, (ϕ_1, λ_1) and (ϕ_1, λ_1), is calculated as follows:

$$r \arccos (\sin \phi_1 \sin \phi_2 + \cos \phi_1 \cos \phi_2 \cos (\lambda_1 - \lambda_2)) \qquad (6.16)$$

where r is the assumed radius of Earth. This is often referred to as the **great circle distance**, as it takes into account the curvature of the sphere. Returning to Figure 6.3, London is shown at approximately (51.53, 0) and Los Angeles is about at (34.54, −118.64), so the distance between the two cities is 5,434 miles. This can be confirmed using (6.16) with an assumed radius of the

Figure 6.2 Distance in two-dimensional space.

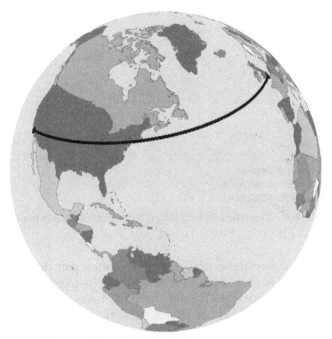

Figure 6.3   Great circle distance on a sphere.

earth of 3,963 miles ($r = 3{,}963$). Note that degrees must first be converted to radians in order to apply (6.16).

It is not uncommon to see examples where people have derived distances using locations reported in latitude and longitude (three-dimensional space), but then use Euclidean distance, (6.1). Clearly, this is problematic, as Euclidean distance assumes a Cartesian coordinate system (two-dimensional space), not a sphere. Errors will no doubt result in this case, and become more significant the further locations are from each other.

6.3.3   Planar Distance

In contrast to spherical distance, planar distance does not take into account Earth's curvature because it corresponds to two-dimensional space. Much attention in this chapter has already been devoted to planar distance, and the Euclidean metric in particular. Further, in Chapter 3 we also discussed **rectilinear distance**, also a planar distance. However, there are other conceivable paths of travel. If we must travel in a vehicle, as an example, then our movement will more than likely be confined to the road network. This will not necessarily conform to either Euclidean (e.g., straight line) or rectilinear (e.g., east-west or north-south movement) paths of travel between two locations. Thus, on a network, distance must be computed between locations in

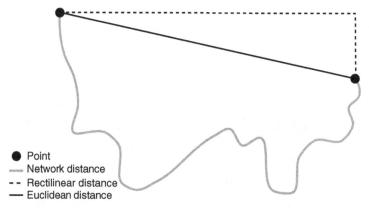

Figure 6.4   Depiction of Euclidean, rectilinear, and network distances.

order to ensure complete accuracy (often as shortest path distance). Of course a street network is also needed for distance assessment between locations. These three planar distances are illustrated in Figure 6.4.

What about cases where no street network is available for evaluation, or when travel is not confined to the street network? In these cases, distance metrics like Euclidean and rectilinear are needed, though there are cases where they do actually mimic street networks. There is another, more generalized distance metric as well, the so-called l_p metric for calculating distance between two locations (x_1, y_1) and (x_2, y_2):

$$\left(|x_1 - x_2|^p + |y_1 - y_2|^p\right)^{1/p} \tag{6.17}$$

This is considered more general because rectilinear and Euclidean distance measures are special cases. Specifically, rectilinear results when $p = 1$, $(|x_1 - x_2|^1 + |y_1 - y_2|^1)^{1/1} = |x_1 - x_2| + |y_1 - y_2|$, and Euclidean is defined when $p = 2$, $(|x_1 - x_2|^2 + |y_1 - y_2|^2)^{1/2} = ((x_1 - x_2)^2 + (y_1 - y_2)^2)^{1/2}$.

In summary, this section has highlighted that it is often necessary to project the three-dimensional Earth into two dimensions, but doing so leads to a distortion of shape or area. No projection can preserve both shape and area. Additionally, this section has reviewed different distance measures, depending on whether a sphere is used (three-dimensional) or a coordinate system (two-dimensional). For location analysis, these insights are important, but so too are the implications of their use in different contexts.

6.4   MODELING APPLICATION

Assume that a grocery chain has a number of stores in a city and would like to locate a warehouse to serve the stores. This warehouse will allow the

TABLE 6.1   Demand located at points

Point	x-coordinate	y-coordinate	Demand
1	10	5	5
2	20	7	2
3	15	12	1
4	30	13	5
5	23	17	7
6	5	17	9
7	12	22	6
8	17	25	3

chain to achieve greater efficiency in the distribution of goods to the stores, as this warehouse will also allow purchases from suppliers to be consolidated and centralized, enabling the chain to receive discounted pricing. The eight store locations are given in Table 6.1 as points in two-dimensional space, and are shown in Figure 6.5. The demand reported in Table 6.1 for each store represents shipments per week anticipated from the warehouse. The problem is to identify the best location for this warehouse. Any location in the region is possible, and efficiency is to be measured as a function of Euclidean distance travel.

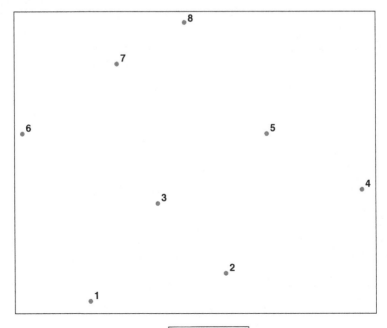

Figure 6.5   Demand points in two-dimensional space.

6.4.1 Solution Using Commercial Software

It is possible to solve this Weber problem using some commercial optimization software packages. Using the information provided in Table 6.1, the algebraic statement of this problem, (6.2), is the following:

$$
\begin{aligned}
Minimize \quad & 5((X - 10)^2 + (Y - 5)^2)^{0.5} + 2((X - 20)^2 + (Y - 7)^2)^{0.5} \\
& + ((X - 15)^2 + (Y - 12)^2)^{0.5} + 5((X - 30)^2 + (Y - 13)^2)^{0.5} \\
& + 7((X - 23)^2 + (Y - 17)^2)^{0.5} + 9((X - 5)^2 + (Y - 17)^2)^{0.5} \\
& + 6((X - 12)^2 + (Y - 22)^2)^{0.5} + 3((X - 17)^2 + (Y - 25)^2)^{0.5}
\end{aligned}
$$

There are two decision variables in this model, X and Y, which correspond to the location coordinates of the warehouse to be sited, (X, Y). This objective is nonlinear because the decision variables are members of functions raised to a power.

Figure 6.6 gives the LINGO specification of this optimization model (doing this requires a license for the nonlinear solver). One note regarding this specification is the use of XX and YY for the decision variables. This was done because LINGO is not case sensitive, so a completely different variable name was needed to avoid confusion with the x-coordinate and y-coordinate parameters used to specify demand points.

Solving this problem in LINGO finds that the warehouse should be located at (14.73769, 16.77792), which results in an objective value or total weighted distance of 375.5624. This required 10 iterations to solve in LINGO. The solution report notes that this is a local optima, but since this problem is convex, we know that this local minima is the global minima. The optimal facility location for the Weber problem is shown in Figure 6.7.

```
! Weber Problem;

Sets:
 Points /1..8 /: x,y,a;
EndSets

Data:
 x = 10, 20, 15, 30, 23, 5, 12, 17;
 y = 5, 7, 12, 13, 17, 17, 22, 25;
 a = 5, 2, 1, 5, 7, 9, 6, 3;
EndData

Min = @Sum(points(i): a(i)*((XX-x(i))^2 + (YY-y(i))^2)^0.5 );

End
```

Figure 6.6 Weber problem structured in LINGO.

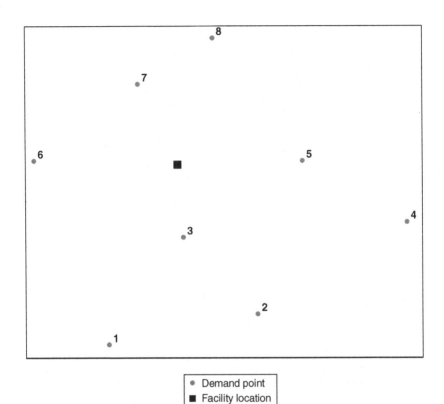

Figure 6.7   Optimal facility location.

6.4.2   Iterative Solution

As mentioned previously, the Weber problem can also be solved optimally using the Weiszfeld algorithm. In fact, the Weiszfeld algorithm is the most commonly used approach for solving this problem. In order to illustrate the application of the Weiszfeld algorithm to the siting of our warehouse, it is now applied to the demand information summarized in Table 6.1. The initial estimate of the facility location is (5, 5).

A summary of the first 20 iterations of the algorithm is given in Table 6.2. The initial estimate of (5, 5) results in a weighted distance of 638.4293292. The first iteration then improves to (12.57421713, 12.96593909), with a weighted distance of 398.9156435. By the twentieth iteration, the facility location is at (14.73767539, 16.7779226), having a weighted distance of 375.5624113. In terms of the objective value, convergence could be declared after nine iterations (tolerance of 0.0001); however, the algorithm was continued to show its convergence toward the optimal location of (14.73769, 16.77792).

TABLE 6.2   First 10 iterations of the Weiszfeld algorithm

Iteration	X	Y	Objective
0	5	5	638.4293292
1	12.57421713	12.96593909	398.9156435
2	13.85614749	15.2356567	379.4804752
3	14.36206314	16.15595835	376.2291958
4	14.57491767	16.53475045	375.6711215
5	14.6652709	16.68533972	375.5798528
6	14.70422452	16.74374364	375.5652432
7	14.72151531	16.76589479	375.5628932
8	14.7294988	16.77405754	375.5625017
9	14.73335629	16.77692693	375.5624312
10	14.73530952	16.77784768	375.5624165
11	14.73634274	16.77808376	375.5624129
12	14.73691013	16.77810018	375.5624118
13	14.73723109	16.77806029	375.5624115
14	14.73741674	16.77801648	375.5624113
15	14.73752583	16.77798219	375.5624113
16	14.73759065	16.77795835	375.5624113
17	14.73762945	16.77794268	375.5624113
18	14.73765279	16.7779327	375.5624113
19	14.73766687	16.77792646	375.5624113
20	14.73767539	16.7779226	375.5624113

6.5   ADVANCED TOPICS

It should be obvious by now that there are many different types of single-facility location problems, like the one-center problem, single-facility maximum coverage. Although not covered in this chapter, we will see that they are special cases of the multifacility problems reviewed later in the text. It is probably fair to say that the Weber problem, where Euclidean distance travel is considered, has been the subject of much interest and application for various reasons. Other single-facility location variants, however, can be important and applicable, depending on the siting context. Thus, one advanced topic is examining variants of single-facility location in the plane. A second advanced topic is the fallacy of the centroid. The centroid is probably the most commonly suggested model for locating a point. Industrial location texts even suggest it as an appropriate siting technique. In fact, many consider the Weber problem and the centroid problem to be essentially equivalent! But this is patently false, and is placed into perspective later in this section. A third advanced topic is the Weber problem on a sphere. A final advanced topic is an extension of the Weber problem that accounts for continuously distributed demand.

6.5.1 Variants of Planar Single Facility Location

There are, in fact, many variants of single-facility location in two-dimensional space, so the Weber problem relying on Euclidean distance travel is not the only way that spatial proximity can be accounted for. In this section, we limit our discussion to only two such variants given space limitations, though there are many more. One variant we have already discussed is where travel is made according to rectilinear movement (see Figure 6.4). Formally, the single facility location problem with rectilinear distance travel is:

$$Minimize \quad \sum_{i=1}^{n} a_i \left(|X - x_i| + |Y - y_i|\right) \qquad (6.18)$$

Given that attention was given to this problem in Chapter 3, our discussion here will be brief. This function is nonlinear due to the absolute value function in (6.18). As with the nonlinear Weber problem, it is also possible to solve this problem directly as a nonlinear function using commercial optimization software such as LINGO. However, as shown in Chapter 3, it is also possible to reformulate the problem using only linear functions. Further, specialized approaches do exist for solving this problem optimally.

Another problem variant we will discuss is limiting potential facility sites to discrete locations. That is, what if after suitability analysis we find that only a finite number of discrete locations are acceptable for siting the facility? How does our single facility location problem change? To answer this question, we first need to define some additional notation:

$j =$ index of potential facility sites $(j = 1, 2, 3, \ldots, m)$

$d_{ij} =$ distance between demand i and potential facility site j

$F_j = \sum_{i=1}^{n} a_i d_{ij}$, the weighted distance associated with locating at site j

As defined, the distance measure can be any metric desired, Euclidean, rectilinear, network, and so on. This single-point location problem can then be structured as the following optimization model:

$$\underset{j}{Min} \; F_j \qquad (6.19)$$

Since the number of sites is finite, the weighted distance of each site j serving all demand can be computed in advance, which is F_j. By enumeration, we can then select the site j with the lowest F_j value. This enumeration task is not very burdensome, as there are only m sites to evaluate. This is one case in location modeling where enumeration is both expedient and appropriate.

6.5.2 Fallacy of the Centroid

It may be apparent that the above section did not include any mention of single-facility location using the centroid. When looking for a centrally located point in space, many people suggest, "Why not site at the centroid?" Of course this seems like a reasonable approach. But the important question to ask is, What is the underlying problem for which the centroid is the solution? The centroid, $(\bar{X}, \bar{Y})$, is actually the solution to the following optimization problem:

$$\text{Minimize} \quad \sum_{i=1}^{n} a_i \left[\left((\bar{X} - x_i)^2 + (\bar{Y} - y_i)^2 \right)^{1/2} \right]^2 \tag{6.20}$$

Given our previous discussion of Euclidean distance and the Weber problem, it is obvious that (6.20) minimizes the weighted Euclidean distance squared function. This simplifies to the following:

$$\text{Minimize} \quad \sum_{i=1}^{n} a_i \left((\bar{X} - x_i)^2 + (\bar{Y} - y_i)^2 \right) \tag{6.21}$$

As was done previously for the Weber problem, it is possible to apply calculus to this function, taking derivatives with respect to the unknown variables $\bar{X}$ and $\bar{Y}$ and solving for the extremum. If this is done, it turns out that the optimal solution to (6.20), and (6.21) is

$$(\bar{X}, \bar{Y}) = \left(\frac{\sum_{i=1}^{n} a_i x_i}{\sum_{i=1}^{n} a_i}, \frac{\sum_{i=1}^{n} a_i y_i}{\sum_{i=1}^{n} a_i} \right) \tag{6.22}$$

In contrast to the derivative of the Weber point, it is possible to isolate the unknown variables in this case in order to specify a closed-form solution to (6.20). Thus, the centroid is not mathematically messy, and is somewhat convenient from an analytical perspective. The **fallacy of the centroid** is that it does not minimize weighted distance, but, rather, minimizes "weighted distance-squared."

One need only compare the derivatives of the two different models to see this—for example, (6.22) and (6.8). It should not be a surprise that the optimal location to each problem is in fact different. That is, the centroid is not an optimal point for a problem involving the minimization of weighted distance, (6.2). The more critical question is, what is the spatial interpretation of distance-squared, and is this something that should be optimized? For geographical analysis, there is no meaningful interpretation of distance-squared, so the significance of the centroid is questionable.

6.5.3 Location on a Sphere

In this chapter we have gone to some effort to highlight the fact that a two-dimensional coordinate system cannot accurately depict the three-dimensional surface of the earth, except when the region of interest is somewhat small. If we are interested in siting a facility to serve a large region, perhaps multiple states or countries, then the use of the Weber problem will be problematic due to projection issues (see section 6.3). Fortunately, it is possible to define the Weber problem on the sphere as follows:

$$\textit{Minimize} \quad \sum_{i=1}^{n} a_i \left[r \arccos \left(\sin \phi \sin \phi_i + \cos \phi \cos \phi_i \cos (\lambda - \lambda_i) \right) \right]$$

$$(6.23)$$

where

$$r = \text{assumed radius of Earth}$$
$$i = \text{index of demand points } (i = 1, 2, 3, \ldots, n)$$
$$a_i = \text{demand at point } i$$
$$(\phi_i, \lambda_i) = \text{latitude and longitude of demand point } i$$
$$(\phi, \lambda) = \text{location to site facility}$$

This unconstrained model, (6.23), involves finding the optimal facility location (ϕ, λ) on the earth's surface that minimizes the sum of weighted great circle arc distances to the facility. Algorithms for solving this specialized problem have been developed, but are not reviewed here due to space limitations.

6.5.4 Continuously Distributed Demand

Up to this point in the chapter, demand has been assumed to be discrete, existing only a points in space. In looking across a city, however, it is possible to think of demand as a smooth surface, rather than discrete points of demand. As an example, Figure 6.8 depicts a continuous surface for a small geographical area representing hourly demand for coffee. This surface begins at the perimeter of the area at zero and reaches a peak demand of 3 per unit area toward the center of the region. The Weber problem with continuously

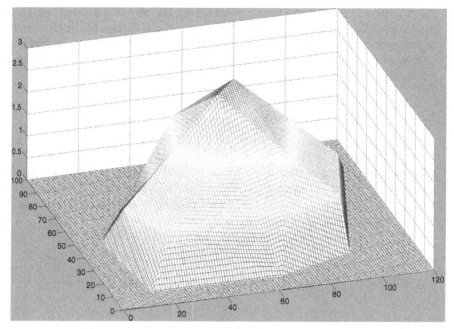

Figure 6.8 Continuously distributed demand surface.

distributed demand can be defined as a function of the facility located at point (X, Y):

$$Minimize \int_s^t \int_u^v g(x, y)\, d(x, y, X, Y)\, dx\, dy \qquad (6.24)$$

where

$$g(x, y) = \text{function of demand at point } (x, y)$$
$$d(x, y, X, Y) = ((X - x)^2 + (Y - y)^2)^{1/2}$$
$$s, t, u, \text{ and } v \text{ define boundary positions of the region}$$

This is a model that cannot be solved analytically; however, it is possible to approach it using an iterative process or a method of enumeration. For example, we can evaluate (6.24) at numerous locations across the region. If we do this, we can plot the three-dimensional surface of (6.24) for various locations, (x, y). The result is a cost surface, or weighted distance surface, and is shown in Figure 6.9 using the demand surface given in Figure 6.8. The cost or objective surface is somewhat bowl-shaped, with the lowest cost

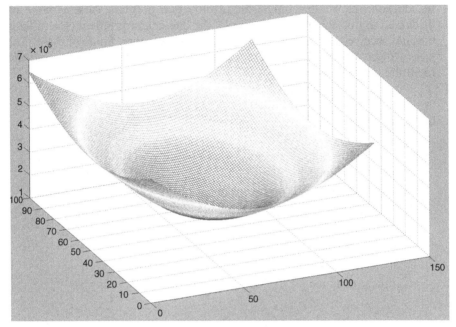

Figure 6.9   Cost surface.

or best locations tending toward the center and the higher costs toward the periphery. We can then identify the best location as the lowest point on surface with respect to the z-axis.

For locating a single facility on a plane, using either continuously distributed demand or discrete demand points, it is relatively easy to characterize the entire cost surface, as done in Figure 6.9, instead of identifying only the optimal point. This allows a planner or decision maker to understand the impact of moving away from the point considered to be optimal.

6.6   SUMMARY

This chapter has introduced the problem of locating a single facility, where the facility is point-based. There are many types of point-based facilities, including break-of-bulk distribution centers and solid-waste incinerators. Considerable attention was given to the single-facility location problem, assuming Euclidean distance travel in two-dimensional space (the Weber problem). For many reasons, this problem has been widely utilized to support location decision making. This chapter also discussed several variants of the single-facility location problem, including the use of different distance measures, siting on a three-dimensional surface, and representing demand as a continuous surface.

In addition, many other single-facility location problem variants were not discussed in this chapter. For example, the one-center problem (see problem 6.8) has received considerable attention in the literature. Some of these problems will be discussed later in this text within the context of siting multiple facilities simultaneously.

6.7   TERMS

map projection
Euclidean distance
continuous space *vs.* discrete space
weber problem
Weiszfeld algorithm
coordinate system
great circle distance
rectilinear distance

6.8   REFERENCES

Weber, A. 1909. *Uber den standort der Industrien* (Tubingen). Translated by C.J. Friedrich as *Theory of the Location of Industries* (Chicago: University of Chicago Press, 1929).

Weiszfeld, E.V. 1937. Sur le point pour lequal la somme des distances de n points donnes est minmum. *The Tohoku Mathematical Journal* 4:335–386.

Wesolowsky, G. 1993. The Weber problem: History and procedures. *Location Science* 1:5–24.

6.9   EXERCISES

6.1. Suppose that you have been asked to locate a bus transit garage that will be the location for parking busses overnight, cleaning busses after use, performing mechanical maintenance, and routine inspection. Buses are used along predefined routes. When they are finished, they will have to return to the transit garage. Describe why this is a central facility location problem with discrete demand points.

6.2. The city of Trainopolis has a railroad that cuts right through the city. Unfortunately, all of the crossings are at grade. So whenever a train passes through town, traffic across the tracks is completely blocked for 15 minutes or more. The city wishes to build an overpass, so that there will always be an available route to get to the hospital for the side of town that has no hospital. Suggest a strategy to locate the overpass. Formulate a model to support this strategy.

6.3. The public administrator of Podunk is interested in locating a recycling facility. Garbage collection vehicles will travel to and from their collection areas and the recycling facility. Recyclables will be separated into paper and cardboard, aluminum, glass, yard wastes, and other items. Paper and cardboard will be transported to a paper company for recycling. The same will happen for aluminum and glass wastes. The city will compost the yard waste, at the city's own facility outside of town. All other waste will be transported to a sanitary landfill. Formulate a model for the location of a recycling center in order to minimize appropriate transportation costs. Define all notations used and define the purpose of each term of the model. Use the rectilinear distance metric.

6.4. The classic Weber problem is not sensitive to varying site costs. Suppose that there is one main road in the area and one can site a facility anywhere along the road at a cost of H. Further assume that site costs decrease as a linear function of the distance from the road (slope of $-\beta$). Formulate a Weber model with site costs, such that the objective is to find the location that minimizes the present value of site and transportation costs. Define all notation used.

6.5. Compute the great circle arc distance between Bismarck, North Dakota, and Galveston, Texas, using the following information. Also compute the Euclidean distance given the Mercator coordinates. Compare the two distance values and calculate the percentage of error involved.

City	x, y (miles)	Latitude, Longitude (decimal degrees)
Bismarck, ND	−6966, 2112	N46.81, W100.8
Galveston, TX	−6554, 3654	N29.27, W94.87

6.6. For the following 3 demand locations, solve for three iterations of the Weiszfeld algorithm, starting at the point 15, 15.

Demand	X	Y	Weight
1	0	0	5
2	30	0	3
3	0	40	4

6.7. The grocery chain discussed in section 6.4, with information summarized in Table 6.1, realizes that rectilinear distances may be more appropriate given the orientation of its street network. Specify and solve this variant in LINGO. How does the facility location change, compared to the use of Euclidean distance?

6.8. A town administrator is interested in locating a facility that is central to everyone. Although weighted distance is important, the administrator has expressed interest in minimizing the distance to the furthest demand point in the town. Since the town is arranged along a grid network of roads, the administrator is happy with using the rectilinear distance measure. Formulate a model to find the optimal location of the facility. Note that this type of problem is called a *center* problem, and the administrator is interested in finding the one-center location using rectilinear distance measure.

6.9. There are two large retail stores that are to be served by a warehouse. The first store needs to be supplied by 20 truck trips a month (approximately one truck load each weekday of the month) and the second by 10 truck trips a month (or about one truck load every other workday of the month). The first store is located at milepost 10 along a straight highway and the second store is located at milepost 30. Find the Weber point. Does this location differ from the centroid? What is the difference between these two solutions in terms of weighted distance?

CHAPTER 7

LINE-BASED LOCATION

7.0 INTRODUCTION

The previous chapter introduced the notion of a single point-based facility, where the task was to site a facility in order to optimize a stated efficiency measure, such as maximizing access or minimizing cost. Of course, the facility may not be point-based in many cases, but instead could be line-1 or area-based. This chapter will focus on line-based single-facility location, and area-based facilities will be addressed in Chapter 8. Examples of a line-based facility include a bus transit route, a rail line, a highway or street, a bike path, a hiking trail, a wildlife corridor, a canal, a package delivery route, or an electricity transmission line, among others. Thus, the line-based facility might be a path, route, passageway, or corridor. It is common to know in advance a beginning location or an ending location for the facility, or even both the beginning and ending locations. In the siting or design of the line-based facility, there are a host of criteria that might impact what the best shape and direction should be, including cost/time of movement along the facility, impact on the environment, access issues, danger to people, and so on. We can define this problem within two general contexts: (1) routing along an existing network, and (2) routing across a continuous landscape. We will begin this chapter by analyzing the problem within the context of an existing network. In the GIScience section, we examine the requirements of siting in continuous space, discussing the process of moving from a raster layer to a discrete network representation. In the advanced topics section, we discuss how to account for path width in a continuous space domain, as well as a specially constrained form of the shortest path problem.

7.1   MOTIVATION AND PROBLEM DEFINITION

As already suggested, a line-based facility could represent a **path** or a **corridor**. If the facility is a path, this might be a route along a road network for laying a fiber-optic cable. Another example of a path could be the route taken by a business in delivering goods to customers. If the facility is a corridor, this might be a route for a pipeline to deliver fuel from a refinery to a metropolitan area. Another example is a wildlife corridor, where land is protected in order to provide a natural connection on the landscape for animals to migrate and move between two larger areas of habitat. Whether a path or a corridor, what we have is a line-based facility forming a passageway between two otherwise separated locations. This could be along a street/road network or simply across the surface of the earth.

The problem of locating a line-based facility is as old as mankind, as even hunters and gathers had to develop trails between their encampments, with an attempt to make them as short as possible while circumnavigating obstacles such as cliffs and fast-moving rivers. The problem is much the same today, except that the landscape contains many new types of obstacles, including restricted zoning, incompatible land uses, critical habitat, and varying costs. Locating a line-based facility can be an involved process, requiring an environmental impact study, significant public review, resolution of contention among different interest groups, estimating user demand, reliability assessment, and so on. It has even been described as a wicked planning problem in some contexts. As an example, in southern California there are plans to extend a tollway (highway 241) in Orange County. The Foothill/Eastern Transportation Corridor Agency chose a route (out of 6 identified alternatives) that bisects a park and cuts across the habitat of 10 endangered species. This plan was immediately met with opposition from a number of public interest groups, threatening to sue and tie up the proposed plan in court for years. In review, the California Coastal Commission refused to give approval for the project. This example underscores the importance of being able to identify the best and most suitable routing alternatives from which to make a choice. A less contentious example is a bus route established by a local transit agency. Given the desire to reduce congestion and other negative externalities, public transit exists to get people into and out of major destination areas within an urban region, like the central business district, efficiently. Routes serving these destinations need to be structured so that they are well used and profitable. Thus, at issue is what streets the route should take and where access stops should be located, in addition to decisions regarding vehicle type, scheduling, and safety considerations.

The problem stemming from these examples is to locate a single line-based facility. The facility in one of the previous examples was a highway, so issues to be addressed would include costs to acquire land and build the infrastructure, impacts on the environment, and public acceptance. For transit planning, there is a need for route efficiency as well as sufficient ridership. A general single-facility location problem can therefore be stated as follows:

Site a line-based facility as efficiently as possible in order to connect two locations.

Again, this problem could involve locating a path, route, or corridor. Further, we have couched the problem in terms of connecting two areas, although it could be more generalized. We now move on to formalizing these concepts and the basic problem.

7.2 MATHEMATICAL REPRESENTATION

In line-based facility location, the emphasis might be on either a path or a corridor. In a technical sense, a path and a corridor can be viewed as representing different contexts from the perspective that a path suggests, in many instances, the siting of the facility on an existing network. Often, this network is composed of street/road segments and intersections. In contrast, a corridor is typically less confined and more open in terms of being able to be routed almost anywhere on the landscape in theory. Perhaps a good characterization would be that a path-oriented situation is likely discrete (restricted to a defined network), whereas a corridor application is likely continuous (capable of being directed through any part of a region).

Given this context, we begin by reviewing the problem of locating a path along a discrete **network** between an origin (or starting point) and a destination (or ending point). Therefore, it is assumed that we have an existing network through which a path, or line-based facility, is needed. Later in the chapter we return to the corridor context, where the key issue is how to create a representative network and model the continuous space problem using a discrete network. Thus, conventional methods for modeling path and corridor location both involve a network. Networks, in general, comprise a set of nodes and a set of arcs. For example, nodes may represent towns of a state and arcs represent major highway connections between towns. On a different scale, nodes could represent every street intersection in a city where the arcs are the connecting street segments. For a network, each arc connects two nodes and can be either directed or undirected, meaning that travel can go either way on an arc (undirected) or only one way (directed). An example of an undirected network is shown in Figure 7.1. There are six nodes (labeled A through F) and nine arcs (labeled 1 through 9). Arcs in the network generally have attributes, as is shown in Table 7.1 for this network. Nodes, too, can

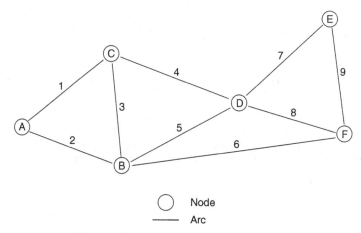

Figure 7.1   Network of nodes and arcs.

have attributes, as indicated in Table 7.2 for this network. From a spatial perspective, network topology is an important feature. In particular, we want to know whether it is possible to get from one node to another, and what path(s) would be involved in such travel. One data structure that is often used in network analysis is a node-arc incidence list, and is summarized for this network in Table 7.3.

With the network, and associated information corresponding to features of this network, it is now possible to structure the problem of line-based facility location in mathematical terms.

7.2.1 Shortest-Path Model

Efficiency is a major resonating need in line-based facility location. As an example, the path desired might be the one that incurs the least time in

TABLE 7.1   Arc attributes

Arc	Cost	Capacity
1	5	30
2	6	30
3	4	8
4	5	7
5	3	12
6	9	14
7	2	11
8	5	7
9	2	22

TABLE 7.2 Node attributes

Nodes	Population	Amenities
A	24	High
B	12	Low
C	19	Medium
D	6	Low
E	17	Low
F	39	High

traveling from one specified location to another. It may be, as another example, that one seeks the least-cost corridor connecting two locations. In either case, the objective is often to find a least-cost route, though deriving cost estimates might be complex and somewhat contentious in certain circumstances. Given this, it is possible to structure the location of a line-based facility as a **shortest-path problem**.

Consider the following notation:

i = index of nodes in the network (j and k also used to index nodes)
Ω_i = set of nodes connected directly to node i by an arc (i, j)
d_{ij} = length/cost of arc (i, j)
s = node corresponding to origin of path
t = node corresponding to terminal point of path

$$X_{ij} = \begin{cases} 1 & \text{if path traverses arc } (i, j) \\ 0 & \text{otherwise.} \end{cases}$$

A few comments about some of the introduced notation is in order. First, s and t specify the beginning and ending locations, respectively, of the line-based facility to be identified. Second, information about which nodes are

TABLE 7.3 Node-arc incidence list

Nodes	Arcs
A	1, 2
B	2, 3, 5, 6
C	1, 3, 4
D	4, 5, 7, 8
E	7, 9
F	6, 8, 9

directly connected to a given node i is captured in the set Ω_i. This is precisely the information inferred from network topology, and happens to be summarized in Table 7.3 for the network shown in Figure 7.1, as an example. Finally, decisions in this case correspond to whether or not each individual arc is to be included on the path.

Given decisions about arcs, X_{ij}, and derived costs for including an arc on a path, d_{ij}, a measure of route efficiency is the sum of the costs for arcs chosen for the path as follows:

$$\sum_i \sum_{j \in \Omega_i} d_{ij} X_{ij} \tag{7.1}$$

Since the decision variables are either 0 or 1 in value, this sum is the cost for only those arcs that have been chosen for the path, and is what we would like to minimize. There are a number of important conditions that need to be maintained as well. The first is that the path must begin and end at specified locations s and t, respectively. If we consider s, then we want the path to originate at node s, so an arc beginning with node s must be selected. This is accomplished mathematically in the following way:

$$\sum_{j \in \Omega_s} X_{sj} = 1 \tag{7.2}$$

Thus, exactly one of the arcs leading away from node s is to be selected. A similar type of function can be structured for the path ending at node t. A final condition for ensuring path structure is to maintain connectivity between selected arcs. That is, any node along the path, other than s or t, must have exactly one incoming arc and one outgoing arc selected. This is often referred to as *conservation of flow*. Alternatively, nodes not along the path must have no incoming arc and no outgoing arc selected. This can be stipulated mathematically for a given node k as

$$\sum_{i \in \Omega_k} X_{ik} - \sum_{j \in \Omega_k} X_{kj} = 0 \tag{7.3}$$

Given these notation and functional specifications, the shortest path problem can be summarized as follows:

$$\textit{Minimize} \sum_i \sum_{j \in \Omega_i} d_{ij} X_{ij} \tag{7.4}$$

Subject to:

$$\sum_{j \in \Omega_s} X_{sj} = 1 \tag{7.5}$$

$$\sum_{i \in \Omega_t} X_{it} = 1 \tag{7.6}$$

$$\sum_{i \in \Omega_k} X_{ik} - \sum_{j \in \Omega_k} X_{kj} = 0 \quad \forall k \neq s, t \tag{7.7}$$

$$X_{ij} = \{0 \ 1\} \quad \forall (i, j) \tag{7.8}$$

The objective, (7.4), minimizes the total cost of arcs chosen for the path. Constraint (7.5) establishes that one arc incident to the origin node s must be chosen, thus connecting the path to the point of origin. Constraint (7.6) maintains that one arc ending at the destination node t is selected. Constraint (7.7) ensures that if an arc is chosen that leads to node k, then an arc will be chosen that leads away from node k. It also ensures that if no arc is chosen leading to node k, then no arc can be chosen leading away from node k. Finally, integer restrictions are imposed in constraint (7.8).

This model is an integer-linear program, and was first suggested by Dantzig (1957). It seeks to find the path or route of least cost, and has been the subject of continued research.

7.2.2 Exact Solution Approach

The shortest-path problem has been the subject of considerable research over the last five decades, given its broad and diverse applicability. In fact, most of the focus has been devoted to the development of specialized algorithms for optimally solving the shortest path problem on a network, and many approaches exist. This effectively eliminates the need to solve the problem using commercial linear programming software such as LINGO. One of the more prominent approaches was developed by Dijkstra (1959).

Dijkstra's algorithm is based upon the assumption that all arc costs are non-negative in value. However, a specialized algorithm has been designed for the case when some arc costs are negative (Ford 1956). In path and corridor location, we can reasonably assume that each arc has a cost or impact value that is greater than zero, so we can rely on the shortest-path algorithm of Dijkstra. To describe the algorithm, consider the following notation:

T = set of nodes that are candidates for the "next closest node" to the origin

$\hat{D}(k)$ = computed distance to node k from the origin

$P(k)$ = predecessor node in the path from s to k

u = set of nodes that have not been placed into set T

The **Dijkstra algorithm** starts at the origin node, s, and seeks to identify nodes in order of increasing distance from the origin. At any point during the algorithm, the candidates for the "next closest node" to the origin are listed in set T, and the distances to those nodes are given as $\hat{D}(.)$. The *Dijkstra shortest-path algorithm* consists of the following steps:

Step 0: Identify beginning node s and ending node t. Initialize all nodes as "unlabeled by placing them into set u." Let $\hat{D}(s) = 0$, $T=\{s\}$ and $u = u - \{s\}$

Step 1: Select the node in the T with the smallest value $D(.)$. Let this be called node k. Set $T = T - \{k\}$ and mark node k as labeled. If $k = s$ then set $P(k) =$ "stop."

Step 2: For each arc(k, j):

(a)   If $j \in T$ and $\hat{D}(k) + d_{kj} \leq \hat{D}(j)$, then let $\hat{D}(j) = \hat{D}(k) + d_{kj}$ and $P(j) = k$.

(b)   If $j \notin T$ and $j \in u$, then let $\hat{D}(j) = \hat{D}(k) + d_{kj}$, $P(j) = k$, $T = T + \{j\}$ and $u = u - \{j\}$

Step 3: If node t has been labeled, the shortest path to t has been found with distance $\hat{D}(t)$. Otherwise go to step 4.

Step 4: If $T = \{\}$, stop, as network is not fully connected. Otherwise, go to step 1.

The Dijkstra algorithm is known as a *labeling approach* and can be easily programmed to solve problems on large networks. The algorithm as described also allows us to identify the shortest path, once node t has been labeled. This is accomplished through the use of the labels $P(.)$. Specifically, the label $P(t)$ will indicate the preceding node to node t in the path. Suppose that $P(t) = B$, indicating that node B is the node in the path just before node t is reached. We can backtrack from node B by going to node $P(B)$. By recursively backtracking nodes in the path, we will eventually reach the origin where $P(s) =$ "stop."

In summary, this section has focused on the shortest-path problem assuming a network exists. This is essentially a discrete space problem. This problem can be solved by linear programming or by a specialized algorithm, and enables us to identify a line-based facility, connecting one location to another, that is the most efficient.

7.3   GISCIENCE

Now we turn our attention to the case where the line-based facility is a corridor, to be routed potentially anywhere on the landscape. As such, corridor routing reflects a continuous space siting problem. Often, the approach taken is to transform the problem from a field view of geographic space to a discrete, network representation. Thus, considerable work involves defining the network and deriving attributes associated with the network. GIS and associated functionality is essential in this process.

The problem of locating a corridor is typically broken down into five components of analysis:

1. Decide what type of data is the most meaningful in terms of routing a corridor. Collect these data for the area of analysis.
2. Derive suitability layer(s), indicating the relative compatibility of routing a corridor through each location.
3. Define a network of possible transitions across the landscape, where the costs of the network arcs are related to the suitability of the area the arcs traverse.
4. Utilize a shortest-path algorithm, or other appropriate model, to identify the route of least impact and/or cost.
5. Analyze possible route alternatives.

In the remainder of this section, these components of analysis will be described in more detail, but will largely focus on defining the network (component 3). The first component involves the collection of appropriate data to support the routing of a corridor. Possible factors influencing corridor location include:

- Soils type
- Slope
- Land use type—residential, commercial, industrial, farmland, open space, parks, etc.
- Land cover—vegetation type, presence of structures, etc.
- Presence of historical elements
- Biological elements—type of habitat, species presence, endangered or threatened species, sensitive habitat, etc.
- Transportation elements—existing roads, pipelines, transmission lines, etc.
- Land ownership

It is important to collect data that can be used to estimate the suitability or compatibility of devoting a specific piece of land for the purpose of supporting a corridor, as well as costs of using that land. The second component corresponds to the use of suitability analysis, the topic of Chapter 5. The aim is to estimate for cell i a compatibility measure, z_i', and a construction/cost impact, z_i''. These two competing measures can then be weighted and combined to form a composite suitability value s_i for cell i, where $s_i = w_1 z_i' + w_2 z_i''$ (w_1 and w_2 are the weights for compatibility and cost, respectively). This should be done such that a high suitability score represents high impact/cost, and a low score represents a low impact/cost. The reason for this is to make the shortest path problem contextually meaningful.

7.3.1 Defining the Network

Few have approached the problem of delineating a path across the land-scape using GIS without first deciding on an appropriate data model (i.e., field vs. object). Virtually everyone who has worked on a corridor location problem starts with a raster data structure, although some have used tri-angular and hexagonal tessellations. This is a logical choice, as some data usually exist as a raster layer or image. Second, digital elevation models are also used, and are typically available as a raster layer. The third reason is that the raster format is a convenient data structure for assessing suitabil-ity (see Chapter 5), facilitating the evaluation of aligning a route across a given cell.

Given an underlying raster representation of space, it is possible to derive associated nodes and corresponding arcs of travel. As an example, consider the raster of four rows and four columns shown in Figure 7.2. Illustrated is a network for this raster layer, where each node coincides with each raster

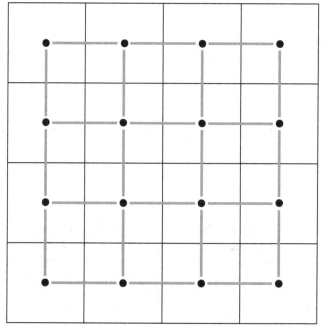

Figure 7.2 Orthogonal network overlaid on a raster layer.

cell. Further, arcs connect adjacent cells in the east-west and north-south directions. This is called an *orthogonal network* because all arcs are either parallel or perpendicular in direction.

The basic idea is that a path will go from cell center to cell center. We can define the "length" of an arc as a function of the impact or suitability values of the cells that are associated with the arc:

$$t_{i,j} = \frac{s_i + s_j}{2} \tag{7.9}$$

where $t_{i,j}$ is a measure of suitability and/or cost to traverse from cell i to neighboring cell j. Essentially, this is the average composite suitability value of the two cells incident to arc (i, j). As an example, Figure 7.3 shows a path through this network, beginning from cell 14 and ending at cell 8. The cost of this path can be derived arc by arc based on (7.9), as follows:

$$t_{14,15} + t_{15,11} + t_{11,7} + t_{7,8} = \frac{1}{2}(s_{14} + s_{15})$$

$$+ \frac{1}{2}(s_{15} + s_{11}) + \frac{1}{2}(s_{11} + s_7) + \frac{1}{2}(s_7 + s_8) \tag{7.10}$$

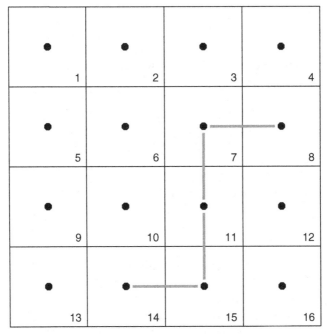

Figure 7.3 Path through an orthogonal network.

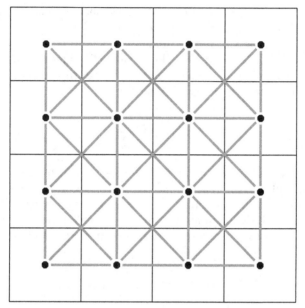

Figure 7.4   Network of orthogonal and diagonal arcs.

This is equivalent, after simplification, to

$$\frac{1}{2}s_{14} + s_{15} + s_{11} + s_7 + \frac{1}{2}s_8 \tag{7.11}$$

Thus, the length of this path is essentially one half of the suitability score of the origin cell, plus one half of the suitability score of the destination cell, plus the suitability scores of all cells traversed in between along the path.

It should be apparent, however, that the orthogonal network is very restrictive. It may be desirable to move in a more direct trajectory between the origin and destination. For example, Figure 7.4 depicts a network that includes orthogonal and diagonal arcs. An issue that arises is how to treat varying lengths of arcs.[1] A logical approach is to explicitly account for distance. Thus, the impact of an arc can be estimated in terms of cost and distance as follows:

$$t_{i,j} = d^i_{i,j}s_i + d^j_{i,j}s_j \tag{7.12}$$

where $d^i_{i,j}$ is the distance of the arc connecting cells i and j falling within cell i.

---

[1] A diagonal arc would have a length of $\sqrt{2}$ (or 1.4142) in a unit cell. So, some approximations assume $t_{i,j} = 1.4142^{(s_i + s_j)}/2$, which is the convention used in ArcGIS for computing the diagonal cost of an arc.

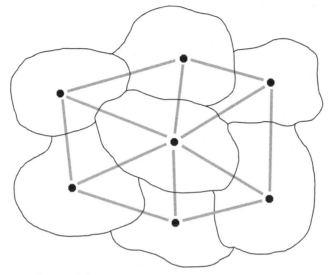

Figure 7.5   Network structure for a polygon layer.

Worth mentioning is that the underlying spatial representation need not be a raster in order to create an associated network structure. Consider the polygons shown in Figure 7.5. A node is identified for each polygon and adjacent polygons are connected by an arc. Costs can be estimated using (7.12), as done for a raster layer. However, there could be cases where the connecting arc (path segment) intersects multiple polygons (or raster cells), as shown in Figure 7.6. This requires a simple extension of (7.12). We return to this as an advanced topic later in the chapter.

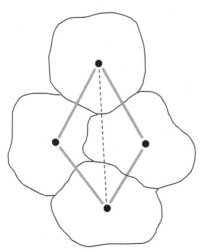

Figure 7.6   Multiple polygon intersections of an arc.

7.4 MODELING APPLICATION

In order to illustrate line-based single facility location for both a path and corridor, two different applications are utilized in this section. The path application assumes a network is given, and proceeds to focus on the identification of the shortest or least-cost route. The corridor application begins with a field view of space, or, more specifically, a raster data layer, then proceeds to structure an underlying network in which the shortest-path problem can be used to find the best alignment for the corridor.

7.4.1 Path

A company has structured a representative network through which it can transport goods produced at its factory in one city to its distribution warehouse in another city. The network shown in Figure 7.1 represents the possibilities, with associated arc travel costs given in Table 7.1. The factory is located at node A, so $s = A$, and the warehouse is at node F, meaning $t = F$. Thus, the goal is to identify an efficient path connecting nodes A and F through the network.

The shortest-path problem defined in (7.4) through (7.8) can be algebraically stated given this possible transportation system and beginning and ending locations as follows:

Minimize $\quad 6X_{AB} + 5X_{AC} + 6X_{BA} + 4X_{BC} + 3X_{BD} + 9X_{BF} + 5X_{CA}$

$$+ 4X_{CB} + 5X_{CD} + 3X_{DB} + 5X_{DC} + 2X_{DE} + 5X_{DF} + 2X_{ED}$$

$$+ 2X_{EF} + 9X_{FB} + 5X_{FD} + 2X_{FE} + 2X_{DE} + 5X_{DF} + 2X_{ED}$$

$$+ 2X_{EF} + 9X_{FB} + 5X_{FD} + 2X_{FE}$$

Subject to:

$X_{AB} + X_{AC} = 1$

$X_{BF} + X_{DF} + X_{EF} = 1$

$X_{AB} + X_{CB} + X_{DB} + X_{FB} - X_{BA} - X_{BC} - XBD - X_{BF} = 0$

$X_{AC} + X_{BC} + X_{DC} - X_{CA} - X_{CB} - X_{CD} = 0$

$X_{BD} + X_{CD} + X_{ED} + X_{FD} - X_{DB} - X_{DC} - X_{DE} - X_{DF} = 0$

$X_{DE} + X_{FE} - X_{ED} - X_{EF} = 0$

$X_{AB} = \{0, 1\}, X_{AC} = \{0, 1\}, X_{BA} = \{0, 1\}, X_{BC} = \{0, 1\}, X_{BD} = \{0, 1\},$

$X_{BF} = \{0, 1\}, X_{CA} = \{0, 1\}, X_{CB} = \{0, 1\}, X_{CD} = \{0, 1\}, X_{DB} = \{0, 1\},$

$X_{DC} = \{0, 1\}, X_{DE} = \{0, 1\}, X_{DF} = \{0, 1\}, X_{ED} = \{0, 1\}, X_{EF} = \{0, 1\},$

$X_{FB} = \{0, 1\}, X_{FD} = \{0, 1\}, X_{FE} = \{0, 1\}$

This model has 18 arc path decision variables because the arcs are undirected. Note that each undirected arc is represented by two variables. For example, X_{ED} represents travel from node E to D along arc (E,D), and X_{DE} represents travel on arc (E,D) from node D to E. There are six major constraints, one specifying the path beginning (node A), one specifying the path ending (node F) and four ensuring that incoming arc activity is the same as outgoing arc activity. This problem can be specified using LINGO, as depicted in Figure 7.7. The form of the model is presented so that it follows the

```
! Shortest Path Problem;
MODEL:
SETS:
 Nodes /A,B,C,D,E,F/ ;
 Mat(Nodes,Nodes) : d, omeg, X ;
ENDSETS

! Objective - minimize total path cost;
MIN = @SUM( Mat(i,j)| omeg(i,j) #EQ# 1 : d(i,j) * X(i,j) );

! Beginning node (A) included on path;
@Sum( Nodes(j) | omeg(1,j) #EQ# 1 : X(1,j) ) = 1 ;

! Ending node (F) included on path;
@Sum( Nodes(i) | omeg(6,i) #EQ# 1 : X(i,6) ) = 1 ;

! Number of in arcs equal number of out arcs;
@FOR( Nodes(k) | (k #NE# 1) #AND# (k #NE# 6) :
 @SUM( Nodes(i) | omeg(k,i) #EQ# 1 : X(i,k) ) -
 @SUM( Nodes(j) | omeg(k,j) #EQ# 1 : X(k,j) ) = 0);

! Integer restrictions on variables;
@FOR(Mat(i,j)| omeg(i,j) #EQ# 1 : @BIN( X(i,j)) );

! Input data and parameters;
DATA:
 d =        0, 6, 5, 0, 0, 0,
            6, 0, 4, 3, 0, 9,
            5, 4, 0, 5, 0, 0,
            0, 3, 5, 0, 2, 5,
            0, 0, 0, 2, 0, 2,
            0, 9, 0, 5, 2, 0;
 omeg =     0, 1, 1, 0, 0, 0,
            1, 0, 1, 1, 0, 1,
            1, 1, 0, 1, 0, 0,
            0, 1, 1, 0, 1, 1,
            0, 0, 0, 1, 0, 1,
            0, 1, 0, 1, 1, 0;
ENDDATA
END
```

Figure 7.7 Shortest-path problem structured in LINGO.

structure of the previous algebraic statement. The data for this model are specified at the bottom of the LINGO file. Note that comparison of the LINGO structured model to the previous algebraic statement is possible using "LINGO→Generate→Display model" pull-down menus (or Ctrl+G) in LINGO.

The LINGO solution indicates that the shortest path has a total cost of 13. The arcs included in the path are $X_{AB} = X_{BD} = X_{DE} = X_{EF} = 1$, and are depicted in Figure 7.8.

As noted previously, the Dijkstra shortest path algorithm also can be applied directly to solve this problem. The major steps are summarized in Figure 7.9 for applying the Dijkstra algorithm to solve for the shortest path through the network shown in Figure 7.1, given $s = A$ and $t = F$. Iteration 1 begins with initialization (step 0), where all nodes and arcs are unlabeled and the set T is initialized as $T = \{A\}$. Next, node A is labeled and removed from T (step 1). Following this is the evaluation of arcs connecting the newly labeled node to an unlabeled node (step 2). Candidates in this iteration includes arc (A, B), with a total distance from A of 6 ($\hat{D}(A) = 6$), and arc (A, C), with a total distance from A of 5 ($\hat{D}(C) = 5$). Both nodes B and C are then added to the T.

In the next iteration, the node in T with the lowest distance $\hat{D}(.)$ value is node C with $\hat{D}(C) = 5$. Node C is then removed from T. All arcs connected to node C (i.e., (C, A), (C, B), and (C, D) are evaluated, and node D is added to set T with $\hat{D}(D) = 10$. Since node F has not been labeled and T contains elements, we must return to step 1.

This brings us to the third iteration, where B is selected from T with the lowest $\hat{D}(.)$ value of 6. It is then removed from T and labeled.

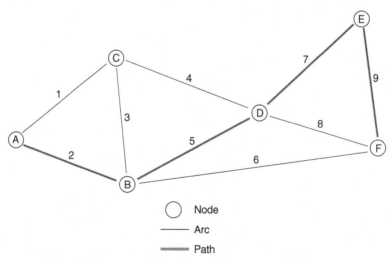

Figure 7.8 Shortest-path solution.

Iteration 1:
- All nodes are set as unlabeled.
- Set $\hat{D}(A) = 0$, $T = \{A\}$, and $P(A) = $ "stop."
- Select A in T with lowest $\hat{D}(.) = 0$; label A and set $T = T - \{A\}$.
- Consider arcs (A, B) and (A, C).
- Set $\hat{D}(B) = \hat{D}(A) + 6 = 6$, $T = T + \{B\}$ and $P(B) = A$.
- Set $\hat{D}(C) = \hat{D}(A) + 5 = 5$, $T = T + \{C\}$ and $P(C) = A$.
- F not labeled and T contains elements, so go back to step 1.

Iteration 2:
- Select C in T with lowest $\hat{D}(.) = 5$; label C and set $T = T - \{C\}$.
- Consider arcs (C, A), (C, B) and (C, D).
- Set $\hat{D}(D) = \hat{D}(C) + 5 = 10$, $T = T + \{D\}$ and $P(D) = C$.
- F not labeled and T contains elements, so go back to step 1.

Iteration 3:
- Select B in T with lowest $\hat{D}(.) = 6$; label B and set $T = T - \{B\}$.
- Consider arcs (B, C), (B, D) and (B, F).
- Reset $\hat{D}(D) = \hat{D}(B) + 3 = 9$ and $P(D) = B$.
- Set $\hat{D}(F) = \hat{D}(B) + 9 = 15$, $T = T + \{F\}$, and $P(F) = B$.
- F not labeled and T contains elements, so go back to step 1.

Iteration 4:
- Select D in T with lowest $\hat{D}(.) = 9$, label D and set $T = T - \{D\}$.
- Consider arcs (D, B), (D, C), (D, E) and (D, F).
- Set $\hat{D}(E) = \hat{D}(D) + 2 = 11$, $T = T + \{E\}$ and $P(E) = D$.
- Reset $\hat{D}(F) = \hat{D}(D) + 5 = 14$ and $P(F) = D$.
- F not labeled and T contains elements, so go back to step 1.

Iteration 5:
- Select E in T with lowest $\hat{D}(.) = 11$, label E, and set $T = T - \{E\}$.
- Consider arcs (E, D) and (E, F).
- Reset $\hat{D}(F) = \hat{D}(E) + 2 = 13$ and $P(F) = E$.
- F not labeled, and T contains elements, so go back to step 1.

Iteration 6:
- Select F in T with lowest $\hat{D}(.) = 13$ and label F.
- F is labeled, so stop. Algorithm terminates with a path from A to F. Use $P(.)$ labels to backtrack shortest route.

Figure 7.9   Dijkstra algorithm summary for the 6 node, 9 arc problem.

All arcs connected to node B are considered for updating node distance values.

In this iteration, node D is reset with a distance of 9 (i.e., $\hat{D}(D) = 9$) and node F is given a distance value of 15. Now nodes A, B, and C have been labeled. Since F has yet to be labeled and T is not empty, we return to step 1 for another iteration. In the fourth iteration, node D is selected from T and is labeled. It is then removed from T. Then the distance to node E can be set at

11 and the distance to node F is reset to 14 associated from arcs connected to node D. In the fifth iteration, node E is selected from T with the lowest distance value of 11. It is removed from T and labeled. In this iteration, the distance to node F is reset again to 13.

Finally, in the sixth iteration, node F is selected from T with the lowest distance $\hat{D}(.)$ value of 13. Node F is labeled and the algorithm is finished. Thus, at that point the shortest path has been found, and it corresponds to that shown in Figure 7.8.

7.4.2 Corridor Siting in ArcGIS

Of course, it is possible to solve for a line-based single facility in GIS using shortest-path solution techniques. Thus, we could have identified the shortest path for the network in Figure 7.1 solely in ArcGIS, as an example. In this section we go beyond merely solving for a shortest path, and detail how GIS can be used to site a corridor across a landscape. This involves deriving the network from a continuously distributed field. In our case here, we begin with a raster layer, then specify a network structure. Once we have a network structure with associated suitability measures for arcs, it is possible to solve for a shortest path, or rather, site the corridor.

The objective of the planning problem now approached is to site a power transmission corridor connecting a power generation facility to a nearby urban area. The region of interest is represented by the 20×20 raster depicted in Figure 7.10, with each cell being 1×1 km in size. Suitability values for each raster cell are classified from 0 to 10 and 99. The lower the value, the more suitable the cell is for the corridor. A value of 99 indicates highly unsuitable, and is meant to effectively exclude that cell from the located corridor. The corridor is to begin at location s (lower-left-hand corner) and end at location t (upper-right-hand corner), as shown in Figure 7.10.

The solution for the corridor location problem using the suitability raster given in Figure 7.10 can be easily identified using ArcGIS. Specifically, ArcGIS will automatically generate an $r = 1$ network (orthogonal plus diagonal moves) and identify a shortest path from a specified origin cell to a specified destination cell. To do this, it is necessary to have three raster data layers: one indicating the source cell, one indicating the destination cell, and the third representing the suitability values of each cell. In ArcToolbox under Spatial Analyst Tools, it is necessary to use the *cost-distance* and *cost-path* functions in the *Distance* folder.[2] Using the *cost-distance* function first, it is possible to generate the path distances to all other cells from a source cell. The output from this process is a raster of path distances.

---

[2] It is also possible to access this functionality in ArcGIS through the Spatial Analyst Toolbar ("View→Toolbars") instead of ArcToolbox. Through the Spatial Analyst Toolbar, it is required that you select "Spatial Analyst→Distance→Cost Weighted" and "Spatial Analyst→Distance→Shortest Path" options.

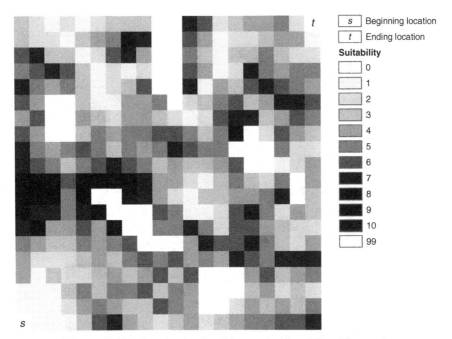

Figure 7.10   Landscape for siting a corridor (20 × 20 raster).

Then using the *cost-path* function, the shortest path to a specified destination cell can be identified and generated. Figure 7.11 superimposes the shortest path, or corridor, over the suitability raster. The total cost of this corridor is 8249.14. Note that to analyze paths with higher r-values requires special programming.

7.5   ADVANCED TOPICS

Solving any geographic problem requires some form of abstraction, as discussed throughout the text. It is literally impossible to represent every aspect of a problem. Nevertheless, it is important to minimize distortion and error to the greatest extent possible. In corridor analysis, one can better model route design with more movement options across the landscape, as well as a more accurate accounting of the impact zone of a corridor segment. For path optimization, it was mentioned that other models existed to support efficient route design. Such variants often arise because of additional constraining conditions or the need to address other, nonmodeled, considerations. As advanced topics in this chapter we first look at expanding network representation and accounting for corridor width and then discuss two shortest-path problem variants: constrained shortest path and gateway shortest paths.

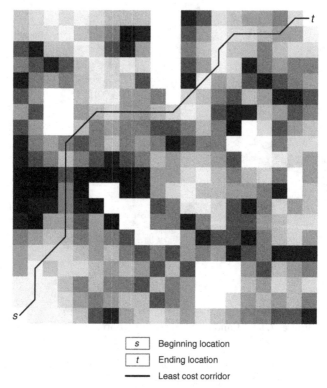

Figure 7.11   Optimal corridor from s to t.

7.5.1 Expanding the Network

It is possible to consider an expanded network for a raster layer beyond the orthogonal and diagonal networks depicted in Figures 7.2 and 7.4. For example, Figure 7.12 maintains the orthogonal and diagonal arcs (the so-called *queen's network*), but includes additional neighboring arcs. There are 8 such new arcs for each cell/node. Thus, the network is expanded from a maximum of 8 arcs per node to a maximum of 16 arcs per node. This expansion results in a larger underlying network and additional computation time needed for solving the shortest-path problem, but it also results in lower levels of distortion error. Network **distortion error** in this context refers to the situation where arc directions are limited. Such limits on the number of possible directions an arc may take from a given node tends to result in longer path lengths than would be the case in moving across the actual landscape. The network shown in Figure 7.12 enables shorter, more efficient paths to be identified as compared to the networks in Figures 7.2 or 7.4. The reason for this is that more arc options exist, thereby reducing

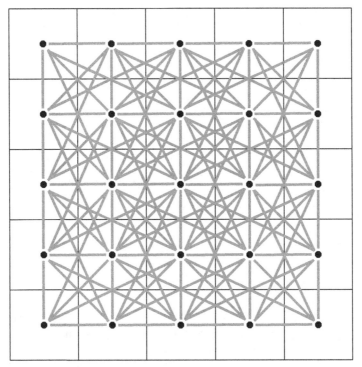

Figure 7.12   Expanded network ($r = 2$).

the potential for distortion error. This potential for error is illustrated in Figure 7.13, where Figure 7.13a shows a path through the orthogonal network arcs in contrast to a potential arc used in Figure 7.2. A similar situation is shown in Figure 7.13b for the orthogonal plus diagonal network (Figure 7.4). If the potential arc shown in either case is used in the least-cost route, then distortion error would exist when that arc is not included. As a result, there would be distortion error because of the inability of the structured network to more accurately approximate the true optimal path of the corridor. Of course it is possible to further expand the network beyond that shown in Figure 7.12 as well.

A general characterization of network structure associated with a raster layer can now be summarized. We can refer to r as the radius of cells around a given cell. For example, the orthogonal network would represent $r = 0$. The orthogonal and diagonal network would represent $r = 1$. The set of cells for $r = 2$ includes those cells that are $r = 0$ and 1 plus those cells that form a second ring of cells around a given cell. Thus, $r = 2$ reflects the network shown in Figure 7.12. Networks of $r = 3$ and beyond simply extend outward to include more direct connection with a cell and nearby cells. Huber and Church

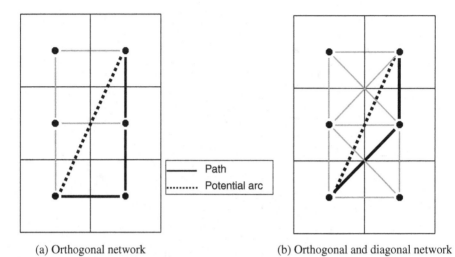

(a) Orthogonal network   (b) Orthogonal and diagonal network

Figure 7.13   Corridor path cost distortion.

(1985) suggest that the best trade-off in accuracy of network representation and ease of computation is struck with the $r = 3$ system, reducing errors of distortion to below 1 percent on average.

Of course, an expanded network means that we also need to account for the complexities of estimating arc cost. As mentioned previously, if an arc between two cells crosses, or intersects, other cells, then this must be accounted for in suitability assessment of the potential path segment. An extension of (7.12) that includes any incident cells is as follows:

$$t_{i,j} = \sum_{k \in \Psi_{ij}} d_{i,j}^k s_k \qquad (7.13)$$

where Ψ_{ij} is the set of cells crossed by an arc connecting cells i and j, and $d_{i,j}^k$ is the length of the portion of arc (i, j) crossing raster cell k. With this general form of the arc suitability cost, we can easily expand the definition of the network in order to make it as accurate as needed for any application.

There is another issue that needs to be discussed within the context of problem abstraction. This involves the corridor footprint, or impact zone. Figure 7.14 shows the diagonal arc between cells 1 and 4. If this arc is included on the path, it will actually have some width, w, associated with it. Most corridors have some type of width, for example, a highway might have a right-of-way that is hundreds of feet wide. To this point, width has not been accounted for in the suitability measure of a path segment. However, it is

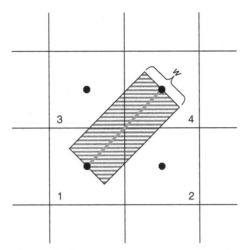

Figure 7.14   Depicting a corridor footprint.

clear in Figure 7.14 that a diagonal arc and the footprint of a corridor actually traipses through cells 2 and 3 in this case, not just cells 1 and 4. But, the suitability measures (7.9) through (7.13) do not account for any arc impact on cells that are intersected, because they are assumed to be a line of zero width. This means that the impact of an arc, like that of the diagonal arc from 1 to 4, needs to account for width. An extension of the previous measures is as follows:

$$t_{i,j} = \sum_{k \in \Psi_{ij}} a_{i,j}^k s_k \qquad (7.14)$$

where $a_{i,j}^k$ is the area associated with arc (i, j) impacting raster cell k. Equation (7.14) sums all of the suitability scores of each cell intersected by a corridor arc of fixed width, where each suitability value is weighted by the area of the corridor footprint in that cell. Deriving $a_{i,j}^k$ is precisely the type of detailed analysis that GIS enables.

7.5.2 Shortest-Path Variants

As mentioned previously, there are many different types of shortest-path problems. These variants typically address aspatial and spatial conditions, timing considerations, beginning/ending requirements, and so on. Beyond this, it has been found that for planning purposes the single shortest path may not only be of interest, but also alternative optima (other paths with the same cost/impact), or paths perhaps only slightly longer. Thus, methods for identifying many shortest paths have been necessary.

We begin first by discussing a basic version of a constrained shortest-path problem. What if we wish to explicitly address certain types of concerns in path or corridor siting? For example, although our suitability measure addresses both impact and cost, we might want to ensure that the identified corridor does not have a total impact on a particular species or habitat type beyond a stated limit, Γ. If the impact for each arc is a_{ij}, then it is possible to structure a constraining condition on the acceptable path. Thus, we can extend the shortest path problem defined in (7.4) through (7.8):

$$Minimize \quad \sum_i \sum_{j \in \Omega_i} d_{ij} X_{ij} \tag{7.15}$$

Subject to:

$$\sum_{j \in \Omega_s} X_{sj} = 1 \tag{7.16}$$

$$\sum_{i \in \Omega_t} X_{it} = 1 \tag{7.17}$$

$$\sum_{i \in \Omega_k} X_{ik} - \sum_{j \in \Omega_k} X_{kj} = 0 \quad \forall k \neq s, t \tag{7.18}$$

$$\sum_i \sum_{j \in \Omega_i} a_{ij} X_{ij} \leq \Gamma \tag{7.19}$$

$$X_{ij} = \{0, 1\} \quad \forall (i, j) \tag{7.20}$$

As previously described, the objective, (7.15), minimizes the total cost of arcs chosen for the path and constraints (7.16) to (7.18) ensure a path is structured between nodes s and t. Constraint (7.19) is a new addition, imposing a limit on the path impact as a function of arc attributes. Finally, integer restrictions are imposed in constraints (7.20).

Another shortest variant could involve a spatial constraint. For example, we might want the path to go through one or more intermediate locations between s and t. This intermediate location has been referred to as a *gateway*. Mathematically, this can be imposed by adding a constraint that requires the path to visit a gateway node g. This is accomplished as follows:

$$Minimize \quad \sum_i \sum_{j \in \Omega_i} d_{ij} X_{ij} \tag{7.21}$$

Subject to:

$$\sum_{j \in \Omega_s} X_{sj} = 1 \tag{7.22}$$

$$\sum_{i \in \Omega_t} X_{it} = 1 \tag{7.23}$$

$$\sum_{i \in \Omega_k} X_{ik} - \sum_{j \in \Omega_k} X_{kj} = 0 \quad \forall k \neq s, t \tag{7.24}$$

$$\sum_{i \in \Omega_g} X_{ig} = 1 \tag{7.25}$$

$$X_{ij} = \{0, 1\} \quad \forall (i, j) \tag{7.26}$$

The only constraint that has changed from our original formulation of the shortest-path problem is constraint (7.25), where it requires that the path enter node g. Lombard and Church (1993) described the *gateway shortest-path problem* as an approach for identifying alternative paths. They also provided an approach for solving all gateway paths, and summarize them in comparative terms using the Dijkstra algorithm. Interestingly, the Corridor function in ArcGIS (in the Spatial Analyst toolbox) enables gateway paths to be identified.

Shortest-path problem variants are in no way limited to the two described here. The point, however, is that there are ways to extend line-based single-facility locations beyond the simple shortest-path problem. Such extensions have been approached using specialized algorithms and/or heuristics, and have been structured as mixed integer-linear programs. In the cases where they have been addressed using integer programming, it is worth at least mentioning that certain complications can arise in practice. Specifically, it is possible to satisfy all stipulated constraints (e.g., (7.5) through (7.8)), yet not get an actual path through the network. What happens is that *subtours* end up forming.

For example, consider intermediate nodes i, j and k, each on the "path" and connected only to each other (e.g., $X_{ij} = X_{jk} = X_{ki} = 1$). This is a subtour of the network, and actually satisfies the conservation of flow requirement (e.g., constraints (7.7)), but we do not end up with a path connecting s to t. This means that, in this case, our formulation is missing necessary constraints, the subtour busting constraints. A general subtour busting constraint is as follows:

$$\sum_{(i, j) \in \Delta} X_{ij} \leq |\Delta| - 1 \tag{7.27}$$

where Δ is the set of arcs (i, j) forming a subtour. Thus, inequality (7.27) breaks this subtour. Of course, in a network there are likely many potential subtours, so identifying them in advance is not desirable, and often may not even be feasible. Thus, in practice, path-oriented problems have been approached by first ignoring potential subtours, then adding subtour busting constraints as needed if and when any arise. This means that a path problem might need to be solved many times, even hundreds or thousands, to resolve subtour issues.

7.6   SUMMARY

In this chapter, we have introduced line-based single facility location. It has been shown that the line-based facility might be either a path or a corridor, effectively a route between one location and another. Underlying this problem is generally the assumption that a network of nodes and arcs exists, or can be derived, so the task is to identify a path through the network connecting an origin location to a destination location. The shortest-path problem was suggested as a basic approach for single facility location, and the mathematical model and specialized solution technique (Dijkstra algorithm) for this problem were reviewed. Path and corridor location are important problem contexts, often inextricably tied to GIS because of the ease with which a suitability/cost data layer can be derived. The advanced topics section explored expanding network representation and variants of the basic shortest path problem. The aim of this chapter was to illustrate fundamentals of line-based, single-facility location, as well as highlight the importance of the shortest-path problem and its extensions in geographical planning and analysis.

7.7   TERMS

path
corridor
network
shortest-path problem
Dijkstra algorithm
cost-distance
distortion errors
area-distance
r-based network
path alternatives

7.8 REFERENCES

Dantzig, G. B. 1957. Discrete-variable extremum problems. *Operations Research* 5:266–277.

Dijkstra, E. W. 1959. A note on two problems in connection with graphs. *Numerische Mathematik* 1:269–271.

Ford, L. R. 1956. *Network flow theory*. Technical Report P-932. Santa Monica, CA: Rand Corporation.

Huber, D. L. and R. L. Church. 1985. Transmission corridor location modeling. *Journal of Environmental Engineering* (ASCE) 111:114–130.

Lombard, K., and R. L. Church. 1993. The gateway shortest path problem: Generating alternatives for a corridor location problem. *Geographical Systems* 1: 25–45.

7.9 EXERCISES

7.1. Suppose that you are to locate an oil pipeline across the state of Arizona. List possible data and land-use characteristics that would be important in locating this pipeline.

7.2. Why is it necessary to generate significantly different alternatives for a corridor planning problem?

7.3. Compare and contrast a path vs. a corridor in line-based single-facility location.

7.4. Solve for the shortest path in Figure 7.1 using ArcGIS. What are the necessary steps in doing this? How does the solution compare with that reported in section 7.4?

7.5. Observe the selected route in Figure 7.11. Does this route cross any cells that are high cost? Does the applied model account for these cells of high cost?

7.6. On the island of Hokaido (northern Japan), there is a volcano under constant observation. The government wishes to keep a surveillance camera on a steam vent, which is the most likely area for a mud flow or lava eruption. The camera transmits a live video 24 hours a day. This live video cannot be picked up by a receiver unless it is within the line of sight from the camera's antenna. As the monitoring station is many miles from this observation camera and out of sight, Hitachi engineers have been asked to place repeaters so that the signal can be picked up at the station. Repeaters pick up and retransmit the signal. For the signal to be reached at the station, repeaters need to be placed along a route in which each repeater is within the line of sight of its neighbor repeaters. Suggest a methodology to locate the fewest repeaters, such that the signal can be received at the station and such that no repeater is placed in an area that is dangerous for the engineers to install the system.

7.7. A platoon from the 101st Airborne Rangers has been asked to walk through an enemy-infested area. They will need to leave their starting position at 1100 hours and must arrive at their destination by 2200 hours. They wish to avoid as many insurgent locations as possible. Suggest a methodology to route a path for the Rangers to take.

7.8. Structure and solve a shortest-path problem extension discussed in section 7.5 in LINGO applied to the network shown in Figure 7.1 (and summarized in Tables 7.1 to 7.3). How does the added constraint change the identified path? Do any subtours arise, and if so, how did you address this problem?

CHAPTER 8

AREA-BASED LOCATION

8.0 INTRODUCTION

The two previous chapters discussed two classes of single-facility site selection problems: one was point-based and the other was line-based. The point-based location problem involved the siting of a facility to efficiently serve demand. The line-based location problem dealt with siting a path/corridor from an origin to a destination location. In this chapter, we continue to examine the single-facility siting problem, but shift attention to acquiring a subregion of land, or rather, area-based location. This area may be contiguous or noncontiguous, involving the selection of multiple land parcels. Three variations of the area-based location problem are considered in detail: *knapsack*, *threshold,* and *shape*. Two fundamental concepts, *adjacency* and *contiguity*, are discussed in the GIScience section. The application section highlights differences in model characteristics as well as the importance of GIS in measuring lengths of shared edge for adjacent parcels. The chapter ends with the advanced topic of formulating an area-based selection model that keeps all selected parcels in a connected cluster.

8.1 PROBLEM DEFINITION AND MOTIVATION

A fundamental geographic planning problem involves selecting land to acquire for some purpose. There are many contexts where land acquisition is necessary, such as selecting land for a new solid waste disposal site, selecting an area for a large scale industrial facility, building a new residential subdivision, establishing new parks and recreation areas, and by establishing reserves to protect endangered species, to name a few.

In **land acquisition** there are many criteria that are important to consider. Among the most critical are often cost and suitability, but shape, area and proximity, among others, can also be influential factors in what land should be acquired. The idea is to select land for use, development, or preservation, taking into account budgetary and quality issues in the process. As an example, vulnerable biological species must be protected to ensure the existence of ecosystems and plant communities in a region, and this should be done in such as way that costs are kept reasonable. Protection necessarily means acquiring and preserving land where such biological species exist. From this we can distill the following general planning problem:

> *Optimize the selection of multiple land parcels for an intended use, while maintaining stipulated conditions on acquisition.*

Given this definition of the area selection problem, one might want to minimize costs, maximize benefits, remain within a budget, satisfy regulatory standards, and so on. In the sections that follow, a number of different approaches are defined and structured to support the problem of area selection.

8.2   MATHEMATICAL REPRESENTATION

In order to formulate a model for area-based location planning, we first need the following mathematical notation and decision variables:

i = index of land parcels
b_i = benefit associated with parcel i
c_i = cost to acquire parcel i

$$X_i = \begin{cases} 1 & \text{if parcel } i \text{ acquired} \\ 0 & \text{otherwise} \end{cases}$$

The index i corresponds to individual land parcels that could be acquired. At a minimum, it is assumed that benefit and cost information, b_i and c_i respectively, can be derived for planning purposes. Such information is typically managed and/or derived using GIS, as discussed in previous chapters. Thus, b_1 and c_1 are known, or could be determined, for parcel 1, b_2 and c_2 are known, or could be determined, for parcel 2, and so on. Finally, related to area-based location, there is a decision variable for each parcel of land, X_i, corresponding to whether parcel i is acquired or not.

The conservation of plant species highlighted in the previous section could be approached along these lines by specifically detailing the benefits to individual plant species. As an example, if we assume that the various plant species are distinguished by the index k (that is, k is the index of plant species), then we could define $\hat{b}_{ik}$ to be the benefit to species k of conserving land parcel i. Given this, our decision variable, X_i, would correspond to preserving and/or otherwise safeguarding the species that are present in parcel i.

The most basic area-based location approach involves the use of overlay for suitability analysis. The concepts of overlay and suitability analysis were developed over a hundred years ago in order to support planning. As detailed in Chapter 5, overlay is a process involving co-registered spatial information layers that are combined in some way in order to produce a composite suitability layer. In this case, the composite layer would represent values associated with selecting land for the desired purpose. We can then use this composite suitability layer as a guide in helping us select specific parcels for purchase or protection. As an example, if we are interested in those land parcels satisfying $b_i \geq \Gamma_b$ and $c_i \leq \Gamma_c$, where Γ_b and Γ_c are specified thresholds that must be maintained, then the composite suitability layer would indicate those parcels meeting these conditions and this would be the land to acquire for the intended purposes.

For reserve design, as another example, overlay would be applied to identify land to be acquired for species preservation. This land would satisfy stipulated suitability criteria, and would therefore comprise the land to acquire. Also discussed in Chapter 5 was that the overlay approach could be used in facility selection through the use of map algebra functions in GIS. An important issue arising from the overlay approach, however, is that typically too many parcels satisfy basic conditions/thresholds. This means that planners and decision makers must choose from among a set of suitable parcels in order to develop an acquisition plan. Deciding which of the feasible parcels to select can be quite a complex task. As a result, an optimization model is needed to assist in making the plan.

As we will now see, there are many possible area selection optimization models. Here, three particular types of area-based location models are reviewed: knapsack, threshold, and shape.

8.2.1 Knapsack Model

A basic category of area-based location is the *knapsack* problem, involving the selection of parcels from among a choice set. The problem is one where the maximum derived benefit is sought from the collection of acquired land parcels subject to limitations. The name comes from the analogy to a knapsack (or backpack) that can only hold so many items. One must be able to pack the items in the knapsack, but only the most essential items are to be packed.

The following additional notation will be used in the specification of the **knapsack model** for area selection:

μ = project acquisition budget

With this parameter, we can effectively place a bound on the amount or quantity of land acquired, as it is generally the case that only limited resources

are available. Thus, given a fixed project budget, it is obvious that the total cost
of acquired/selected land cannot exceed this limit. This bound on available
resources in acquiring land can be structured in an optimization model, along
with an objective to maximize an attribute of the area selected, as follows:

$$\textit{Maximize} \quad \sum_i b_i X_i \tag{8.1}$$

Subject to:

$$\sum_i c_i X_i \leq \mu \tag{8.2}$$

$$X_i = \{0, 1\} \quad \forall i \tag{8.3}$$

The objective, (8.1), is to maximize the total benefit of acquired land. Constraint (8.2) limits total land selected by the project budget. Constraints (8.3)
impose integer restrictions on decision variables.

This is referred to as the *knapsack model* because of the bounding condition
imposed by constraint (8.2), along with the objective, (8.1), seeking the
greatest benefit possible. Such a model has been a sole or primary feature of
many land-use planning approaches (see Davis et al. 1996).

8.2.2 Threshold Model

A somewhat different area-based approach for selecting parcels from among
a candidate set of sites is the *threshold* problem. In contrast to the knapsack
approach, the idea behind the threshold problem is to minimize cost or impact
while acquiring no less than a specified level or amount of land.

Additional notation for detailing this approach is:

λ = minimum acceptable project benefit

In contrast to the knapsack approach, the bound here is on a minimal level of
activity. This can be structured as an optimization model as follows:

$$\textit{Minimize} \quad \sum_i c_i X_i \tag{8.4}$$

Subject to:

$$\sum_i b_i X_i \geq \lambda \tag{8.5}$$

$$X_i = \{0, 1\} \quad \forall i \tag{8.6}$$

The objective, (8.4), is to minimize the total cost of acquired land. Constraint (8.5) requires a minimum total benefit of the selected area. Constraints (8.6) impose integer restrictions on decision variables.

This is referred to as the **threshold model** because of the lower bounds stipulated in constraint (8.5) and the objective, (8.4), of minimizing costs. This model has also been a sole or primary feature of many land-use planning approaches (see Davis et al. 1996).

The threshold model can also be stated so that it handles specific needs separately. Recall that we defined $\hat{b}_{ik}$ as the benefit associated with element k in the purchase or conservation of land parcel i. We can structure individual conditions for each element k as follows:

$$\sum_i \hat{b}_{ik} X_i \geq \lambda_k \qquad (8.7)$$

where λ_k is the minimum requirement for element k in the area selected. Basically, the minimum threshold of benefits would account for each requirement separately. Constraint (8.5) in the threshold model would be replaced with constraint (8.7).

8.2.3 Shape Model

A feature of the knapsack and threshold models is that they are inherently aspatial in terms of the criteria employed to select land parcels. Although parcels are geographically located, the data supporting such decisions are spatial, and attributes are often spatially autocorrelated, there is nothing about how land is being selected that relies on spatial relationships. It should not be a surprise, then, that other approaches exist, oriented toward addressing spatial criteria. One such approach for area-based location is to take into account shape properties of the land selected. In contrast to the previous approaches, the **shape model** explicitly requires that certain spatial relationships are considered in the land parcel selection process.

Spatial configuration, or *shape*, has been recognized as a difficult concept to define in land acquisition (area selection), but nevertheless is important to address in some way. Driving this importance is no doubt that some land uses require a contiguous land area for planned activities. A complication is that *shape* is a nebulous term. Some researchers view compact, contiguous configurations of land as important. Given this view, focusing on the total perimeter of acquired land is a meaningful shape property. The rationale is that minimizing perimeter necessarily encourages compactness and promotes contiguity. For example, if total area is held constant, a circle is the shape that is clearly the most compact (and has the smallest perimeter). Recent research in nature reserve design, as an example, suggests that spatially cohesive lands acquired to protect species from invasion or undesirable biotic interaction are important. Thus, compactness is often a central concern in land acquisition. A popular approach for addressing shape is through the optimization of resulting perimeter.

In the context of area-based location, **perimeter** is the resulting exterior edge of acquired parcels. Specifically, an exterior edge is defined by one parcel being selected and an adjacent parcel that is not selected. As an example, nine land parcels are shown in Figure 8.1. Three parcels (2, 4 and 5) are selected for acquisition in this case, and the resulting perimeter of the area is highlighted in Figure 8.1.

Additional notation for defining this model is as follows:

Ψ = set of parcels on region boundary
p_{ij} = edge length shared by parcels i and j
p_{ii} = length of perimeter of parcel i that is not shared with other parcels
Ω_i = set of all parcels that are adjacent to parcel i

$$E_{ij}^+ = \begin{cases} 1 & \text{if } X_i = 1 \text{ and } X_j = 0 \\ 0 & \text{otherwise} \end{cases}$$

$$E_{ij}^- = \begin{cases} 1 & \text{if } X_i = 0 \text{ and } X_j = 1 \\ 0 & \text{otherwise} \end{cases}$$

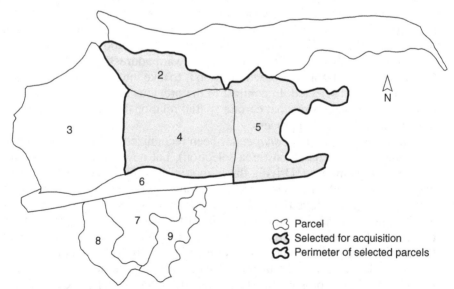

Figure 8.1   Selected land parcels and resulting perimeter.

Of course, the significance of this additional notation and variables is that it enables explicit tracking of spatial relationships between parcels of land. Specifically, it is possible to account for shared parcel boundaries and provide an indicator of when perimeter edge is created. Structuring this for area selection is achieved as follows:

$$Maximize \quad \sum_i b_i X_i \tag{8.8}$$

$$Minimize \quad \sum_i \sum_{j \in \Omega_i} p_{ij} \left(E_{ij}^+ + E_{ij}^- \right) + \sum_{i \in \Psi} p_{ii} X_i \tag{8.9}$$

Subject to:

$$\sum_i c_i X_i \leq \mu \tag{8.10}$$

$$X_i - X_j - E_{ij}^+ + E_{ij}^- = 0 \quad \forall i, j \in \Omega_i \tag{8.11}$$

$$X_i = \{0, 1\} \quad \forall i \tag{8.12}$$

$$E_{ij}^+, E_{ij}^- \geq 0 \quad \forall i, j \in \Omega_i$$

There are two model objectives. The first objective, (8.8), maximizes total benefit, as is done in the knapsack model. The second objective, (8.9), minimizes total perimeter. Constraint (8.10) limits total acquired land by the project budget, as done previously also. Constraints (8.11) track the perimeter resulting from selected land parcels. Constraints (8.12) impose integer and nonnegativity restrictions on decision variables.

The shape model explicitly tracks external edges of the area to be acquired in order to account for perimeter. If two neighboring parcels, i and j, are both selected, then $X_i = X_j = 1$. This forces $E_{ij}^+ = E_{ij}^- = 0$ in constraint (8.11), given the objective of minimizing external edge in (8.9). This is what should happen in this case, because both parcels are selected and no external edge results between these two parcels. A similar situation occurs when neither is selected. When an external edge is produced (only one of the two neighbors is selected), then the edge must be accounted for. This is addressed in the model through constraints (8.11), combined with the minimization objective for total external perimeter. For region boundary parcels, perimeter edge is produced and is accounted for through $\sum_i p_{ii} X_i$.

This is referred to as the *shape model* because the perimeter around acquired land is measured and optimized. Wright et al. (1983) relied on perimeter as a measure of shape in an attempt to encourage a compact assemblage of land.

8.3 GISCIENCE

The data required for the knapsack, threshold, and shape area selection models are inherently spatial, especially the perimeter or edge elements needed for the shape model. To begin, GIS can be relied on to conduct necessary analysis through map algebra operations, identifying suitable land for potential acquisition. A need in applying either the knapsack, threshold or shape model is the associated attribute data. GIS can also be used to derive and manage information layers relating to land costs and benefits, as well as other attribute data. For the shape model, GIS is essential for specifying spatial characteristics of, and relationships between, land parcels. Of course, we have already defined *perimeter* as a primary feature of the shape model, but perimeter is actually a derived attribute of a topological property of land parcels called **adjacency**. If two parcels, or polygons, i and j are in fact adjacent, then a nonzero length boundary between the two areas exists and can be computed. If two areas are not adjacent, then there is no shared boundary. Using the 16 parcels shown in Figure 8.2 as an example, parcels 3 and 7 are adjacent because they share a common boundary. In contrast, parcels 1 and 15 do not share a common boundary or point, so they are not adjacent.

Using GIS, adjacency is examined based on analysis/evaluation of polygon boundaries. Specifically, two polygons are adjacent if they share a common edge or point. Although syntax and command terminology differ between commercial GIS packages, all systems support assessment of adjacency in a layer containing polygons.

As input for the detailed models, the set of polygons adjacent to polygon i is the set Ω_i. We can summarize the assessment of adjacency for the polygons shown in Figure 8.2, as an example, using a table. This is done in Table 8.1, assuming that adjacency reflects a nonzero length shared boundary.

The shape model requires details on which parcels are adjacent to a given parcel i, Ω_i, as well as shared boundary length information, p_{ij}, for edges between adjacent parcels, not to mention identification of boundary parcels Ψ.

1	2	3	4
5	6	7	8
9	10	11	12
13	14	15	16

Figure 8.2 Land parcels for establishing a reserve system.

TABLE 8.1   Adjacency summary (parcels in Figure 8.2)

Polygon	Adjacent Polygons (Ω_i)
1	2, 5
2	1, 3, 6
3	2, 4, 7
4	3, 8
5	1, 6, 9
6	2, 5, 7, 10
7	3, 6, 8, 11
8	4, 7, 12
9	5, 10, 13
10	6, 9, 11, 14
11	7, 10, 12, 15
12	8, 11, 16
13	9, 14
14	10, 13, 15
15	11, 14, 16
16	12, 15

The derivation of p_{ij} for two adjacent polygons i and j is simply the length of the line (or polyline) segment common to both polygons.

Of course the major purpose of deriving p_{ij} is to define perimeter in area selection. Given two adjacent parcels, perimeter is created when one is selected and the other is not. As an example, parcels 3 and 4 in Figure 8.1 create perimeter because parcel 4 is selected as a part of the area but parcel 3 is not selected. Thus, their shared boundary defines part of the perimeter of the selected area.

Adjacency is important in the context of perimeter, but it also reflects connectivity between parcels. That is, if two parcels are adjacent, then they can be viewed as connected as well. As an example, one could walk directly from one parcel to an adjacent parcel. The notion of connectivity between parcels brings us to another important topological property: *contiguity*. Formally defined, **contiguity** is the property that describes two locations as being connectable or reachable from each other. In area selection, contiguity often has to do with explaining the relationship between acquired land. Two selected polygons i and j are said to be contiguous if there is an uninterrupted path between them, where *uninterrupted* means other selected polygons. That is, one could move from i to an adjacent selected polygon, then to another adjacent selected polygon, then another, etc. until polygon j is reached. If this is not possible, then the selected area is noncontiguous. To illustrate this property, the selected parcels (2, 4, and 5) in Figure 8.1 are an example of a contiguous area. However, what if parcels 1, 6 and 8 are selected instead? In this case, it would not be possible to move between selected parcels to reach other selected parcels, as there are no selected parcels connecting parcel 1 to parcels 6 and 8.

8.4 MODELING APPLICATION

The area-based location problem examined here is to establish a nature reserve. This is not very different than selecting parcels for other purposes, like agribusiness, industrial complexes, and shopping malls, except that the area requirements are often larger in land acquisition for nature reserves. The 16 land parcels depicted in Figure 8.2 are considered for acquisition. The planning objective is to acquire one or more of these land parcels for the reserve network, subject to satisfying specified constraints in order to preserve/protect threatened species. Constraints could include cost, suitability, area (or area by species or element), contiguity, and/or shape. Each parcel is 1 km × 1 km in size, and adjacent parcels are those sharing a nonzero length edge, summarized in Table 8.1. A decision variable corresponds to each land parcel and whether the parcel is to be included in the reserve network (i.e., $X_i = 1$) or not (i.e., $X_i = 0$).

Benefit and cost information for this example is given in Figure 8.3. GIS is used to derive expected benefit if a parcel is included in the reserve system, taking into account other relevant attribute layers. This is also the case for derived parcel costs.

Given this information, the problem involves selecting parcels to include in the reserve system. It is assumed that all parcels could be acquired, so all therefore satisfy minimum suitability requirements. Suppose, however, this was not necessarily the case. If it is assumed that benefit represents the suitability criterion of interest and a minimum value of $\Gamma_b = 13$ is imposed, the suitable parcels emerging from an overlay approach would be all parcels except 10, 12, and 16. If the total cost of acquiring these parcels, \$50,800,

19.4	16.0	14.3	15.7
15.8	13.7	13.0	14.1
16.3	12.6	15.4	11.5
13.4	16.8	13.4	10.9

(a)

5.1	2.1	4.4	4.9
3.2	3.8	2.3	5.1
2.2	5.1	6.4	1.8
1.9	4.3	5.1	5.3

(b)

Figure 8.3 Benefit and cost information derived for land parcels.

exceeds our budget, then too many parcels have been identified and we need further assistance in deciding which parcels to include in the reserve system. This is precisely why optimization approaches are essential in area selection.

8.4.1 Knapsack Model Application

The knapsack model is now used to assist in the process of area selection. If we assume each parcel is possible to acquire, the idea would be to maximize the total derived benefit of land selected without exceeding an expenditure budget. In this case, the budget limit is established at \$24,000, so $\mu = 24$.

An important aspect of using an optimization approach is making the connection between the abstract specification of the model and its realization when actual coefficient values and decision variables are used. The algebraic knapsack model specification for this application instance is the following:

$$\text{Maximize} \quad 19.4\, X_1 + 16.0\, X_2 + 14.3\, X_3 + 15.7\, X_4 + 15.8\, X_5 + 13.7\, X_6$$
$$+ 13.0\, X_7 + 14.1\, X_8 + 16.3 X_9 + 12.6\, X_{10} + 15.4\, X_{11} + 11.5\, X_{12}$$
$$+ 13.4\, X_{13} + 16.8\, X_{14} + 13.4\, X_{15} + 10.9\, X_{16}$$

Subject to:

$$5.1\, X_1 + 2.1\, X_2 + 4.4\, X_3 + 4.9\, X_4 + 3.2\, X_5 + 3.8\, X_6 + 2.3\, X_7 + 5.1\, X_8$$
$$+ 2.2\, X_9 + 5.1\, X_{10} + 6.4\, X_{11} + 1.8\, X_{12} + 1.9\, X_{13} + 4.3\, X_{14} + 5.1\, X_{15}$$
$$+ 5.3\, X_{16} \leq 24$$
$$X_1 = \{0,\ 1\},\ \ X_2 = \{0,\ 1\},\ \ X_3 = \{0,\ 1\},\ \ X_4 = \{0,\ 1\},\ \ X_5 = \{0,\ 1\},$$
$$X_6 = \{0,\ 1\},\ \ X_7 = \{0,\ 1\},\ \ X_8 = \{0,\ 1\},\ \ X_9 = \{0,\ 1\},\ \ X_{10} = \{0,\ 1\},$$
$$X_{11} = \{0,\ 1\},\ \ X_{12} = \{0,\ 1\},\ \ X_{13} = \{0,\ 1\},\ \ X_{14} = \{0,\ 1\},$$
$$X_{15} = \{0,\ 1\},\ \ X_{16} = \{0,\ 1\}$$

This problem can be solved using commercial integer programming software or specialized solution techniques. Consistent with previous chapters, LINGO is utilized for model solution. There are two basic ways in which this problem can be specified in LINGO. The first is to enter the objective and constraints as depicted above, following the syntax rules of LINGO. The second is to specify the data separately and give the model in an algebraic form. The latter approach is used here. The problem is specified in an algebraic form using LINGO syntax, and is shown in Figure 8.4. This is consistent with the knapsack formulation shown in (8.1) to (8.3).

```
MODEL:
! Knapsack problem - LINGO format;

SETS:
   Units / 1..16 / : X, b, c;
ENDSETS

DATA:
 b = 19.4 16.0 14.3 15.7 15.8 13.7 13.0 14.1
     16.3 12.6 15.4 11.5 13.4 16.8 13.4 10.9;

 c = 5.1 2.1 4.4 4.9 3.2 3.8 2.3 5.1 2.2 5.1
     6.4 1.8 1.9 4.3 5.1 5.3;

ENDDATA

! Objective;
MAX = @SUM(Units(I) : b(I) * X(I) );

! Constraints ;
@SUM(Units(I) : c(I) * X(I) ) <= 24;

!Integer restrictions;
@FOR( Units(I) : @BIN( X(I) ));

End
```

Figure 8.4   Knapsack problem structured in LINGO.

Solving this application using LINGO indicates that the optimal solution is 122.2 (total benefit), with $X_1 = X_2 = X_5 = X_7 = X_9 = X_{12} = X_{13} = X_{14} = 1$ and $X_3 = X_4 = X_6 = X_8 = X_{10} = X_{11} = X_{15} = X_{16} = 0$. This solution is depicted in Figure 8.5, identifying parcels to be acquired. In general, high derived benefit parcels are selected, but not in all cases. For example, parcel 12 is selected, with a benefit of 11.5, but not parcel 11, having a much higher benefit value of 15.4. No doubt the budget constraint comes into play; in this case, parcel 12 has a low cost ($1,800), whereas parcel 11 has a cost of $6,400.

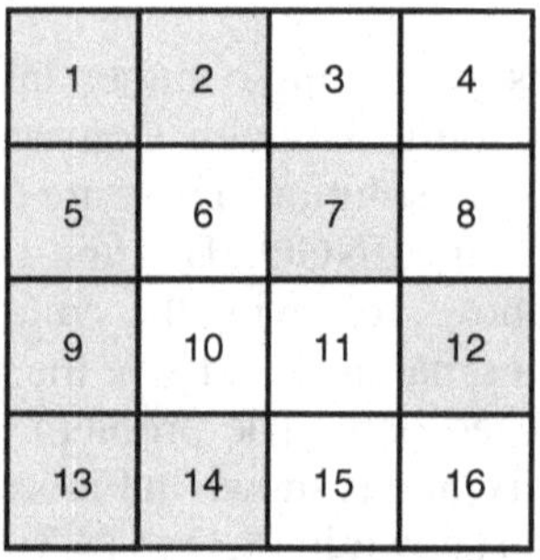

1	2	3	4
5	6	7	8
9	10	11	12
13	14	15	16

Figure 8.5   Land parcels selected using knapsack model.

8.4.2 Threshold Model Application

An alternative area selection approach is the threshold model. Relative to our example, the goal for the threshold approach would be to acquire parcels so that the derived benefit is no less than some total specified value, but doing so in such a way that cost is minimal. Again, there are 16 decision variables related to whether a parcel is selected or not selected. Here it is assumed that a total benefit of at least 110 (i.e., $\lambda = 110$) is necessary.

The specific algebraic threshold model specification for this application instance is as follows:

Minimize $5.1\ X_1 + 2.1\ X_2 + 4.4\ X_3 + 4.9\ X_4 + 3.2\ X_5 + 3.8\ X_6 + 2.3\ X_7$

$$+ 5.1\ X_8 + 2.2\ X_9 + 5.1\ X_{10} + 6.4\ X_{11} + 1.8\ X_{12} + 1.9\ X_{13} + 4.3\ X_{14}$$

$$+ 5.1\ X_{15} + 5.3\ X_{16}$$

Subject to:

$19.4\ X_1 + 16.0\ X_2 + 14.3\ X_3 + 15.7\ X_4 + 15.8\ X_5 + 13.7\ X_6 + 13.0\ X_7$

$$+ 14.1\ X_8 + 16.3\ X_9 + 12.6\ X_{10} + 15.4\ X_{11} + 11.5\ X_{12} + 13.4\ X_{13}$$

$$+ 16.8\ X_{14} + 13.4\ X_{15} + 10.9\ X_{16} \geq 110$$

$X_1 = \{0,\ 1\},\ X_2 = \{0,\ 1\},\ X_3 = \{0,\ 1\},\ X_4 = \{0,\ 1\},\ X_5 = \{0,\ 1\},$

$X_6 = \{0,\ 1\},\ X_7 = \{0,\ 1\},\ X_8 = \{0,\ 1\},\ X_9 = \{0,\ 1\},\ X_{10} = \{0,\ 1\},$

$X_{11} = \{0,\ 1\},\ X_{12} = \{0,\ 1\},\ X_{13} = \{0,\ 1\},\ X_{14} = \{0,\ 1\},$

$X_{15} = \{0,\ 1\},\ X_{16} = \{0,\ 1\}$

The problem specification in LINGO syntax is provided in Figure 8.6. This is consistent with the formulation given in (8.4) to (8.6).

The optimal solution for the threshold model is shown in Figure 8.7. Of note is that this selection of parcels differs slightly from that identified using the knapsack approach. It should not be a surprise that mostly low-cost parcels were acquired. The interesting change in this case is that parcel 12, with a cost of $1,800, is not included. The threshold solution has a total cost of $21,100, whereas the total cost of the knapsack solution is $22,900, yet both are above the threshold benefit of 110.

8.4.3 Shape Model Application

In order to apply the third area selection approach, the shape model, we first need to recall that it has two objectives. This makes it a multiobjective

```
MODEL:
! Threshold problem - LINGO format;

SETS:
   Units / 1..16 / : X, b, c;
ENDSETS

DATA:
 b = 19.4 16.0 14.3 15.7 15.8 13.7 13.0 14.1
       16.3 12.6 15.4 11.5 13.4 16.8 13.4 10.9;

 c = 5.1 2.1 4.4 4.9 3.2 3.8 2.3 5.1 2.2 5.1
       6.4 1.8 1.9 4.3 5.1 5.3;

ENDDATA

! Objective;
MIN = @SUM( Units(I) : c(I) * X(I) );

! Constraints ;
@SUM( Units(I) : b(I) * X(I) ) >= 110;

!Integer restrictions;
@FOR( Units(I) : @BIN( X(I) ));

End
```

Figure 8.6   Threshold problem structured in LINGO.

optimization problem and requires consideration as to how the objectives are to be dealt with in application. As done in previous chapters, we elect to use the weighting method to handle the two objectives. Doing this requires the following additional parameter:

w = importance weight for perimeter objective

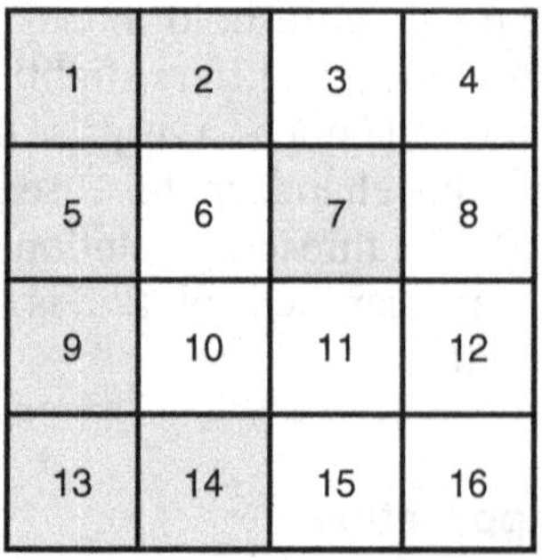

Figure 8.7   Land parcels selected using threshold model.

This weight parameter can then be used to treat the two objectives as a linear combination. Specifically, this weighted combination is as follows:

$$Maximize \quad (1 - w) \sum_i b_i X_i - w \left[\sum_i \sum_{j \in \Omega_i} p_{ij} \left(E_{ij}^+ + E_{ij}^- \right) + \sum_{i \in \Psi} p_{ii} X_i \right]$$

(8.13)

The shape model incorporates two objectives as a weighted linear combination. This is known as the *weighting method* in multiobjective optimization. Varying the weight, w, offers the potential to find noninferior, or trade-off, solutions. Such solutions represent differing decision-making preferences related to the importance of the structured problem objectives, (8.8) and (8.9).

As noted in the previous section, the approaches examined thus far are aspatial with respect to the criteria employed to select land parcels. An approach that explicitly takes into account spatial relationships in area selection is the shape model. Again, it is assumed that parcels are 1×1 km and that neighboring parcels are those sharing a nonzero length edge. It is further assumed that the value of the shape objective weight is $w = 0.4$.

The specific algebraic shape model specification for this application instance is as follows:

$$Maximize \quad 0.6 \, (19.4 \, X_1 + 16.0 \, X_2 + 14.3 \, X_3 + 15.7 \, X_4 + 15.8 \, X_5$$
$$+ \, 13.7 \, X_6 + 13.0 \, X_7 + 14.1 \, X_8 + 16.3 \, X_9 + 12.6 \, X_{10} + 15.4 \, X_{11}$$
$$+ \, 11.5 \, X_{12} + 13.4 \, X_{13} + 16.8 \, X_{14} + 13.4 \, X_{15} + 10.9 \, X_{16})$$
$$- \, 0.4 \, (EP_{1,2} + EN_{1,2} + EP_{1,5} + EN_{1,5} + EP_{2,3} + EN_{2,3} + EP_{2,6}$$
$$+ \, EN_{2,6} + EP_{3,4} + EN_{3,4} + EP_{3,7} + EN_{3,7} + EP_{4,8} + EN_{4,8} + EP_{5,6}$$
$$+ \, EN_{5,6} + EP_{5,9} + EN_{5,9} + EP_{6,7} + EN_{6,7} + EP_{6,10} + EN_{6,10} + EP_{7,8}$$
$$+ \, EN_{7,8} + EP_{7,11} + EN_{7,11} + EP_{8,12} + EN_{8,12} + EP_{9,10}$$
$$+ \, EN_{9,10} + EP_{9,13} + EN_{9,13} + EP_{10,11} + EN_{10,11} + EP_{10,14} + EN_{10,14}$$
$$+ \, EP_{11,12} + EN_{11,12} + EP_{11,15} + EN_{11,15} + EP_{12,16} + EN_{12,16}$$
$$+ \, EP_{13,14} + EN_{13,14} + EP_{14,15} + EN_{14,15} + EP_{15,16} + EN_{15,16} + 2 \, X_1$$
$$+ \, X_2 + X_3 + 2X_4 + X_5 + X_8 + X_9 + X_{12} + 2X_{13} + X_{14} + X_{15} + 2X_{16})$$

Subject to:

$$5.1 \, X_1 + 2.1 \, X_2 + 4.4 \, X_3 + 4.9 \, X_4 + 3.2 \, X_5 + 3.8 \, X_6 + 2.3 \, X_7 + 5.1 \, X_8$$
$$+ \, 2.2 \, X_9 + 5.1 \, X_{10} + 6.4 \, X_{11} + 1.8 \, X_{12} + 1.9 \, X_{13} + 4.3 \, X_{14} + 5.1 \, X_{15}$$
$$+ \, 5.3 \, X_{16} \leq 24$$

$$X_1 - X_2 + EP_{1,2} - EN_{1,2} = 0 \qquad X_7 - X_{11} + EP_{7,11} - EN_{7,11} = 0$$
$$X_1 - X_5 + EP_{1,5} - EN_{1,5} = 0 \qquad X_8 - X_{12} + EP_{8,12} - EN_{8,12} = 0$$
$$X_2 - X_3 + EP_{2,3} - EN_{2,3} = 0 \qquad X_9 - X_{10} + EP_{9,10} - EN_{9,10} = 0$$
$$X_2 - X_6 + EP_{2,6} - EN_{2,6} = 0 \qquad X_9 - X_{13} + EP_{9,13} - EN_{9,13} = 0$$
$$X_3 - X_4 + EP_{3,4} - EN_{3,4} = 0 \qquad X_{10} - X_{11} + EP_{10,11} - EN_{10,11} = 0$$
$$X_3 - X_7 + EP_{3,7} - EN_{3,7} = 0 \qquad X_{10} - X_{14} + EP_{10,14} - EN_{10,14} = 0$$
$$X_4 - X_8 + EP_{4,8} - EN_{4,8} = 0 \qquad X_{11} - X_{12} + EP_{11,12} - EN_{11,12} = 0$$
$$X_5 - X_6 + EP_{5,6} - EN_{5,6} = 0 \qquad X_{11} - X_{15} + EP_{11,15} - EN_{11,15} = 0$$
$$X_5 - X_9 + EP_{5,9} - EN_{5,9} = 0 \qquad X_{12} - X_{16} + EP_{12,16} - EN_{12,16} = 0$$
$$X_6 - X_7 + EP_{6,7} - EN_{6,7} = 0 \qquad X_{13} - X_{14} + EP_{13,14} - EN_{13,14} = 0$$
$$X_6 - X_{10} + EP_{6,10} - EN_{6,10} = 0 \qquad X_{14} - X_{15} + EP_{14,15} - EN_{14,15} = 0$$
$$X_7 - X_8 + EP_{7,8} - EN_{7,8} = 0 \qquad X_{15} - X_{16} + EP_{15,16} - EN_{15,16} = 0$$

$$X_1 = \{0, \ 1\}, X_2 = \{0, \ 1\}, X_3 = \{0, \ 1\}, X_4 = \{0, \ 1\}, X_5 = \{0, \ 1\},$$

$$X_6 = \{0, \ 1\}, X_7 = \{0, \ 1\}, X_8 = \{0, \ 1\}, X_9 = \{0, \ 1\}, X_{10} = \{0, \ 1\},$$

$$X_{11} = \{0, \ 1\}, X_{12} = \{0, \ 1\}, X_{13} = \{0, \ 1\}, X_{14} = \{0, \ 1\}, X_{15} = \{0, \ 1\},$$

$$X_{16} = \{0, \ 1\}EP_{1,2} \geq 0, EN_{1,2} \geq 0, EP_{1,5} \geq 0, EN_{1,5} \geq 0, EP_{2,3} \geq 0,$$

$$EN_{2,3} \geq 0, EP_{2,6} \geq 0, EN_{2,6} \geq 0, EP_{3,4} \geq 0, EN_{3,4} \geq 0, EP_{3,7} \geq 0,$$

$$EN_{3,7} \geq 0, EP_{4,8} \geq 0, EN_{4,8} \geq 0, EP_{5,6} \geq 0, EN_{5,6} \geq 0, EP_{5,9} \geq 0,$$

$$EN_{5,9} \geq 0, EP_{6,7} \geq 0, EN_{6,7} \geq 0, EP_{6,10} \geq 0, EN_{6,10} \geq 0, EP_{7,8} \geq 0,$$

$$EN_{7,8} \geq 0, EP_{7,11} \geq 0, EN_{7,11} \geq 0, EP_{8,12} \geq 0, EN_{8,12} \geq 0, EP_{9,10} \geq 0,$$

$$EN_{9,10} \geq 0, EP_{9,13} \geq 0, EN_{9,13} \geq 0, EP_{10,11} \geq 0, EN_{10,11} \geq 0,$$

$$EP_{10,14} \geq 0, EN_{10,14} \geq 0, EP_{11,12} \geq 0, EN_{11,12} \geq 0, EP_{11,15} \geq 0,$$

$$EN_{11,15} \geq 0, EP_{12,16} \geq 0, EN_{12,16} \geq 0, EP_{13,14} \geq 0, EN_{13,14} \geq 0,$$

$$EP_{14,15} \geq 0, EN_{14,15} \geq 0, EP_{15,16} \geq 0, EN_{15,16} \geq 0$$

The problem specification in LINGO syntax is provided in Figure 8.8.

Parcels to be acquired using the shape model are identified in Figure 8.9. The total benefit for this solution is 119.1, with a total cost of $22,400. The total external perimeter associated with selected parcels is 18 km, given that a parcel boundary is 1 km in length. Comparatively, the shape solution has a greater total benefit than the threshold solution, but at a slightly higher total cost. While not entirely contiguous (e.g., parcel 12), this configuration of land is fairly compact. Relative to the knapsack solution, the configuration shown in Figure 8.5 for the shape model is more contiguous, with only slightly less total benefit and lower total cost.

```
MODEL:
!Shape problem - LINGO format;

SETS:
 Units / 1..16 / : X, b, c, r;
 MaxAdj / 1..4 /;
 Mat(Units,Units) : EN, EP;
 Mat2(Units, MaxAdj) : a;
ENDSETS

DATA:
 b = 19.4 16.0 14.3 15.7 15.8 13.7 13.0 14.1
     16.3 12.6 15.4 11.5 13.4 16.8 13.4 10.9;

 c = 5.1 2.1 4.4 4.9 3.2 3.8 2.3 5.1 2.2 5.1
     6.4 1.8 1.9 4.3 5.1 5.3;

 w =    0.4;
 a =    2 5 0 0
        1 3 6 0
        2 4 7 0
        3 8 0 0
        1 6 9 0
        2 5 7 10
        3 6 8 11
        4 7 12 0
        5 10 13 0
        6 9 11 14
        7 10 12 15
        8 11 16 0
        9 14 0 0
        10 13 15 0
        11 14 16 0
        12 15 0 0;
 r = 2 1 1 2 1 0 0 1 1 0 0 1 2 1 1 2;
END DATA

!Objective;
MAX = (1-w)*O1 - w*O2;

!Define objectives;
O1 - @SUM(Units(I) : b(I) * X(I) ) = 0;
O2 - @SUM(Mat2(I,J)| a(I,J) #GT# 0 : EP(I, a(I,J)) + EN(I, a(I,J)) ) +
@SUM(Units(I) : r(I) * X(I) ) = 0;

!Constraints;
@SUM(Units(I) : c(I) * X(I) ) <= 24;

@For(Mat2(I,J)| a(I,J) #GT# 0 : X(I) - X(a(I,J)) - EP(I, a(I,J)) + EN(I,a(I,J))  =
0);

!Integer restrictions;
@FOR( Units(I) : @BIN( X(I) ));

End
```

Figure 8.8 Shape problem structured in LINGO.

8.5   ADVANCED TOPICS

Recognizing that it is possible to add greater spatial specificity in area-based location, an advanced topic in this chapter is detailing an approach to account for contiguity explicitly. Of course, doing this creates challenges, both in terms of mathematical representation and computational complexity.

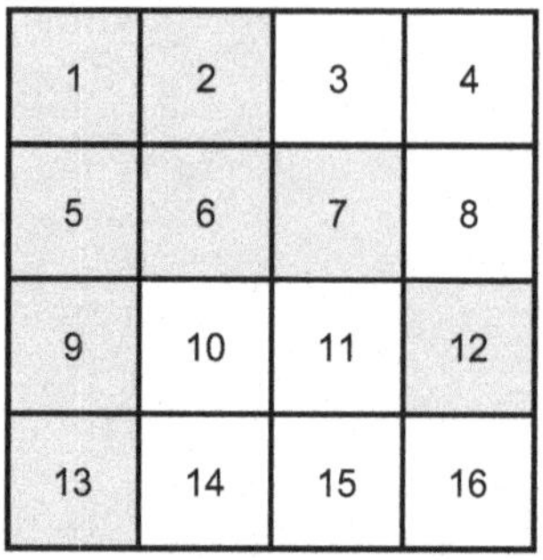

Figure 8.9   Land parcels selected using shape model ($w = 0.4$).

Another category of area selection is called the *contiguity* model. Mentioned previously was the importance of shape considerations in the acquisition of land, and contiguity was noted as being related to shape. Contiguity relative to land acquisition is where any selected parcel can be traveled to from a given parcel without leaving acquired land parcels. Selected parcels in Figure 8.8 show a contiguous subregion (with one exception, where unit 12 only touches unit 7 and does not share an edge). It may be important in a planning context to ensure that acquired land is contiguous. If this is the case, none of the models detailed thus far will guarantee such an outcome.

We need the following notation to add contiguity considerations to the previously formulated models:

m = large number (at least the total number of parcels)

Z_{ij} = path flow between parcel i and j

$$V_i = \begin{cases} 1 & \text{if parcel } i \text{ selected as a root} \\ 0 & \text{otherwise} \end{cases}$$

$$\text{Maximize} \quad \sum_i b_i X_i \tag{8.14}$$

Subject to:

$$\sum_i c_i X_i \leq \mu \tag{8.15}$$

$$\sum_{j \in \Omega_i} Z_{ij} - \sum_{j \in \Omega_i} Z_{ji} \geq X_i - m\,V_i \quad \forall i \tag{8.16}$$

$$\sum_i V_i = 1 \tag{8.17}$$

$$\sum_{j \in \Omega_i} Z_{ij} \le (m - 1) X_i \quad \forall i \tag{8.18}$$

$$V_i \le X_i \quad \forall i \tag{8.19}$$

$$X_i = \{0, 1\} \quad \forall i \tag{8.20}$$

$$V_i = \{0, 1\} \quad \forall i$$

$$Z_{ij} \ge 0 \quad \forall i, j$$

The objective, (8.14), is to maximize the benefit of acquired land. Constraint (8.15) limits total acquired land by the project budget. Thus far, this is nothing other than the knapsack model. Conditions imposing contiguity between selected parcels are structured in constraints (8.16) to (8.19). These constraints establish a root parcel to be acquired, then enforce connectivity between selected parcels and the root parcel. Constraints (8.20) impose integer restrictions and nonnegativity requirements on decision variables.

Interpreting the contiguity constraints in the context of the reserve design application, Constraints (8.16) for parcel 7 would be as follows:

$$Z_{7,6} + Z_{7,8} + Z_{7,3} + Z_{7,11} - Z_{6,7} - Z_{8,7} - Z_{3,7} - Z_{11,7} \ge X_7 - 16V_7$$

The realization of constraints (8.18) for parcel 7 would be:

$$Z_{7,6} + Z_{7,8} + Z_{7,3} + Z_{7,11} \le 15X_7$$

Finally, constraints (8.19) for parcel 7 would be:

$$V_7 \le X_7$$

Constraints similar to these would be needed for each parcel. These constraints, in addition to Constraint (8.16) establishing one sink, ensure a contiguous configuration of acquired parcels.

This model has also been a sole or primary feature of recent land use planning approaches, including that of Wu and Murray (2007).

8.6 SUMMARY

Area-based location continues to be challenging because of the desire to better represent complex spatial relationships in planning models. The shape model not only attempted to explicitly address spatial configuration, but also provided the capacity to identify trade-offs between perimeter importance and total benefit associated with the selection of parcels. Though only briefly mentioned in the chapter, these two concerns represent multiple objectives in the optimization model. Their integration in the shape model as a weighted linear function is but one way to address multiple objectives. Further, only one weighting value was considered here. It is typically the case that the entire range of weighting values is considered in practice as other unique solutions may exist, and likely would be of interest as planning alternatives. In addition, other approaches exist for finding trade-off, or nondominated, solutions, such as the constraint method.

In addition to mathematical complexities like multiple objectives, increasing attention has been turned to different measures of shape and explicitly addressing contiguity issues. The advanced topic illustrated how the incorporation of spatial and topological properties, like contiguity, are not only challenging, but require greater mathematical sophistication and the explicit use of GIS (see Wu and Murray 2008).

8.7 TERMS

land-use acquisition
knapsack model
threshold model
shape model
perimeter
adjacency
contiguity

8.8 REFERENCES

Davis, F. W., D. M. Stoms, R. L. Church, W. J. Okin, and K. N. Johnson. 1996. Selecting biodiversity management areas. In *Sierra Nevada Ecosystem Project: Final report to Congress*. Davis: University of California.

Wright, J., C. ReVelle, J. Cohon. 1983. A multiobjective integer programming model for the land acquisition problem. *Regional Science and Urban Economics* 13:31–53.

Wu, X., and A. T. Murray. 2007. Spatial contiguity optimization in land acquisition. *Journal of Land Use Science* 2:243–256.

Wu, X., and A. T. Murray. 2008. A new approach to quantifying spatial contiguity using graph theory and spatial interaction. *International Journal of Geographical Information Science* 22.

8.9 EXERCISES

8.1. Nature Conservancy is interested in acquiring land to protect the endangered mission blue butterfly (*Icaricia icarioides missionensis*). It needs a minimum area of land to protect this species, and has a limited budget for purchasing land. Can you suggest an optimization model to support this decision-making problem?

8.2. Compute the total area for the following shapes. Also compute the total perimeter of each area object. How do these shapes compare with respect to area and perimeter?

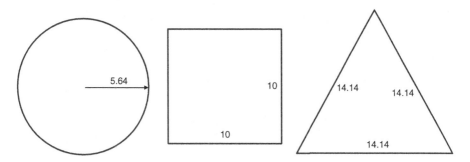

8.3. Suppose that for the land-acquisition problems addressed in this chapter, there was a requirement that units 10, 12, and 16 could *not* be selected. How could the knapsack and threshold models be altered to incorporate this additional requirement (i.e., $X_{10} = X_{12} = X_{16} = 0$)? Do the results change if such conditions are included in the optimization models?

8.4. Explore how shape model solutions change if the weight w is varied between 0 and 1. Do you expect a change? What is the rationale behind any identified changes?

CHAPTER 9

COVERAGE

9.0 INTRODUCTION

The first two parts of this text discussed the theory of location analysis, GIS and model building fundamentals, and various modeling approaches for addressing what are generally single facility location problems. In essence we have set the stage for being able to now address more combinatorically difficult location problems. Part 3 of this text covers three different classes of multisite location problems.

We introduced the third law of location science (LLS3) in Chapter 1: *Sites of an optimal multisite pattern must be selected simultaneously rather than independently, one at a time.* The combinatorics of even the most simple multiple-facility problems are daunting. For example, assume there are m sites where p facilities could be located. The number of unique **combinations** for such a configuration of facilities is $m!/p! \, (m - p)!$. If there are 86 potential sites for locating 11 facilities, this means that there are 24,464,362,713,336 combinations possible (over 24 trillion!). Examining each of the 24+ trillion spatial configurations using a process of enumeration would be so time consuming that it would be impossible. For all intents and purposes, enumeration is relegated to problems where the number of possible alternatives is small in number.

The question, then, is, how do we analyze problems involving the location of multiple facilities? The answer is to employ mathematical modeling. Optimization models have been a mainstay in location analysis work for the past 40+ years. Here we show how optimization can be used to locate a set of service facilities, where **standards-based service** is defined in terms of some type of spatial standard. Examples of spatial standards include a maximal acceptable response time in responding to a call for emergency service like fire or EMS, the audible range of an emergency warning siren alerting the public of approaching severe weather, the maximum distance out to which radar can detect objects/phenomena (e.g., Doppler radar), to name but a few. Spatial standards are akin to the notion of *range* in central place theory, as a facility providing some sort of service has a distance based range beyond which it is either impossible or considerably less desirable to serve demand. Two of the most prominent standards-based (or coverage) location models are the **location set covering problem** (LSCP) and the **maximal covering location problem** (MCLP). These two problems will be detailed in the sections that follow. Advanced topics explored in this chapter include other models for addressing issues of backup coverage, service availability, and spatial representation. Many planning applications have been pursued using coverage location models: nature reserve design, cell tower siting, air quality monitoring, fire station location, groundwater monitoring, banking, and many other important issues.

9.1 PROBLEM DEFINITION AND MOTIVATION

Providing fire and emergency medical services (EMS) is big business. The city of Los Angeles, for example, operates a fire department composed of 103 stations, approximately 3,800 personneling, a population of about 4 million people spread over some 470 square miles. This department keeps 1,045 firefighters on duty at all times. Including the police, Los Angeles spends more than $1 billion per year on public safety. The Los Angeles Fire Department responds to both EMS and fire emergencies, which amounted to more than 715,000 emergency service calls in 2004. As another example, the city of Hong Kong handles more than 35,000 fire calls and close to 600,000 EMS calls each year, maintaining nearly 600 firetrucks and 250 ambulances housed at 109 stations. Even smaller towns operate multiple stations and have a sizable payroll. For example, Culver City, California, has a population of 30,000 people and is served by three fire stations. Whatever the size, this means that it is very important to be as efficient as possible in providing emergency services, or the costs would be even higher.

One problem faced by many communities is where to locate fire stations. Even though most people do not want to live next to a station, they do want fire protection services nearby. The value of fire protection services is time critical. If a crew at a station takes more than 10 minutes to reach a structure fire, there is a significant chance that the fire will consume major portions or even all of the structure, threatening lives and property. Most fires can be easily extinguished when response is timely, assuming that the mixture of equipment and crew is sufficient. The trick is to respond quickly, before a fire gets out of control. To protect people and property, it is necessary to establish a network of stations with appropriate equipment so areas of a city can be reached from their nearest station within a short distance. For example, some communities stipulate no more than 1.5 miles, or a maximum response time of 6 minutes.[1] If a station is within a maximum response distance or time of a neighborhood, then the station is "covering" that neighborhood. Thus, we can establish a standard with respect to travel distance or response time in this situation.

Another issue faced in the case of fire suppression is providing the public service in a fiscally efficient manner. As already noted, even a small town or city might have more than one fire station because of the need for timely response when a fire does break out. However, too many fire stations can be unsustainable, as a station typically costs $2 million or more plus the cost of firefighting personnel. Thus, given a performance standard associated with service provision, city planners seek to site multiple fire stations in an efficient manner.

9.1.1 Complete Coverage

Again considering the issue of firefighting and emergency medical service, suppose that we are interested in providing **complete coverage** to a region. Viewing the fire station as a facility, we can state our standards-based planning problem in a somewhat generic form with respect to service and efficiency as follows:

> Find the minimum number of facilities and their locations such that all neighborhoods are covered within the maximal distance or time standard.

The requirement, then, is that all neighborhoods (or areas) are served, or covered, by located facilities, where coverage is defined in terms of a maximal distance or time standard. Essentially, a demand area is covered if it is within a maximal distance or time standard of a facility. System efficiency is accounted for in this case through the goal to minimize the number of needed facilities to cover or serve all neighborhoods.

This planning problem is called the *location set covering problem* (LSCP) and was proposed in a spatial context by Toregas et al. (1971). The LSCP is based on the assumption that the cost of building a facility does not vary appreciably across a city or town. The rationale for this is that the cost of a facility is often much less than the costs of the labor needed to provide the service. For example, a fire station costs approximately $2 million to develop and build, but the costs of operation may exceed that amount each year!

---

[1] Such requirements can be driven by the insurance industry as well, as the insurance industry has written fire insurance policies for over a hundred years. They rate municipalities in their level of fire protection service and then set premiums based on this level of service. One of the main factors is geographical coverage. Guidelines state that dense urban areas should have a fire station within three-quarters of a mile, and less-dense suburban areas should have a station within a mile and a half for suitable coverage.

Thus, the individual facility and site costs, while significant, often do not vary substantially and are relatively small when compared to overall system operations cost, so the number of facilities is an important efficiency measure of geographical facility arrangement.

9.1.2 Maximal Coverage

Suppose that for a given **maximal service** distance or time standard, that the number of facilities needed for complete coverage is too many for a city to afford. This predicament is common for public agencies. One must ask, just how much coverage can be provided with a limited number of facilities? If coverage levels could be high using a limited number of facilities, then it might be more acceptable to leave only a few areas served at a distance beyond the standard, while covering a high proportion of the demand within the standard. For example, geographically, it might be possible to cover 90 percent of demand if only a few facilities are sited, in contrast to covering the entire region with many more facilities. Thus, a second standards-based location problem is the following:

> Locate a prespecified number of facilities such that coverage within a maximal service distance or time is maximized.

This problem recognizes the realities of financial limitations, yet offers the potential to do the best with the resources available. System efficiency in this case is to maximize what demand can be covered when using a limited number of facilities. This problem is called the *maximal covering location problem* (MCLP). It was introduced in Church and ReVelle (1974). It makes sense to use a model like the LSCP if resources are sufficient. But when resources are limited, then the MCLP is more appropriate. Again, the focus of the MCLP is to use our facility resources to the maximal extent possible, by providing service-based coverage to the largest amount of demand.

9.2 MATHEMATICAL REPRESENTATION

One important issue in mathematically formalizing the LSCP and MCLP is the measurement of demand for service. A region of analysis is typically divided into small spatial units, or polygons. Each unit is a geographically contiguous area, and could represent a city, a policing precinct, a fire response zone, or even a neighborhood. For a given planning problem, there may be hundreds or thousands of such units. It is generally assumed that the spatial extent of each demand unit is relatively small, when compared to the maximal service distance or travel time standard. Note that the facility may provide the service to the unit (e.g., fire station response) or the service may be provided at the facility (e.g., treatment at a heath care center).

A second issue is where the facilities can potentially be located. We assume that site suitability analysis has been carried out in advance, so only a finite set of potential facility locations will be considered. Note, however, that there are approaches for dealing with standards-based problems if facilities can be located anywhere in space (e.g., continuous space).

Consider the following notation:

j = index of potential facility sites where $j = 1, 2, \ldots, m$
i = index demand units where $i = 1, 2, \ldots, n$
$a_{ij} = \begin{cases} 1, & \text{if facility located at site } j \text{ covers demand unit } i \\ 0, & \text{if not} \end{cases}$

It is assumed that we can determine which units can be provided coverage by a facility-specific site. This means that we can then define a_{ij} accordingly. More discussion on this is left for later in the chapter.

What remains now is to define decision variables associated with whether or not a facility is located at a given potential site j:

$X_j = \begin{cases} 1, & \text{if a facility is located at potential site } j \\ 0, & \text{otherwise} \end{cases}$

Selection of a given site j is represented by a binary (or integer) variable, where the value of the variable represents whether the site is selected for facility placement or not. The LSCP and MCLP can now be formally specified.

9.2.1   Complete Coverage

The LSCP (location set covering problem) already described is to choose the smallest set of sites such that each demand unit is covered at least once. The binary decision variables can be used to mathematically structure an optimization model for this problem. The objective is to minimize the number of sites chosen. This can be stated mathematically as:

$$Minimize \quad X_1 + X_2 + \ldots + X_m \tag{9.1}$$

This objective, given the binary values of the decision variables, will be the sum of ones (associated with the sites that are selected) and zeroes (associated with the sites that are not selected). Thus, it will equal the total number of selected sites.

We can rewrite (9.1) in an equivalent form using summation notation:

$$Minimize \quad \sum_{j=1}^{m} X_j \tag{9.2}$$

The constraints for the LSCP must ensure that the selection of sites cover each demand unit. For unit i, the requirement is that at least one site that provides coverage is selected. Mathematically, this can be stated as:

$$a_{i1}X_1 + a_{i2}X_2 + \ldots + a_{im}X_m \geq 1 \tag{9.3}$$

Of course, this equation will be somewhat simplified once the values of each a_{ij} are defined in application, as all zero-valued coefficients will effectively drop out of the equation. For example, if sites 3, 5, and 7 can cover demand i, then equation (9.3) would be $X_3 + X_5 + X_7 \geq 1$, upon inserting the values of a_{ij}. This means that for the constraint to be met, at least one of the sites 3, 5, or 7 must be selected for demand i to be covered, which is the purpose of the constraint. Rewriting inequality (9.3) in a summation format yields the following:

$$\sum_{j=1}^{m} a_{ij}X_j \geq 1 \tag{9.4}$$

Altogether, the complete model for the LSCP is

$$Minimize \quad \sum_{j=1}^{m} X_j \tag{9.5}$$

Subject to:

$$\sum_{j=1}^{m} a_{ij}X_j \geq 1 \quad \text{for each } i = 1, 2, \ldots, n \tag{9.6}$$

$$X_j = \{0, 1\} \quad \text{for each } j = 1, 2, \ldots, m \tag{9.7}$$

The objective of the LSCP, (9.5), minimizes the number of facilities selected. Constraints (9.6) specify that each demand unit i must be covered by at least one located facility. Finally, constraints (9.7) impose integer restrictions on the decision variables.

The above model minimizes the number of sites selected so that each unit is covered by one or more selected facility sites. The model is relatively small in terms of mathematical structure as there is one constraint for each demand unit and one decision variable for each site that may be selected. Thus, there are n constraints and m variables, plus integer restrictions on decision variables. Note that the LSCP incorporates a linear objective function and linear constraints, with the exception of the integer restrictions on the variables. Thus, it is an integer-linear programming model.

9.2.2 Maximal Coverage

The LSCP specifies that all demand units are to be covered, which assumes that sufficient resources exist to locate all necessary facilities to achieve this. What if there are budgetary limitations? What if a city simply cannot afford to build and maintain the number of facilities needed for complete coverage? If this is the case, then another modeling approach is necessary, one that seeks to do the best possible job with the level of resources available. With respect to standards based modeling, the goal would be to maximize coverage provided by a specified number of facilities, and this was defined as MCLP.

For the maximal covering problem, service is not guaranteed, as it is now conditional upon whether a facility is located in order to provide service to an area within the stipulated standard. Thus, we need to be able to distinguish between whether coverage has been provided or not to a given demand unit. To do this, the following decision variables are needed:

$$Y_i = \begin{cases} 1, & \text{if unit } i \text{ is covered by at least one facility} \\ 0, & \text{otherwise} \end{cases}$$

We also need to be able to distinguish the level of demand between spatial units, as demand for services is often heterogeneously distributed across space, as well as specify the number of facilities that we can afford to site. Accordingly, consider the following two model parameters:

$g_i = $ service demand in unit i
$p = $ number of facilities to locate

A model for maximal covering using this additional notation can be structured as follows:

$$\text{Maximize} \quad \sum_{i=1}^{n} g_i Y_i \tag{9.8}$$

Subject to:

$$\sum_{j=1}^{m} a_{ij} X_j \geq Y_i \quad \text{for each } i = 1, 2, \ldots, n \tag{9.9}$$

$$\sum_{j} X_j = p \tag{9.10}$$

$$X_j = \{0, 1\} \quad \text{for each } j = 1, 2, \ldots, m \tag{9.11}$$

$$Y_i = \{0, 1\} \quad \text{for each } i = 1, 2, \ldots, n$$

The objective of the MCLP, (9.8), is to maximize the amount of covered demand. Constraints (9.9) define whether coverage has been provided to a given demand i based upon the location decisions. Constraints (9.10) specify that p facilities are to be located. Integer restrictions on the siting and coverage variables are stipulated in constraints (9.11). Structurally, the MCLP works in the following way. Given the orientation of the objective, if demand unit i is provided coverage, then the decision variable Y_i will be equal to 1 and the objective will count the demand in unit i, g_i, as covered. If a unit is not covered, then the associated Y_i variable will be zero and the objective will not count the demand of that unit as being covered.

Coverage is accounted for in (9.9), because if $\sum_j a_{ij} X_j$ is zero, then no facilities have been located in order to cover unit i, When this happens, the value of the decision variable Y_i will be constrained to equal zero, indicating that demand unit i has not been covered. If, however, $\sum_j a_{ij} X_j$ is greater than or equal to 1, then one or more facilities have been sited that cover demand unit i and the variable Y_i can then equal 1, indicating that it is covered. This set of constraints, (9.9), then translates site decisions X_j into whether coverage is provided to a given demand i (i.e., Y_i equals 1 if covered, or 0 if not). The sense of the objective will ensure that if a demand is covered, its associated Y_i variable will be forced to equal 1.

The LSCP and the MCLP have both been solved by a variety of optimal and heuristic techniques. In many cases, general-purpose integer-linear programming software packages, such as LINGO, have be used to efficiently solve these problems optimally.

9.3   GISCIENCE

A critical issue in applying models like the LSCP or the MCLP is obtaining and/or deriving the data to support the model. This is not to say that it is the only issue, but, nonetheless the role of model setup and data support is important. For both the LSCP and the MCLP, there are three major items needed for a specific problem instance, and GIS plays a central role in organizing and deriving such data. These three data elements are: (1) the set of demand units to be served, (2) the set of feasible facility sites, and (3) the service coverage capabilities for facilities/units.

Demand units could represent a range of geographies, including zipcodes, fire response zones or neighborhoods. In many location studies Census-based geographical units are used, such as blocks, block groups or tracts. Historically, point representations of demand units have been utilized, often centroids of demand polygons. In fact, any spatial unit could be considered: point, line, polygon, circle, ellipse, arc. One is only limited by the capabilities of the GIS. Though this is an important detail that can impact analysis, it has ultimately been left to the analyst to decide what spatial representation of demand units is most appropriate for the study at hand.

Potential facility sites often are dictated by available land, proximity to infrastructure, and other constraining conditions. It is precisely this context that the GIS based methodologies detailed in Chapter 5 (suitability analysis) are applied, and from this the set of feasible facility sites is derived. There are circumstances, however, where such detailed feasibility analysis is not pursued. In strategic planning, where one wants to get a general idea of how many facilities can serve a region or estimate budget needs for a siting project, analysts may allow facilities to be located anywhere in space (e.g., continuous space). Alternatively, some studies simply allow facilities to be located at centroids of demand units. Thus, potential facility sites are either identified using a GIS-based suitability analysis process or some other defendable approach, giving a discrete set of possible locations for facilities.

The final data element that needs to be derived is the service coverage capabilities of each possible facility site. Specifically, this task refers to determining the values of the a_{ij} coverage matrix. If the coverage standard is based on distance, then a spatial query identifying those units covered by a facility at site j can be structured. In some cases this may be a kind of buffer analysis. If the standard is based on a travel time, then travel times are needed to delineate the coverage area associated with a given site. There are several ways in which this can be done, from using a road network and determining paths of shortest travel time between each facility and all other demand units to collecting travel data. Coverage areas drawn around a facility are likely to be irregular polygons, and may be contiguous or noncontiguous. Ultimately, what is derived can be summarized in terms of a coverage table or matrix like that presented in Table 9.1 corresponding to the demand units and sites indicated in Figure 9.1. Table 9.1 is an organized presentation of the a_{ij} matrix indicating which sites cover each demand unit. For example, we see that demand unit G would be covered, or served, by facilities located at sites 1 and 2, that is, $a_{G1} = 1$ and $a_{G2} = 1$. Note that sites 3 through 9 cannot cover demand unit G, so $a_{G3} = a_{G4} = ... = a_{G9} = 0$. It is worth highlighting that there is no assumed regularity of shape for a coverage region emanating from site j, as a given region may be regular, irregular, contiguous, or noncontiguous, depending on how

TABLE 9.1   Demand coverage by sites

Demand	Site 1	Site 2	Site 3	Site 4	Site 5	Site 6	Site 7	Site 8	Site 9
A	0	0	0	0	1	1	0	0	0
B	0	0	0	0	0	1	1	1	1
C	0	0	0	0	0	0	1	1	1
D	0	0	0	1	1	1	0	1	0
E	1	1	0	0	0	0	0	1	1
F	0	1	1	1	0	0	0	0	0
G	1	1	0	0	0	0	0	0	0

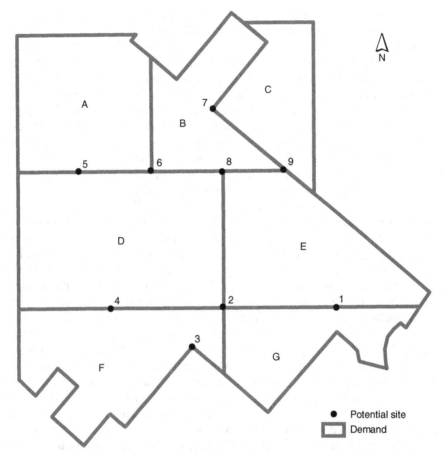

Figure 9.1   Demand units to be served and potential facility sites.

service is provided. Such conditions can be easily handled within the context of GIS.

A final point regarding GIS is that once a model is solved, another essential feature is the capability to display selected facility sites, facility service areas, and covered demand units. This enables further analysis and evaluation to take place, and may even lead to problem alteration and/or modification of coverage parameters.

9.4   MODELING APPLICATION

In this section, the LSCP and the MCLP are utilized for fire station location planning. We apply these two models to the region depicted in Figure 9.1 involving nine sites and seven demand areas where the coverage matrix is as specified in Table 9.1. The intent is to use the two models to identify the best multiple-facility siting configurations involving standards-based coverage. Linear programming and/or linear programming with branch and bound is used for model solution, accessed through LINGO.

9.4.1 LSCP

Suppose that we are interested in covering each demand unit depicted in Figure 9.1 with a fire station using the LSCP model. The coverage capabilities of each potential station location are summarized in Table 9.1. Specifically, the cover matrix indicates which potential facility sites cover each demand unit. The goal is to suitably cover the seven demand units with the fewest number of needed facilities. The generic algebraic statement of the LSCP, (9.5) to (9.7), can be interpreted mathematically for this problem application given the data inputs as follows:

$$Minimize \quad X_1 + X_2 + X_3 + X_4 + X_5 + X_6 + X_7 + X_8 + X_9$$

Subject to

$$X_5 + X_6 \geq 1$$
$$X_6 + X_7 + X_8 \geq 1$$
$$X_7 + X_9 \geq 1$$
$$X_2 + X_4 + X_5 + X_6 + X_8 \geq 1$$
$$X_1 + X_2 + X_8 + X_9 \geq 1$$
$$X_2 + X_3 + X_4 \geq 1$$
$$X_1 + X_2 \geq 1$$
$$X_1 = \{0, 1\}, \ X_2 = \{0, 1\}, \ X_3 = \{0, 1\}, \ X_4 = \{0, 1\}, \ X_5 = \{0, 1\}$$
$$X_6 = \{0, 1\}, \ X_7 = \{0, 1\}, \ X_8 = \{0, 1\}, \ X_9 = \{0, 1\}$$

In order to solve this model using LINGO, we first need to translate the problem to its LINGO equivalent format, and this is given in Figure 9.2. In the LINGO specification of the LSCP, notice that basic set-up is done first, where sets and variables are defined and input data are provided. After this is done, the objective is defined and constraints are stipulated. Solving the LSCP finds that three facilities are necessary for providing coverage to each demand unit. The solution is $X_2 = X_6 = X_9 = 1$, and all other variables are equal to zero. The configuration of selected facilities using the LSCP is shown in Figure 9.3.

```
! Location Set Covering Problem;
MODEL:
SETS:
 sites /1..9/: X ;
 units /A,B,C,D,E,F,G/;
 coverage(units,sites): a ;
ENDSETS

DATA:
 a =  0 0 0 0 1 1 0 0 0
      0 0 0 0 0 1 1 1 1
      0 0 0 0 0 0 1 1 1
      0 0 0 1 1 1 0 1 0
      1 1 0 0 0 0 0 1 1
      0 1 1 1 0 0 0 0 0
      1 1 0 0 0 0 0 0 0;

ENDDATA

! Objective: Minimize the number of facilities selected;
 MIN = @SUM(sites(j): X(j));

! Constraints: Ensure that each demand is covered;
 @FOR(units(i):
  @SUM(sites(j): a(i,j)*X(j)) >= 1;);

! Binary constraints;
 @FOR (sites(j): @BIN(X(j)));

END
```

Figure 9.2 LINGO specification of the LSCP.

9.4.2 MCLP

As detailed previously, an issue arises in using the LSCP when budgetary limits fall short of what is needed for complete coverage. If this is the case, the MCLP is appropriate because it seeks an optimal configuration of facilities that covers as much of the demand to be served as possible. Returning to the demand region shown in Figure 9.1, if the region can only afford two fire stations, then the solution identified using the LSCP is not feasible. Thus, the MCLP is needed. Demand for each unit is specified in Table 9.2 and represents an estimate of the number of fire response calls anticipated over a period of time. This estimate is an attribute of the demand polygons and can be derived from parcel data on buildings and improvements, as well as historical data on building fires. Given the coverage capabilities of each potential station site summarized in Table 9.1, and the demand data given in Table 9.2, the algebraic statement of the MCLP, (9.8) to (9.11), can be

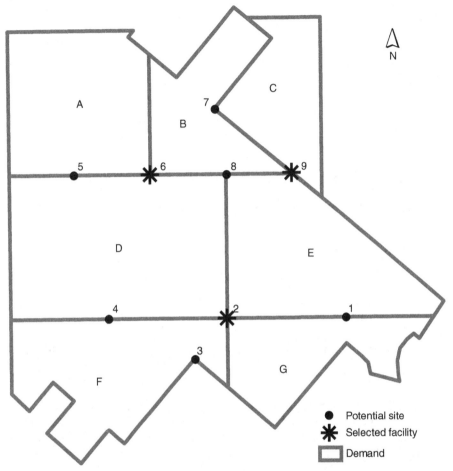

Figure 9.3   Optimal LSCP facility configuration.

TABLE 9.2   Demand unit attributes

Demand	Expected calls (g_i)
A	4
B	6
C	9
D	3
E	9
F	8
G	6

interpreted mathematically as follows:

$$Maximize \quad 4Y_A + 6Y_B + 9Y_C + 3Y_D + 9Y_E + 8Y_F + 6Y_G$$

Subject to:

$$X_5 + X_6 \geq Y_A$$
$$X_6 + X_7 + X_8 \geq Y_B$$
$$X_7 + X_9 \geq Y_C$$
$$X_2 + X_4 + X_5 + X_6 + X_8 \geq Y_D$$
$$X_1 + X_2 + X_8 + X_9 \geq Y_E$$
$$X_2 + X_3 + X_4 \geq Y_F$$
$$X_1 + X_2 \geq Y_G$$
$$X_1 + X_2 + X_3 + X_4 + X_5 + X_6 + X_7 + X_8 + X_9 = 2$$
$$X_1 = \{0, 1\}, \ X_2 = \{0, 1\}, \ X_3 = \{0, 1\}, \ X_4 = \{0, 1\}, \ X_5 = \{0, 1\}$$
$$X_6 = \{0, 1\}, \ X_7 = \{0, 1\}, \ X_8 = \{0, 1\}, \ X_9 = \{0, 1\}$$
$$Y_A = \{0, 1\}, \ Y_B = \{0, 1\}, \ Y_C = \{0, 1\}, \ Y_D = \{0, 1\}, \ Y_E = \{0, 1\},$$
$$Y_F = \{0, 1\}, \ Y_G = \{0, 1\}$$

Again, solving this model using LINGO requires translation of the problem into a LINGO equivalent format. This is provided in Figure 9.4. The LINGO specification of the MCLP is similar to that of the LSCP except for a few additional data values and variables, namely g_i and Y_i. Given that three facilities are needed for complete coverage, the MCLP is evaluated for the case where only two facilities are to be located. The optimal solution is $X_2 = X_8 = 1$ and all other facility siting variables are equal to zero. The configuration of selected facilities identified using the MCLP is shown in Figure 9.5. Of the 45 total expected service calls for fire response, it is possible to cover 41 within the stipulated standard when two facilities are sited. Thus, $Y_A = 0$ and is the only demand area not capable of being suitably covered by the sited facilities, which means that all other Y_i are equal to 1.

9.5 ADVANCED TOPICS

The literature reports many examples of how the LSCP and MCLP have been extended in order to address various issues in application. A few such issues are detailed in this chapter as advanced topics in standards-based location modeling: backup coverage, service availability, and spatial representation.

```
! Maximal Covering Location Problem;
MODEL:
SETS:
 sites /1..9/: X ;
 units /A,B,C,D,E,F,G/: g, Y ;
 coverage(units,sites): a ;
ENDSETS

DATA:
 a =  0 0 0 0 0 1 1 0 0 0
      0 0 0 0 0 0 1 1 1 1
      0 0 0 0 0 0 0 1 1 1
      0 0 0 1 1 1 0 1 0
      1 1 0 0 0 0 0 1 1
      0 1 1 1 0 0 0 0 0
      1 1 0 0 0 0 0 0 0;

 g = 4 6 9 3 9 8 6;

ENDDATA

! Objective: Minimize the number of facilities selected;
 MAX = @SUM(units(i): g(i)*Y(i));

! Constraints: Ensure that each demand is covered;
 @FOR(units(i):
  @SUM(sites(j): a(i,j)*X(j)) - Y(i) >= 0;);

! Constraints: Locate specified number of facilities;
 @SUM(sites(j): X(j)) = 2;

! Binary constraints;
 @FOR (sites(j): @BIN(X(j)));
 @FOR (units(i): @BIN(Y(i)));

END
```

Figure 9.4 LINGO specification of the MCLP.

9.5.1 Backup Coverage

As reviewed previously, the LSCP seeks to minimize the number of facilities needed to provide coverage to all demand for service, yet there is motivation for emphasizing multiple coverage of an area, rather than only coverage by a single facility. This may be achievable, but requires a more comprehensive model. In essence, the problem definition of the LSCP could be further enhanced:

Locate the fewest number of facilities needed to cover each demand unit at least once, but cover demand units a second time to the greatest extent possible.

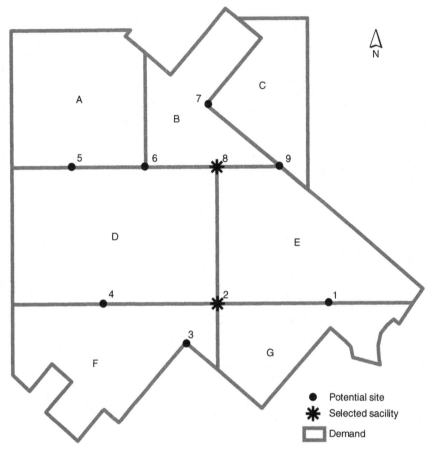

Figure 9.5 Optimal MCLP facility configuration ($p = 2$).

What is desired in this case is to cover each demand unit once, then to the extent possible ensure that facilities are configured so as to maximize demand units covered twice. This assumes that there is system flexibility. It turns out that such flexibility is typically characteristic of coverage models, so we would expect that there exist multiple optima and we are interested in the solution that can cover the most demand twice. The following additional decision variables are needed to specify this model extension:

$$U_i = \begin{cases} 1, & \text{if demand } i \text{ is covered by more than one facility} \\ 0, & \text{otherwise} \end{cases}$$

This variable will be used to account for demand units being provided double coverage. The associated model for achieving this is

$$Maximize \quad \sum_i U_i \qquad (9.12)$$

Subject to:

$$\sum_j a_{ij} X_j \geq 1 + U_i \quad \forall i \tag{9.13}$$

$$\sum_j X_j = p \tag{9.14}$$

$$X_j = \{0, 1\} \quad \forall j \tag{9.15}$$

$$U_i \leq 1 \quad \forall i$$

The objective (9.12) maximizes the number of units covered a second time. If demand i is provided coverage once, then the decision variable U_i will be forced to equal zero and the objective will not count unit i as being provided a second level of coverage. If a unit is covered twice, then the associated U_i variable will be 1 in value, and the objective will count that unit as being covered a second time.

Constraints (9.13) perform two functions: ensure that each unit is covered at least once and account for the case that a unit is covered twice. For example, $\sum_j a_{ij} X_j$ must be greater than or equal to the value of $1 + U_i$. Since U_i can be 0 or 1, the lowest combined value of $1 + U_i$ is one. Thus, at least $\sum_j a_{ij} X_j \geq 1$, which means that each unit must be covered at least once. The only way U_i can be one is when $\sum_j a_{ij} X_j \geq 2$, which means that the unit has been covered at least a second time.

Constraint (9.14) is like that used in the MCLP and establishes that exactly p facilities be sited. The value of p must be set at a value that is equal to or greater than the minimum number of facilities needed for coverage of all demand (identified by using the LSCP). Thus, this new model could be used to identify the best of the multiple optimal solutions, identifying the solution that covers the most units a second time after covering everything once.

This has been called a *backup coverage model* and was effectively introduced in Daskin and Stern (1981). Additional coverage levels for a demand unit, when provided at no additional facility cost, yield greater flexibility in management. For example, if the equipment at one facility is out of service, then an alternate facility can still provide service within the coverage standard. The presence of backup coverage is a property that should be sought and optimized, if it can be achieved at no additional cost.

9.5.2 Service Availability

The reality is that sometimes service may not be available from a facility. Calls for firefighting units are often spread far enough apart in time that a crew receives a call, responds to that call, and then returns to the station before another call is received in the service area of that station. In fact, most crew time is spent at the station, waiting and preparing for the next call. Calls for EMS response, however, are far more frequent and can easily take an hour or more to handle. The most critical component is the time it takes to get paramedics to the scene (i.e., response time). The total time to handle a call includes the response time, the time to stabilize the patient, the time to transport the patient to the hospital, and the time to ready the ambulance for another call. The time to handle a call may also include the time to reposition the vehicle at its home base or dispatch location.

The basic question is, what happens when the ambulance serving an area is busy when the next call comes in? If another vehicle is free and within the coverage area of the call, a response will provide service within the standard. If the closest available ambulance is farther away than the service time standard, then that call will be served, but not within the desired service time. This circumstance should be avoided, if possible. Thus, we need to keep track of the potential busyness of an ambulance in order to assess actual coverage. If facilities may be busy, then coverage is a function of spatial proximity and service availability, necessitating a new problem definition:

> Locate the fewest number of facilities needed to cover each demand unit at a specified level of service availability.

This means that facility busyness must be explicitly considered in the model.

One of the methods used to estimate the time it takes to serve all demand in an area is to multiply the demand times service time. Given an estimate of needed service time, the busyness of k facilities serving demand i can be estimated as follows:

$$b_{ik} = \frac{\bar{t} \sum_{l \in M_i} g_l}{24k} \tag{9.16}$$

where

$$\bar{t} = \text{average length of time to service a call (in hours)}$$
$$M_i = \text{demand units in service area centered at unit } i$$

The numerator represents the total hours of service (average service time multiplied by total demand in a local area) and the denominator represents the total hours of service time available, if k units are present in the local area around demand i. The fraction, then, is the average busyness of each facility.

Given an estimate of the busyness of facilities serving the local area around demand i, the probability that at least one facility will be available when a call is received can be estimated. If only one facility is located within service coverage of demand i, then the **probabilistic coverage** covered would be one minus the probability of being busy: $1 - b_{i1}$. For k facilities, this would be

$1 - (b_{ik})^k$. In making this calculation, it is assumed that the availability of each facility is independent of the others and that the difference in the amount of local demand served by facilities outside the local area is equal to the demand outside the local area that is served by facilities within the local area.

If each demand i must be covered with a 90 percent reliability, then the number of facilities serving the local area around i, r_i, needs to be high enough that the probability of being covered equals or exceeds 90 percent. This means that for demand i:

$$r_i = \min \left(k | 1 - (b_{ik})^k \geq .90 \right) \qquad (9.17)$$

Based on the geographical distribution of demand, the number of needed facilities serving each local area, r_i, can be determined in advance by examining increasing values of k. Given this construct, a service availability–oriented coverage model can be structured as follows:

$$Minimize \quad \sum_j X_j \qquad (9.18)$$

Subject to:

$$\sum_j a_{ij} X_j \geq r_i \quad \forall i \qquad (9.19)$$

$$X_j = \{0, 1\} \quad \forall j \qquad (9.20)$$

This model is obviously similar to the LSCP and backup coverage. The objective of this model, (9.18), is to minimize the number of facilities. Constraints (9.19) require coverage of demand i at a specified level, r_i. Integer restrictions on the siting variables are stipulated in constraints (9.20).

This basic model was first proposed by ReVelle and Hogan (1989) and seeks to distribute enough facilities across an area such that there are enough located locally to ensure availability when service is needed, within the coverage standard. This mathematical model is also a form of multi-level set covering, as each demand must be covered at least a specified number times, rather than just once. Many extensions to this model have also been explored in the literature.

9.5.3 Spatial Representation

Our final advanced topic in standards-based location modeling is to examine more closely the issue of representing geographic space. Traditionally, demand has been represented as points in mathematical models. Coverage assessment for points is fairly straightforward as a point is either covered or it is not covered. As an example, Figure 9.6a illustrates the coverage of demand points for both regular and irregular facility service areas. When demand is represented as a line, polygon or other shape, evaluation can be substantially more complicated. For example, Figure 9.6b illustrates coverage of demand polygons for both regular and irregular facility service areas. Some polygons are completely covered, some polygons are not covered at all, and other polygons are covered partially.

The issue is not only that coverage assessment is more complicated when general spatial demand objects (e.g., points, lines, polygons, etc.) are considered. It also raises some important theoretical questions about how we model a particular planning problem. In the case of complete coverage, the application of the LSCP using demand points to represent an area may result in unintended inaccuracies in that coverage of the entire area may not actually be achieved. Alternatively, the LSCP can be applied to demand objects more generally (e.g., lines, polygons, etc.), and define an $a_{ij} = 1$ only when site j can cover the entire demand object i. Doing this means that complete coverage will be achieved. However, this generally results in an excessive number of facilities being required, because the model cannot track partial coverage of nonpoint demand objects. Unfortunately, the actual number of needed facilities in an application of the LSCP can be a function of the method used to model coverage. When a model is sensitive to how spatial data are represented, it is recognized as a **modifiable areal unit problem (MAUP)**, discussed in Chapter 4. The implications are that a mathematical planning model likely needs to be reconceptualized, though this may not actually be possible in some situations. The main issue in applying the LSCP is to account for the coverage of demand in the best possible way, regardless of how the demand units are defined (e.g., points, lines, polygons or other entities).

As an example of enhancing spatial representation in a covering model, consider the following additional notation:

β = percentage of partial coverage considered acceptable to track

$$\hat{a}_{ij} = \begin{cases} 1, & \text{if facility } j \text{ covers at least } \beta\% \text{ of unit } i \\ 0, & \text{if not} \end{cases}$$

$$V_i = \begin{cases} 1, & \text{if complete coverage provided by two or more facilities} \\ 0, & \text{if complete coverage provided by a single facility} \end{cases}$$

What is new here is the ability to track partial coverage of spatial objects, not just those units completely covered, as done using the original a_{ij} matrix approach. Thus, given some specified level of partial coverage β, $\hat{a}_{ij}$ accounts for those units that are covered by facility j at least β percent but less than 100 percent. With this in mind, assuming that $\beta = 50$ percent, it makes sense to consider that a demand unit covered by two facilities at this level would actually be completely covered. Given this, the variable V_i allows for either complete coverage directly of a demand unit i ($V_i = 0$) or complete coverage

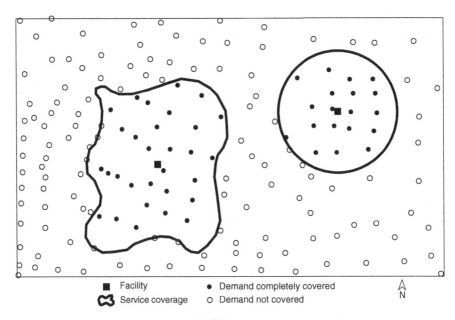

(a) Points

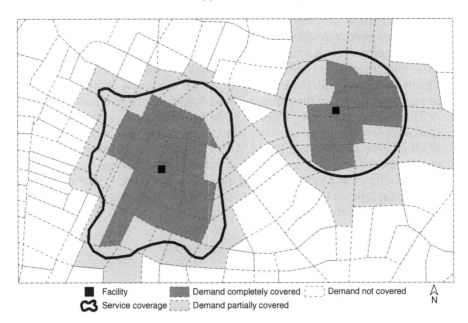

(b) Polygons

Figure 9.6 Demand representation

by multiple facilities that each only partially cover demand i ($V_i = 1$). A model that accounts for the partial coverage of demand objects can be structured as follows:

$$\text{Minimize} \quad \sum_{j=1}^{m} X_j \tag{9.21}$$

Subject to:

$$\sum_{j=1}^{m} a_{ij} X_j \geq 1 - V_i \quad \text{for each } i = 1, 2, \ldots, n \tag{9.22}$$

$$\sum_{j=1}^{m} \hat{a}_{ij} X_j \geq 2V_i \quad \text{for each } i = 1, 2, \ldots, n \tag{9.23}$$

$$X_j = \{0, 1\} \quad \text{for each } j = 1, 2, \ldots, m \tag{9.24}$$

$$V_i = \{0, 1\} \quad \text{for each } i = 1, 2, \ldots, n$$

The objective of this model, (9.21), is to minimize the number of facilities needed, and is equivalent to that of the LSCP. Constraints (9.22) require coverage of demand i directly when $V_i = 0$. Constraints (9.23) require multiple facility coverage of a demand i if direct coverage is not achieved (e.g., $V_i = 1$). Taken together, constraints (9.22) and (9.23) ensure that a demand unit i is either directly covered completely or partially covered by multiple facilities. This is consistent with the intent of the LSCP to provide complete coverage. Integer restrictions on the siting variables are stipulated in constraints (9.24).

This basic model was proposed by Murray (2005) as a means to address spatial representation issues when complete coverage is sought, and reduces or eliminates the effects of the MAUP. The assumption in this model is that complete coverage is provided to demand units by either one facility directly or two facilities at a partial level. In the case where partial coverage by three or more facilities results in complete coverage of a demand unit, then a minor extension of this model is required.

9.6   SUMMARY

In this chapter we have introduced a number of location planning models that involve a service standard, which can be based on a maximal distance or time, or even some other measure. Models that utilize a spatially based service criteria are called *covering models*. Several model constructs were introduced in this chapter, including set covering, maximal covering, backup covering, service availability, and spatial representation. Applications of these types of models have included siting cell phone towers, fire stations, emergency warning sirens, fire lookout stations, bus stops, and security monitors, just to name a few. Many applications of such models require rich, detailed geographic data to work from, especially when attempting to identify feasible sites, characterize demand areas, and derive coverage. GIS provides an ideal framework to support location planning and analysis where coverage standards are a feature of the model.

9.7 TERMS

$\binom{m}{p}$, combinations

standards-based service

location set covering problem

maximal covering location problem

covering

complete coverage

maximal coverage

probabilistic coverage

spatial representation

9.8 REFERENCES

Church, R., and C. ReVelle. 1974. The maximal covering location problem. *Papers of the Regional Science Association* 32:101–118.

Daskin, M. S., and E. H. Stern. 1981. A hierarchical objective set covering model for emergency medical service vehicle deployment. *Transportation Science* 15:137–149.

Murray A. T. 2005. Geography in coverage modeling: Exploiting spatial structure to address complementary partial service of areas. *Annals of the Association of American Geographers* 95(4):761–772.

ReVelle, C. S., and K. Hogan. 1989. The maximum availability location problem. *Transportation Science* 23:192–200.

Toregas, C., R. Swain, C. ReVelle, and L. Bergman. 1971. The location of emergency service facilities. *Operations Research* 19:1363–1373.

9.9 EXERCISES

9.1. A city is considering the closure of three fire stations in order to save money. Suggest possible objectives for selecting stations to close. Formulate a model that optimizes savings while meeting as many of your identified objectives as possible.

9.2. A neighborhood of 500 homes in rural Jenkins, Nebraska, does not have fire hydrants. Although there is a fire station a mile away, the neighborhood has higher fire insurance premiums because of the lack of hydrants. The county is considering designing a plan for hydrants for the neighborhood, and has found that every parcel needs to be within 500 feet of a hydrant in order to make the neighborhood qualify for lower premiums. Suggest a model for locating hydrants and connecting pipe.

9.3. Consider the following coverage matrix:

$$
\begin{bmatrix}
1 & 1 & 1 & 0 & 1 & 1 & 0 & 0 \\
1 & 0 & 0 & 0 & 0 & 1 & 0 & 0 \\
1 & 1 & 1 & 0 & 0 & 0 & 1 & 1 \\
0 & 1 & 0 & 0 & 1 & 1 & 0 & 1 \\
0 & 0 & 1 & 0 & 0 & 0 & 1 & 0 \\
0 & 0 & 0 & 0 & 0 & 1 & 1 & 0 \\
0 & 1 & 0 & 0 & 0 & 0 & 1 & 1 \\
0 & 0 & 0 & 1 & 0 & 0 & 0 & 1 \\
1 & 0 & 0 & 1 & 0 & 0 & 0 & 0 \\
0 & 0 & 0 & 1 & 0 & 1 & 0 & 0
\end{bmatrix}
$$

This matrix contains information about 8 sites and 10 demand areas.

(a) Solve a LSCP using LINGO for the above coverage matrix. Which sites are part of the optimal solution?

(b) Look closely at the coverage matrix and argue why site 5 (represented by the fifth column) would not be in any optimal covering solution.

(c) How many sites will be needed if each demand needs to be covered twice, where at most one facility can be located at any site?

9.4. Using the coverage matrix in question 9.4, solve a MCLP using LINGO, where demand for each area is as follows:

$$
\begin{bmatrix}
27 \\
6 \\
9 \\
4 \\
32 \\
1 \\
12 \\
44 \\
3 \\
19
\end{bmatrix}
$$

(a) What is the optimal configuration for $p = 3$?

(b) How does total demand covered vary as the value of p is increased from 1 to 8?

(c) How do these results compare with those identified using the LSCP?

9.5. The state of Florida is planning to develop a number of shelters for evacuees should another hurricane hit the state. Shelters should be located so that there are five shelters within two hours' drive of each major metropolitan area in the state.

(a) Formulate an optimization model for this problem.

(b) The state would also like to consider taking as many people as possible within 30 minutes of a shelter, given that there will always be at least five shelters within two hours' drive. How can this component be added to your planning model?

9.6. There is a problem called the vertex p-center problem, which involves placing p facilities at nodes of a network in order to minimize the furthest distance that a demand point is from its closest facility. Describe how the vertex p-center problem can be solved by solving a series of location set covering problems? (Hint: What if we solved an LSCP problem using a maximum distance of 15 and the optimal solution used five facilities? What, then, could we say if we were searching for an optimal $p = 7$ vertex center solution?)

CHAPTER 10

DISPERSION

10.0 INTRODUCTION

Much of the focus in the book thus far has been on siting facilities so as to minimize costs and maximize access/accessibility. Attention is now given to modeling, where the intent is to avoid concentration or oversaturation in siting facilities. This is referred to as dispersion modeling, as there is an attempt to spread out facilities because of impact concerns. **Dispersion** is necessary when noxious or obnoxious services are sited, such as nuclear power plants, hazardous waste depots, oil refineries, or even when conducting forest harvesting operations, to limit exposure to noise, odor, chemicals, and/or pollution. Dispersion is also important for various consumer services, like siting franchised eateries or medical testing facilities, as a way of ensuring sufficient market area and demand. Finally, dispersion reflects certain observed behavior in different biological species, where plants and/or animals need a minimal territory to breed or live.

Whether the intent is to promote equity, limit excessive impact on any local area, or determine the carrying capacity of a habitat, dispersion models address interfacility relationships in site selection. To this end, a basic class of standards-based dispersion model is detailed in this chapter. In support of such modeling, buffer analysis and containment are reviewed in the GIScience section. The chapter ends by introducing another type of dispersion model in the advanced topics section, where one can explicitly optimize interfacility separation.

10.1 PROBLEM DEFINITION AND MOTIVATION

There are many instances where it is important to disperse located facilities. One situation is where a hazardous or obnoxious facility is being sited, and there is some level of potential community danger or resistance. In this case, there is generally a need for the service (e.g., power generation or waste disposal), but the facility is not viewed as desirable to the local neighborhood. These are often termed *NIMBY* (not in my back yard) services. Another situation arises in the siting of retail or fast-food outlets. There is a need to ensure a sufficient market base for the business enterprise of the individual outlet, but also a desire to site as many outlets as possible on the part of the corporation. To ensure a fair and productive market environment, it is common that outlets obtain exclusivity agreements from a corporation, preventing other outlets from being established in the local area. A final situation relates to flora and fauna, in that certain species have territorial requirements, and are dependent on sufficient exclusive land for their existence. Whatever the case may be, these situations suggest the following location problem:

> Find the maximum weighted number of facilities, and their location, such that no two facilities are within a stipulated minimum distance or travel time of each other.

In this way, the stipulated minimum distance or travel time is much like the service standard detailed in Chapter 9, but differs in that it refers to the spatial relationship between sited facilities. In particular, there was a focus on whether demand was served within the standard in the previous chapter on coverage. However, in this case, we are interested in maintaining standards between located facilities.

Consider a company such as Subway, which allocates franchises. On the one hand, Subway might like to have as many outlets as possible to ensure the greatest overall potential return to the corporation. However, it does not benefit the corporation if franchise outlets are in competition with each other, or if a consumer market is saturated to the point where an individual franchise is not viable. Thus, a strategic planning goal for Subway is to locate shops so that they are readily accessible to consumers, but not to site too many.

A similar situation exists in natural resource management when considering harvesting operations, as harvest scheduling can be viewed as a facility siting problem. Harvesting operations include all activities to support the extraction, or harvest, of timber. Often a decision is made a priori how timber extraction will be performed, such as by selective thinning, clearcut, etc. Thus, harvest scheduling involves making decisions on which areas will be treated and when in order to maximize revenues. However, there are other constraining conditions as well related to operational performance and environmental impacts. Consider the region shown in Figure 10.1 containing 13 management

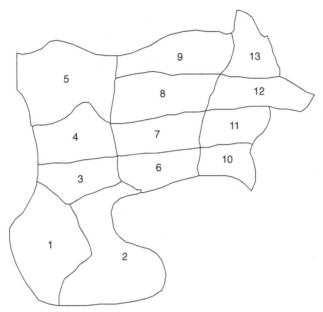

Figure 10.1   Commercial timber production region.

units. The decisions are whether or not each individual unit is to be harvested, but maintaining imposed constraints.

In this case, it turns out that environmental impacts are complicating constraining conditions from a decision-making perspective. Such considerations are important when accounting for wildlife richness, creating habitat favorable to flora and fauna, promoting diversity, maintaining soil and water quality, not exceeding carrying capacity, preserving scenic beauty, and moving toward sustainability more generally. In order to address such concerns implicitly or explicitly, limiting spatial impacts is desired in harvest scheduling models. This has traditionally been approached using dispersion, or adjacency, restrictions. As an example, consider unit 1 in Figure 10.1. An adjacency restriction stipulates that if a unit is harvested, no adjacent units may be harvested. Thus, in this case, if unit 1 is harvested, units 2 and 3 are precluded from being harvested. Similar restrictions exist for each unit. The intent of adjacency restrictions is to disperse harvesting activities. Further, this rationale makes sense intuitively if one is concerned with excessive impact in any local area.

10.2   MATHEMATICAL REPRESENTATION

Recognizing that concentrating facilities/activity too much in any one area might be excessive or harmful, a dispersion model attempts to limit sited activities based on interfacility proximity. Enabling a focus on dispersion is that potential facility sites in conflict with facility site i are known in advance.

This set may be defined based on a distance or travel time standard. For example, say that no two facilities should be located within 2.5 miles of each other. The set of sites that conflict with the choice of site i would then be all potential facility sites within 2.5 miles of site i.

Consider the following notation:

$$i = \text{index of potential facility sites } (j \text{ similarly defined})$$

$$a_{ij} = \begin{cases} 1 & \text{if potential faciltiy site } i \text{ is too close to site } j \\ 0 & \text{if not} \end{cases}$$

Thus, as done previously, the indicator variable a_{ij} is used to identify those sites that conflict with each other, if simultaneously located. Generally, we would rely on GIS functionality to derive the values of a_{ij}. We will now take this notation a step further by viewing sites in conflict as sets. This will be done using the following sets:

$$\Phi_i = \text{set of potential facility sites in conflict with site } i$$

The set is derived based on $\Phi_i = \{ j | a_{ij} = 1 \}$.

Thus, by definition, the set Φ_i comprises those potential facility sites that are within the minimum spatial proximity standard of site i. Of course, the standard must be stipulated in advance, or we would not be able to derive the set.

With the definition of *conflict sets*, the remaining mathematical notation that is needed to detail dispersion models is the following:

$$b_i = \text{benefit associated with siting facility } i$$

$$X_i = \begin{cases} 1 & \text{if facility } i \text{ sited} \\ 0 & \text{otherwise} \end{cases}$$

With this notation, we now have our decision variables associated with each potential facility site, but also the benefit or value of locating at that site. This can be integrated into an objective as follows:

$$Maximize \quad \sum_i b_i X_i \qquad (10.1)$$

In particular, we have an objective to maximize the total weighted benefit of sited facilities. What remains is imposing dispersion standards in the siting of facilities. In what follows, we will see that there are a number of ways to impose such spatial restrictions.

10.2.1 Neighborhood Restrictions

One of the more intuitive ways for imposing restrictions on the spatial proximity of sited facilities is to focus on each facility conflict set Φ_i. An important
observation is that when a facility is located at site i, no facilities in the set
Φ_i may be selected as they would violate proximity restrictions, if located.
Thus, it is possible to structure a single constraint using this set as follows:

$$n_i X_i + \sum_{j \in \Phi_i} X_j \leq n_i \tag{10.2}$$

where

$$n_i = |\Phi_i| = \text{total number of potential facilities in conflict with facility } i$$

Before discussing this constraint, first recognize that a set operator is used to
specify the number of members of a set. Specifically, $||$ indicates the number of
elements, or members, of a set. Thus, n_i corresponds to the number of elements
in the set Φ_i. There is one proximity constraint, (10.2), needed for each site.
The behavior of constraint (10.2) is a function of the value of the variable X_i.
In particular, equation (10.2) simplifies the following when $X_i = 1$:

$$n_i + \sum_{j \in \Phi_i} X_j \leq n_i \tag{10.3}$$

As the right-hand side of this equation is n_i, and the left-hand side is already
equal to n_i, $\sum_{j \in \Phi_i} X_j$ must equal zero in this case. Of course, this is as
intended, because if $X_i = 1$, no facilities should be sited that conflict with
the choice of site i. Alternatively, if site i is not utilized, $X_i = 0$, equation
(10.2) takes the following form:

$$\sum_{j \in \Phi_i} X_j \leq n_i \tag{10.4}$$

In this case, none of the facilities in conflict with site i are prohibited from
being sited, at least with respect to site i. Thus, with both cases the inequality
in (10.2) correctly structures proximity restrictions between a potential site
and other potentially conflicting sites, if they were located. This is referred
to as a *neighborhood restriction*, because of the use of a single constraint
centered on a particular site i.

We can now formulate the basic dispersion model as:

$$Maximize \quad \sum_i b_i X_i \tag{10.5}$$

Subject to:

$$n_i X_i + \sum_{j \in \Phi_i} X_j \leq n_i \quad \forall i \tag{10.6}$$

$$X_i = \{0, 1\} \quad \forall i \tag{10.7}$$

The objective, (10.5), is to maximize the total derived benefit of sited facilities. Constraints (10.6) impose proximity restrictions. Integer requirements are maintained in Constraints (10.7).

We can refer to this formulation as the standards based dispersion problem (also referred to are the anti-covering problem) using neighborhood restrictions, and it has served as a basic model structure in many planning contexts. A review and discussion of this approach can be found in Murray and Church (1996a). An important feature of this model is that a constraint for each potential facility site i is imposed. As suggested in (10.4), no proximity restrictions are imposed when $X_i = 0$. This means that necessary restrictions are imposed elsewhere, as there are n total constraints. A potential issue arising in the application of this formulation structure is that the neighborhood restrictions are not *facet-inducing*, due to the use of a nonbinary coefficient n_i. The implication is that solution approaches like linear programming with branch and bound will spend an exorbitant amount of time in solving this model form to optimality. The propensity to be less than *integer friendly* has led researchers to search for alternate model structures.

10.2.2 Pairwise Restrictions

Given computational considerations in using neighborhood restrictions, there are important reasons for seeking alternative approaches to impose proximity standards in a dispersion model. Another approach for representing restrictions in facility placement is to structure a constraint for each pair of potential facility sites i and j when $a_{ij} = 1$. If $a_{ij} = 1$, then sites i and j are too close to be selected simultaneously. We can prevent selecting both sites, which would create a conflict, using the following inequality:

$$X_i + X_j \leq 1 \tag{10.8}$$

This indicates that any two potential facilities within the proximity standard of each other are limited to, at most, one of them being selected for a facility. In particular, if $X_i = 1$, as an example, then equation (10.8) becomes

$$1 + X_j \leq 1 \tag{10.9}$$

which simplifies to $X_j \leq 0$. Thus, site j is prohibited from being selected for facility placement when $X_i = 1$. Alternatively, if $X_i = 0$, then equation (10.8) becomes:

$$X_j \leq 1 \tag{10.10}$$

In this case, site j remains unbounded in terms of selection for facility placement. That is, a facility can be sited or not, according to inequality (10.10), and this is what should happen when $X_i = 0$. Thus, inequality (10.8) imposes intended proximity standards. All that is needed is identifying all pairwise restrictions. However, this is precisely the information contained in the facility conflict sets Φ_i. Thus, we have all that we need to structure an alternative formulation of the standards-based dispersion problem:

$$\textit{Maximize} \quad \sum_i b_i X_i \tag{10.11}$$

Subject to:

$$X_i + X_j \leq 1 \quad \forall i, j \in \Phi_i \tag{10.12}$$

$$X_i = \{0, 1\} \quad \forall i \tag{10.13}$$

The objective, (10.11), is to maximize the total benefit of sited facilities. Constraints (10.12) prohibit proximal facilities from simultaneously being sited. Constraints (10.13) impose integer restrictions on the decision variables.

We refer to this formulation as the standards-based dispersion problem using pairwise restrictions, because of the use of potential facility site pairs, i and j, in constraints (10.12). This model structure has been utilized in many planning contexts (see Murray and Church 1996b). A practical concern with the pairwise structure is that typically a large number of constraints (10.12) are needed. Specifically, there are $\sum_i n_i / 2$ unique proximity pairs, so a constraint for each pair must be imposed. This may or may not be difficult for a commercial optimization software package, but traditionally it has proven to be an issue in applying standards-based dispersion problems.

10.2.3 Clique Restrictions

An alternative approach for imposing proximity standards is to use *clique restrictions*. A **clique** is a set of potential facility sites that are simultaneously proximal to each other. In fact, the pairwise restriction is a very simple clique where only two locations are considered. In spatial contexts we often find higher-ordered cliques reflecting simultaneous proximity conditions.

Suppose that potential facility sites $i, j,$ and l are simultaneously proximal to each other. This means that sites i and j cannot both have a located facility, or rather $X_i + X_j \leq 1$. It also means that sites i and l cannot both have a located facility, or rather, $X_i + X_l \leq 1$. Finally, it also means that sites j and l cannot both have a located facility, or rather, $X_j + X_l \leq 1$. We can impose all three restrictions simultaneously with a larger clique restriction, in this case:

$$X_i + X_j + X_l \leq 1 \tag{10.14}$$

Thus, with one higher-ordered clique inequality, it is possible to impose what was stipulated using three pairwise restrictions. This is the essence of a clique.

A formal specification of clique restrictions relies on the following notation:

$k =$ index of cliques

$\Psi_k =$ facilities in clique k

This assumes that we can identify all necessary cliques using some approach. Clearly, this is possible, as the simplest clique can readily be found (pairwise). So, assuming that we have identified cliques in advance using GIS, the restriction for clique k can be structured as follows:

$$\sum_{j \in \Psi_k} X_j \leq 1 \tag{10.15}$$

If $\Psi_k = \{i, j, l\}$, as an example, then the clique inequality becomes:

$$X_i + X_j + X_l \leq 1 \tag{10.16}$$

This is precisely what was illustrated in (10.14) for the three pairwise restrictions. More generally, then, we can incorporate clique restrictions into another version of the standards-based dispersion problem:

$$Maximize \quad \sum_i b_i X_i \tag{10.17}$$

Subject to:

$$\sum_{j \in \Psi_k} X_j \leq 1 \quad \forall k \tag{10.18}$$

$$X_i = \{0, 1\} \quad \forall i \tag{10.19}$$

The objective, (10.17), remains to maximize total derived benefit of sited facilities. Constraints (10.18) impose proximity standards using clique restrictions. Integer requirements are maintained in constraints (10.19).

We can refer to this formulation as the standards-based dispersion problem using clique restrictions. This model structure has also been utilized in many planning contexts (see Murray and Church 1996b). There are two important benefits to using cliques in dispersion modeling. One is that the number of required constraints is significantly less than $\sum_i n_i/2$, which is the number of needed pairwise restrictions. The second benefit is that cliques provide desirable mathematical properties, making the problem very amenable to solutions using linear programming–based approaches. That is, cliques are facet-inducing structures, which generally reduce the need for branching and bounding associated with resolving fractions that occur in the relaxed integer program. The challenge with cliques, however, is that an enumeration technique is needed to identify all required restrictions.

10.3 GISCIENCE

In order to apply any of the standards-based dispersion problems detailed in this chapter, there is a need for associated spatial information. This ranges from polygon attributes to spatial proximity of potential facility sites. It should be clear that GIS can readily provide polygon attribute information. Further, using various analysis capabilities of GIS, we can derive facility proximity information. In previous chapters, adjacency was recognized as an important topological property and technical aspects of adjacency determination were discussed. Facility proximity, however, goes beyond adjacency, as potential sites in conflict could be a function of distance or travel time. Given this, proximity is based on distance or travel time buffers. Once this buffer is defined, it is then possible to determine which other potential facility sites are *contained within* the buffer. Thus, in this section we review the two important GIS concepts of *buffering* and *containment* as they relate to supporting standards-based dispersion modeling.

A **buffer** is considered a topological transformation, and can be regular or irregular in shape, as seen in the previous chapter. A buffer can be derived for any vector object, point, line, and/or polygon, or raster cell(s). Most applications of buffering limit the interpretation to an area of regular width around the object, as shown in Figure 10.2, but if a buffer were based on travel time, as an example, this need not be the case in general.

The second concept is **containment**, and it is a topological property (along with adjacency and connectivity, reviewed in Chapter 8). As the term suggests, containment has to do with selecting or identifying those objects spatially located in a defined area. In particular, given a polygon area, it is possible to identify those objects (points, lines, or polygons) contained within that area. An example of containment is shown in Figure 10.3a, where a buffer

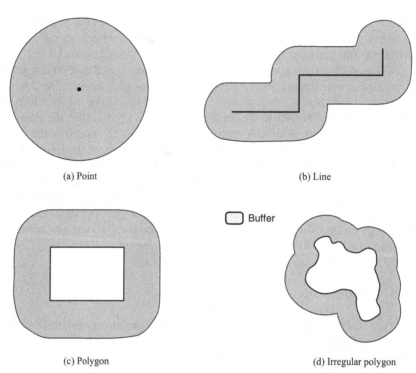

(a) Point

(b) Line

☐ Buffer

(c) Polygon

(d) Irregular polygon

Figure 10.2 Regular-width buffers for vector objects.

has been generated around a parcel and all those parcels within the buffer are highlighted. It is worth noting, however, that many variants are possible in GIS for the selection of objects by location. Another containment approach is identifying all objects within or partially within an area boundary. Such a case is shown in Figure 10.3b. Which variant one should use depends on the analysis endeavor at hand.

Buffering and containment enable dispersion standards to be operationalized and evaluated. A buffer for potential facility site i establishes the conflict zone should a facility be located there. Containment then is used to derive the conflict set for potential facility site i.

10.4 MODELING APPLICATION

In section 10.2, three different forms of the standards-based dispersion problem were formulated. In this section, we will illustrate the use of these models in support of forest planning. The timber production region with 13 management units shown in Figure 10.1 is used for harvest site selection. The planning objective is to identify a harvest schedule that maximizes total benefit. The decisions are whether or not we harvest each management unit i. Thus, the

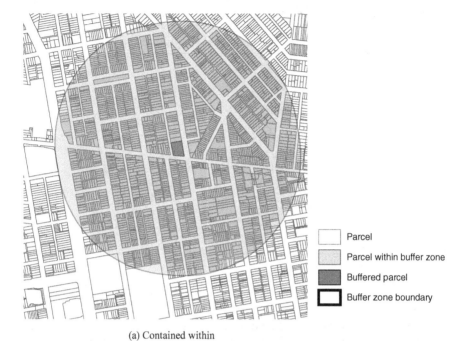

(a) Contained within

(b) Intersecting

Figure 10.3 Residential parcels in parcel buffer zone.

TABLE 10.1 Timber region summary by unit

Polygon	Benefit (b_i) (in \$1,000s)	Adjacent polygons (Φ_i)
1	\$121.38	2, 3
2	\$88.56	1, 3, 6
3	\$11.07	1, 2, 4, 6, 7
4	\$28	3, 5, 6, 7, 8
5	\$29.18	4, 7, 8, 9
6	\$124.18	2, 3, 4, 7, 10, 11
7	\$21.12	3, 4, 5, 6, 8, 10, 11, 12
8	\$47.52	4, 5, 7, 9, 11, 12, 13
9	\$42.26	5, 8, 12, 13
10	\$13.04	6, 7, 11
11	\$17.9	6, 7, 8, 10, 12
12	\$52.89	7, 8, 9, 11, 13
13	\$67.24	8, 9, 12

decision variable X_i is 1 if unit i is harvested and 0 if not. The constraints are to keep local disruption due to harvesting to a minimum. Thus, the harvest activities are to be dispersed, and specifically no two adjacent harvest sites can be harvested at one time.

The needed spatial information is summarized in Table 10.1, obtained using GIS. Benefits are expected economic return associated with the desired harvest regime (thinning, clear-cutting, etc.). The conflict set for each polygon are those units sharing a common point or edge. Of course, these are the adjacent polygons to a management unit. Both benefit and conflict sets are shown in Table 10.1.

With this information, it is now possible to apply the three model forms of the basic dispersion location problem.

10.4.1 Neighborhood Restrictions

The standards-based dispersion problem using neighborhood restrictions is now applied to obtain a forest plan. Again, the needed input information is summarized in Table 10.1. The generic algebraic statement of the model, (10.5) to (10.7), can be interpreted mathematically for this problem application as follows:

$$
\begin{aligned}
Maximize \quad & 121.38\,X_1 + 88.56\,X_2 + 11.07\,X_3 + 28\,X_4 + 29.18\,X_5 \\
& + 124.18\,X_6 + 21.12\,X_7 + 47.52\,X_8 + 42.26\,X_9 \\
& + 13.04\,X_{10} + 17.9\,X_{11} + 52.89\,X_{12} + 67.24\,X_{13}
\end{aligned}
$$

Subject to:

$$2X_1 + X_2 + X_3 \le 2$$

$$3X_2 + X_1 + X_3 + X_6 \le 3$$

$$5X_3 + X_1 + X_2 + X_4 + X_6 + X_7 \le 5$$

$$5X_4 + X_3 + X_5 + X_6 + X_7 + X_8 \le 5$$

$$4X_5 + X_4 + X_7 + X_8 + X_9 \le 4$$

$$6X_6 + X_2 + X_3 + X_4 + X_7 + X_{10} + X_{11} \le 6$$

$$8X_7 + X_3 + X_4 + X_5 + X_6 + X_8 + X_{10} + X_{11} + X_{12} \le 8$$

$$7X_8 + X_4 + X_5 + X_7 + X_9 + X_{11} + X_{12} + X_{13} \le 7$$

$$4X_9 + X_5 + X_8 + X_{12} + X_{13} \le 4$$

$$3X_{10} + X_6 + X_7 + X_{11} \le 3$$

$$5X_{11} + X_6 + X_7 + X_8 + X_{10} + X_{12} \le 5$$

$$5X_{12} + X_7 + X_8 + X_9 + X_{11} + X_{13} \le 5$$

$$3X_{13} + X_8 + X_9 + X_{12} \le 3$$

$$X_1 = \{0, 1\}, \quad X_2 = \{0, 1\}, \quad X_3 = \{0, 1\}, \quad X_4 = \{0, 1\}, \quad X_5 = \{0, 1\},$$

$$X_6 = \{0, 1\}, \quad X_7 = \{0, 1\}, \quad X_8 = \{0, 1\}, \quad X_9 = \{0, 1\}, \quad X_{10} = \{0, 1\},$$

$$X_{11} = \{0, 1\}, \quad X_{12} = \{0, 1\}, \quad X_{13} = \{0, 1\}$$

As expected, there are 13 primary constraints, one for each management unit. The coefficient on the right-hand side of the inequality matches that for the unit variable, and corresponds to the number of conflicting site members, $|\Phi_i|$. As an example, the neighborhood restriction associated with unit 7 has a conflict set of $\Phi_7 = \{3, 4, 5, 6, 8, 10, 11, 12\}$, so $n_7 = |\Phi_7| = 8$. This is precisely what is structured in the seventh constraint of the model.

In order to solve this model using LINGO, it must first be translated to a LINGO equivalent format, and this is given in Figure 10.4. In the LINGO specification, notice that basic set-up is done first, where sets and variables are defined and input data are provided. After this, the objective is defined and constraints are stipulated. Because there are 13 units, when the model is run there are 13 major constraints. Recall that this can be verified using the "LINGO → Generate → Display model" pull down menus (or Ctrl+G).

Solving the model identifies four sites to be harvested, resulting in a total weighted objective value of 341.98, or \$341,980. The decision variable values are $X_1 = X_5 = X_6 = X_{13} = 1$, and all others equal to zero. The spatial configuration of selected units is shown in Figure 10.5.

```
MODEL:
!Standards-based dispersion problem (neighborhood restrictions) - LINGO
format;

SETS:
 Units / 1..13 / : X, b, n;
 MAdj / 1..8 /;
 Mat(Units, MAdj) : a;
ENDSETS

DATA:
 b =  121.38 88.56 11.07 28 29.18 124.18 21.12 47.52 42.26 13.04 17.9
52.89 67.24;
 n =  2 3 5 5 4 6 8 7 4 3 5 5 3;
 a =  2 3   0   0   0   0   0   0
      1 3   6   0   0   0   0   0
      1 2   4   6   7   0   0   0
      3 5   6   7   8   0   0   0
      4 7   8   9   0   0   0   0
      2 3   4   7  10  11   0   0
      3 4   5   6   8  10  11  12
      4 5   7   9  11  12  13   0
      5 8  12  13   0   0   0   0
      6 7  11   0   0   0   0   0
      6 7   8  10  12   0   0   0
      7 8   9  11  13   0   0   0
      8 9  12   0   0   0   0  0;
END DATA

!Objective;
MAX = @SUM(Units(i): b(i)*X(i));

!Constraints;
@For(Units(i): n(i)*X(i) + @SUM(MAdj(j)| a(i,j) #GT# 0 : X(a(i,j))) <=
n(i));

!Integer restrictions;
@FOR( Units(i) : @BIN( X(i) ));

END
```

Figure 10.4 Standards-based dispersion problem (neighborhood restrictions) structured in LINGO.

10.4.2 Pairwise Restrictions

As discussed previously, there are alternative approaches for imposing dispersion requirements. The standards-based dispersion problem using pairwise restrictions is now used to obtain a forest harvest plan. The generic algebraic statement of the model, (10.11) to (10.13), can be interpreted mathematically for this problem application as follows:

$$Maximize \quad 121.38\,X_1 + 88.56\,X_2 + 11.07\,X_3 + 28\,X_4 + 29.18\,X_5$$
$$+ 124.18\,X_6 + 21.12\,X_7 + 47.52\,X_8 + 42.26\,X_9$$
$$+ 13.04\,X_{10} + 17.9\,X_{11} + 52.89\,X_{12} + 67.24\,X_{13}$$

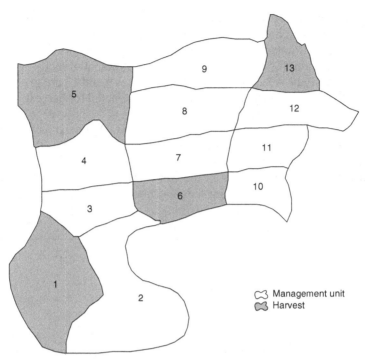

Figure 10.5   Units selected for harvest.

Subject to:

$X_1 + X_2 \leq 1;\ X_1 + X_3 \leq 1;\ X_2 + X_3 \leq 1$

$X_2 + X_6 \leq 1;\ X_3 + X_4 \leq 1;\ X_3 + X_6 \leq 1$

$X_3 + X_7 \leq 1;\ X_4 + X_5 \leq 1;\ X_4 + X_6 \leq 1$

$X_4 + X_7 \leq 1;\ X_4 + X_8 \leq 1;\ X_5 + X_7 \leq 1$

$X_5 + X_8 \leq 1;\ X_5 + X_9 \leq 1;\ X_6 + X_7 \leq 1$

$X_6 + X_{10} \leq 1;\ X_6 + X_{11} \leq 1;\ X_7 + X_8 \leq 1$

$X_7 + X_{10} \leq 1;\ X_7 + X_{11} \leq 1;\ X_7 + X_{12} \leq 1$

$X_8 + X_9 \leq 1;\ X_8 + X_{11} \leq 1;\ X_8 + X_{12} \leq 1$

$X_8 + X_{13} \leq 1;\ X_9 + X_{12} \leq 1;\ X_9 + X_{13} \leq 1$

$X_{10} + X_{11} \leq 1;\ X_{11} + X_{12} \leq 1;\ X_{12} + X_{13} \leq 1$

$X_1 = \{0, 1\},\ X_2 = \{0, 1\},\ X_3 = \{0, 1\},\ X_4 = \{0, 1\},\ X_5 = \{0, 1\},$

$X_6 = \{0, 1\},\ X_7 = \{0, 1\},\ X_8 = \{0, 1\}, X_9 = \{0, 1\},\ X_{10} = \{0, 1\},$

$X_{11} = \{0, 1\},\ X_{12} = \{0, 1\},\ X_{13} = \{0, 1\}$

For this planning problem, there are 30 pairwise dispersion constraints. Thus, the problem has 13 decision variables, one for each management unit, 30 major constraints, and 13 binary integer requirements. The pairwise restrictions account for each case where a pair of potential facility sites cannot simultaneously be selected. As an example, sites 9 and 13 are in conflict with each other, meaning that at most one could be selected for harvest. Thus, there is a constraint for this conflict pair.

Again, in order to solve this model using LINGO, it must first be translated to a LINGO-equivalent format. This is done in Figure 10.6. The objective is defined and constraints are stipulated.

Solving this model results in the same exact solution found when solving the dispersion model using neighborhood constraints. This is what we

```
MODEL:
!Standards-based dispersion problem (pairwise restrictions) - LINGO
format;

SETS:
 Units / 1..13 / : X, b;
 MAdj / 1..8 /;
 Mat(Units, MAdj) : a;
ENDSETS

DATA:
 b =   121.38 88.56 11.07 28 29.18 124.18 21.12 47.52 42.26 13.04 17.9
52.89 67.24;
 a =  2 3  0  0  0  0  0  0
      1 3  6  0  0  0  0  0
      1 2  4  6  7  0  0  0
      3 5  6  7  8  0  0  0
      4 7  8  9  0  0  0  0
      2 3  4  7 10 11  0  0
      3 4  5  6  8 10 11 12
      4 5  7  9 11 12 13  0
      5 8 12 13  0  0  0  0
      6 7 11  0  0  0  0  0
      6 7  8 10 12  0  0  0
      7 8  9 11 13  0  0  0
      8 9 12  0  0  0  0  0;
END DATA

!Objective;
MAX = @SUM(Units(i): b(i) * X(i));

!Constraints;
@For (Mat(i,j)| (a(i,j) #GT# 0) #AND# (a(i,j) #GT# i) : X(i) + X(a(i,j))
<= 1);

!Integer restrictions;
@FOR( Units(i) : @BIN( X(i) ));

END
```

Figure 10.6 Standards-based dispersion problem (pairwise restrictions) structured in LINGO.

expect, and confirms that we are examining the same basic problem. That is, the different constraints have not changed the intent of the model. The objective value is 341.98 (or \$341,980), $X_1 = X_5 = X_6 = X_{13} = 1$, and all other variables are equal to zero. What has changed, however, is that more constraints were needed. That is, there were 30 pairwise restrictions in this case, in contrast to the 13 neighborhood restrictions needed previously.

10.4.3 Clique Restrictions

We now examine the standards-based dispersion problem using clique restrictions for this forest planning problem. The generic algebraic statement of the model, (10.17) to (10.19), can be interpreted mathematically for this problem application as follows:

Maximize $121.38\,X_1 + 88.56\,X_2 + 11.07\,X_3 + 28\,X_4 + 29.18\,X_5$

$+\ 124.18\,X_6 + 21.12\,X_7 + 47.52\,X_8 + 42.26\,X_9$

$+\ 13.04\,X_{10} + 17.9\,X_{11} + 52.89\,X_{12} + 67.24\,X_{13}$

Subject to:

$X_3 + X_4 + X_6 + X_7 \leq 1$

$X_4 + X_5 + X_7 + X_8 \leq 1$

$X_6 + X_7 + X_{10} + X_{11} \leq 1$

$X_7 + X_8 + X_{11} + X_{12} \leq 1$

$X_8 + X_9 + X_{12} + X_{13} \leq 1$

$X_1 + X_2 + X_3 \leq 1$

$X_2 + X_3 + X_6 \leq 1$

$X_5 + X_8 + X_9 \leq 1$

$X_1 = \{0, 1\},\ \ X_2 = \{0, 1\},\ \ X_3 = \{0, 1\},\ \ X_4 = \{0, 1\},\ \ X_5 = \{0, 1\},$

$X_6 = \{0, 1\},\ \ X_7 = \{0, 1\},\ \ X_8 = \{0, 1\},\ X_9 = \{0, 1\},\ \ X_{10} = \{0, 1\},$

$X_{11} = \{0, 1\},\ \ X_{12} = \{0, 1\},\ \ X_{13} = \{0, 1\}$

What is probably most obvious is that only eight clique restrictions are needed in this case. This is substantially less than the 30 pairwise restrictions or the 13 neighborhood restrictions needed in the previously solved cases. Inspection will prove that all conflicts are imposed using this set of constraints.

```
MODEL:
!Standards-based dispersion problem (clique restrictions) - LINGO
format;

SETS:
 Units / 1..13 / : X, b, n;
 MAdj1 / 1..8 /;
 MAdj2 / 1..4 /;
 Mat(MAdj1, MAdj2) : a;
ENDSETS

DATA:
 b =  121.38 88.56 11.07 28 29.18 124.18 21.12 47.52 42.26 13.04 17.9
52.89 67.24;
 a =  3 4  6   7
      4 5  7   8
      6 7 10 11
      7 8 11 12
      8 9 12 13
      1 2  3   0
      2 3  6   0
      5 8  9   0;
END DATA

!Objective;
MAX = @SUM(Units(i): b(i)*X(i));

!Constraints;
@For( MAdj1(i): @SUM( MAdj2(j)| a(i,j) #GT# 0 : X(a(i,j)) ) <= 1);

!Integer restrictions;
@FOR( Units(i) : @BIN( X(i) ));

END
```

Figure 10.7 Standards-based dispersion problem (clique restrictions) structured in LINGO.

The LINGO syntax for this problem application is shown in Figure 10.7. Again, the obtained solution is the same as the previous cases. Thus, all three models identified the same optimal solution.

10.5 ADVANCED TOPICS

Hopefully, you have begun to appreciate the importance of standards-based dispersion, and that there are a number of ways to approach the same basic problem. In this section, we first devote more attention to synthesizing viable approaches for solving larger instances of the dispersion-based location problem. Then we detail an approach to dispersion modeling that requires explicit representation of spatial proximity between all facilities. Interestingly, it can be shown that a standards-based approach can be used to do precisely what is modeled explicitly. Rather than explore this relationship in detail, we leave it as an exercise problem.

10.5.1 Hybrid Restrictions

It may now be evident that there is a trade-off of sorts in structuring standards-based dispersion restrictions. This trade-off has to do with number of constraints and mathematical structure. The neighborhood restrictions require the fewest number of constraints, but may bring about computational difficulties due to the non–facet-inducing structure of the inequalities. Alternatively, pairwise restrictions have good mathematical structure but require the greatest number of constraints, as compared to the number of needed neighborhood or clique constraints. However, the number of needed higher-ordered clique restrictions is smaller than the number of needed pairwise constraints, and the mathematical structure of higher-ordered cliques is substantially better than the structure of pairwise restrictions. Of the three forms, higher-ordered cliques yields the best model. However, it can take considerable computational effort to identify all higher-ordered cliques.

Given the above observations, it may not be surprising that other restriction forms are possible. One approach that has proven effective is to combine neighborhood and higher-ordered clique restrictions, but doing so in a selective way. Suppose that we identify the largest clique containing potential facility site i, referring to it as a maximal clique and denoting it as $\hat{\Psi}_i$. Once we have identified the maximal clique containing each site i, we could then reevaluate the facility conflict set Φ_i with respect to restrictions already imposed in the set of maximal cliques. Specifically, the conflict set can be reduced, eliminating pairs of restrictions already imposed by the maximal cliques restriction for that site. This would results in a modified conflict set, $\hat{\Phi}_i$, with $\hat{n}_i = |\hat{\Phi}_i|$. Of course, $\hat{\Phi}_i \subseteq \Phi_i$, which means that $\hat{n}_i \leq n_i$. It turns out that the smaller $\hat{n}_i$ (or n_i for that matter) can be, the better the structural properties of the neighborhood constraints in a model.

With this modified notation in mind, and the rationale behind it, the combination of neighborhood and maximal clique restrictions represents a hybrid restriction approach. We can incorporate hybrid restrictions in the standards-based dispersion problem as follows:

$$Maximize \quad \sum_i b_i X_i \tag{10.20}$$

Subject to:

$$\hat{n}_i X_i + \sum_{j \in \hat{\Phi}_i} X_j \leq \hat{n}_i \quad \forall i \tag{10.21}$$

$$\sum_{j \in \hat{\Psi}_i} X_j \leq 1 \quad \forall i \tag{10.22}$$

$$X_i = \{0, 1\} \quad \forall i \tag{10.23}$$

The objective, (10.20), remains to maximize total derived benefit of sited facilities. Constraints (10.21) and (10.22) impose proximity standards using modified neighborhood restrictions and maximal clique restrictions. Integer requirements are maintained in constraints (10.23).

This formulation is referred to as the standards-based dispersion problem using hybrid restrictions. This model structure was proposed by Murray and Church (1997). The total number of constraints is $2n$, where n is the total number of potential facility sites. The mathematical structure of hybrid restrictions has been found to be good, reflecting a reasonable trade-off when attempting to keep the total number of constraints relatively small. A benefit of the hybrid restrictions is that identifying them is fairly straightforward, as one must find a maximal clique containing each potential facility site and then modify neighborhood conflict sets accordingly. Thus, we have now demonstrated four model forms for the same basic dispersion problem. At first this might seem excessive, but the structure of a model can determine the ease by which it can be solved. Throughout this text, we have primarily given one formulation for a given problem. However, it is important to note that many problems in location science have been formulated using different, but equivalent, models with an attempt to reduce the computational effort needed to solve the problem.

10.5.2   Max-Min-Min Dispersion

Thus far in this chapter we have detailed multiple ways of approaching one type of dispersion model. That is, the underlying modeling objective was the same, but the way in which dispersion restrictions are viewed and imposed is different.

It probably is no surprise that the fundamental way dispersion is accounted for can differ as well. Suppose that we wish to locate facilities so that they are as far apart as possible, rather than separated by a minimum standard. One form in which we might do this is to maximize the distance of separation between the two closest located facilities. That is, we wish to disperse facilities so that the closest pair of facilities is as far apart as possible. In order to do this, we need to account for the spatial separation between sited facilities explicitly. This could be done with the following term for sites i and j:

$$d_{ij} X_i X_j \tag{10.24}$$

where

d_{ij} = distance or travel time between facilities i and j

If the variables in (10.24) are both one (e.g., $X_i = X_j = 1$), then facilities have been located at both sites. This would then indicate the interfacility distance or travel time, which is what we want to know. Unfortunately, this way of tracking the interfacility distance relationship is nonlinear. However, it is possible to derive a linear transformation of this basic relationship. Consider the following model for maximizing the minimum separation between any two facilities:

$$Maximize \quad Z \tag{10.25}$$

Subject to:

$$Z - m(2 - X_i - X_j) \le d_{ij} \quad \forall i, j > i \tag{10.26}$$

$$\sum_i X_i = p \tag{10.27}$$

$$X_i = \{0, 1\} \quad \forall i$$

$$Z \ge 0 \tag{10.28}$$

where

p = number of facilities to be sited
m = large number
Z = minimum distance separating any two sited facilities

The objective, (10.25), is to maximize the distance between the closest pair of sited facilities. Constraints (10.26) track the distance between facilities, when both are sited. If either or both are selected, then no inter-facility distance is accounted for. Essentially, in constraint (10.26), if either facility i or j has not been selected, then Z is forced to be less than or equal to $d_{ij} + m$. Since m is a very large number, this bound is much larger than what would exist for any constraint (10.26) for which the associated pair of sites have both been selected. This means that the constraint produces an "effective upper bound on Z" only when the associated pair of sites have both been selected. Note that when neither site i nor j has been selected, this bound is even larger, $d_{ij} + 2m$, achieving the same property as if only one of the pair of sites had been selected. Constraints (10.27) specify that p facilities are to be sited. Finally, integer and nonnegativity requirements are stipulated in constraints (10.28).

This is the so called p-dispersion (max-min-min) problem introduced by Kuby (1987) and reformulated in Erkut and Neuman (1991). In contrast to the standards-based approach detailed previously, interfacility proximity is tracked mathematically in this approach. The intent is to maximize the separation between facilities to the greatest extent possible, so this is explicitly optimized.

10.6   SUMMARY

Dispersion is an important concept, and serves as the basis for many public- and private-sector planning problems. The need for dispersed facilities arises in siting hazardous or obnoxious facilities, locating retail, fast-food, and business outlets, and examining species' carrying capacity in a region, among others. A standards-based approach was reviewed in this chapter, because distance and travel time can be assessed in advance for any given standard. Thus, this approach is flexible in the sense that a range of standards could be evaluated.

It is worth pointing out, in summary, that the standards-based dispersion problem is actually recognized by different names in various academic subareas: the node-packing problem (operations research literature), the anti-covering location problem (location science literature) and the stable set problem (mathematics literature), among others. Further, the problem structure is often extended in practice to address a host of complexities, including temporal considerations (e.g., multiple scheduling periods, production flow over time, etc.). Thus, the problem of interest may actually turn out to contain standards-based dispersion as a subproblem.

An important lesson in this chapter is that it often is possible to approach a planning problem in a number of different ways. We might be able to identify different objectives and different constraints, but also alternative ways of imposing constraints. The significance of this is that some approaches may be more advantageous than others, especially in terms of tractability and computational complexity. This is extremely important to keep in mind. There are generally many ways of modeling a particular problem. What we observed for the standards-based dispersion problem was that the underlying modeling objective was the same, but the way in which dispersion restrictions are viewed and imposed can differ. Such differences, particularly in this case, typically have significant implications for computational difficulty when solving for exact solutions. Although the forest planning problem turned out to be fairly easy for LINGO to solve in all cases, this was actually a byproduct of keeping the problem small so as to facilitate understanding. When problems containing hundreds or thousands of sites are examined, the differences in constraint structure become very pronounced. Some constraint forms (e.g., neighborhood and pairwise) simply turn out to be impossible to solve using commercial optimization software, whereas others constraint forms (cliques and hybrid) do enable models to be solved.

10.7   TERMS

dispersion
clique
buffer

containment
anti-covering
carrying capacity
separation
saturation

10.8   REFERENCES

Erkut, E., and S. Neuman. 1991. Comparison of four models for dispersing facilities. *INFOR* 29:68–86.

Kuby, M. 1987. Programming models for facility dispersion: The p-dispersion and maxisum dispersion problems. *Geographical Analysis* 19:315–329.

Murray, A. T., and R. L. Church. 1996a. Constructing and selecting adjacency constraints. *INFOR* 34:232–248.

Murray, A. T., and R. L. Church. 1996b. Analyzing cliques for imposing adjacency restrictions in forest models. *Forest Science* 42:166–175.

Murray, A. T., and R. L. Church. 1997. Facets for node packing. *European Journal of Operational Research* 101:598–608.

10.9   EXERCISES

10.1. Describe and discuss dispersed services/businesses that you have observed in your city. Perhaps you have noticed something about the spatial distribution of a particular chain of stores. What do think are the market area and demand considerations associated with the pattern you observed?

10.2. A city in Arizona has decided to address problems with drinking and drug use by locating treatment centers throughout the city. Can you propose a mathematical model for siting treatment centers so that no two centers are within one-half mile of each other?

10.3. Extract parcels and associated attribute information for some urban region (approximately 9 square miles in size). Assuming that a facility could be located at any parcel, use GIS to determine conflicting sets of parcels when no two facilities can be sited within 1,320 feet of each other.

10.4. Structure and solve the standards-based dispersion problem using hybrid restrictions in LINGO for the forest planning problem explored in this chapter (input data given in Table 10.1).

10.5. Suggest an approach for using the standards-based dispersion model as a tool to find the solution to an associated five facility max-min-min dispersion problem. (*Hint:* Suppose that you solved a standards-based dispersion model using a distance standard of 17 miles and were able to locate seven facilities. What then could you say about the minimum distance possible when siting only five facilities?)

10.6. We are interested in dispersing six facilities so that the sum of distances between all pairs of sited facilities is maximized. Can you formulate this as an optimization problem?

10.7. The mayor of Tomorrow has asked the planning staff of the city to find the vacant parcel within the city that is the furthest distance from all schools and parks, in order to locate a halfway house for rehabilitated drug users and alcoholics. Describe how this problem can be solved using the buffer function within GIS, employing a database containing boundaries of vacant parcels, parks and schools.

CHAPTER 11

LOCATION-ALLOCATION

11.0 INTRODUCTION

Many basic services need to be accessible to the public. Examples include libraries, courts, post offices, vehicle inspection stations, ambulances, solid-waste recycling centers, and many others. In fact, **accessibility** is the most widely used metric in measuring the value of a location in public service delivery. If a service is too far away, then an inordinate amount of time will be spent traveling to/from such services, costing people and business money. The same can be said for commercial activities (e.g., retail outlets) and product supply systems (e.g., warehouses and distribution centers). In this chapter, we continue our focus on the third law of location science, LLS3 (*Sites of an optimal multisite pattern must be selected simultaneously rather than independently, one at a time*), in the design of a system of multiple facilities.

In service system design there is a distinct difference between a system operating one facility and those operating many facilities. Within a system that operates one facility, all customers or demand are served by that single facility (see Chapter 6). However, when a system has more than one facility, then the demand must be divided up between the facilities so as to achieve service provision efficiencies. **Allocation** is the process of determining who is served by which facility. For example, a warehouse system supplies or stocks stores so that distribution costs are minimized. In Chapter 4, several models for analyzing system performance were discussed, and are in essence allocation models as the facility locations were fixed. In contrast to Chapter 4, the subject here involves locating facilities and allocating their services simultaneously. We will begin by defining the basic facilities planning problem involving both location and allocation components. We also present a heuristic approach for solving this model. The GIScience section provides a discussion on data error and uncertainty. Advanced topics in this chapter include a review of a continuous space location-allocation model, structuring a location-allocation model to address variable fixed costs and facility capacities, and a model extension for dealing with one aspect of data uncertainty.

11.1 PROBLEM DEFINITION AND MOTIVATION

The city of Tomorrow would like to encourage its citizens to recycle their solid wastes in order to reduce impacts on the environment. The town council has asked the planning department to locate a number of recycling centers around the city. Although the town council was unanimous in adopting the measure calling for the recycling program, most of the details were left to the planning department to sort out. They have decided that the most cost-efficient plan is to place small recycling centers/kiosks in the parking lots of shopping centers and municipal facilities. For the shopping centers, the city will pay the land owners a fee to house a recycling center, but it will be operated by city personnel. The planning staff has generated a list of feasible municipal facilities and shopping centers, all having sufficient parking lot space and being agreeable to participate. The planning director has indicated that the centers should be as accessible as possible for residents, as this will encourage their use.

The problem here is to locate multiple facilities to serve potential demand in a region. The facility in this case is the recycling center, and the demand is represented as the residents who will take their recyclable wastes to the centers. The goal is to maximize accessibility, so that as many people as possible will bring their wastes to the centers. This general planning problem can be stated as follows:

> Locate a multiple number of facilities and allocate the demand served by these facilities so that the system service is as efficient as possible.

This planning problem is recognized as a location-allocation problem, and is of interest for both the public and business sectors. It can be approached as a continuous space problem, where facilities can be sited anywhere, or as a discrete space problem, where facilities are to be located among a subset of potential predefined sites.

11.2 MATHEMATICAL REPRESENTATION

This definition of the location-allocation problem is necessarily generic, as there are a number of variants of this basic planning context. For the moment, we focus on a discrete version of this problem, and return to continuous space representation later in the chapter.

An important issue in the mathematical specification of a location model is first deciding on an appropriate measure of efficiency to be optimized. For public-service facilities, such as health clinics and post offices, it makes sense to place them so that the facilities are as accessible as possible to the user population. One method of measuring the efficiency of a given configuration of facilities is the total distance or travel time associated with each demand area traveling to their closest facility, multiplied by number of trips originating from that area. This metric is called **weighted distance**, and has already been introduced in Chapter 6 for the single facility Weber problem. The idea is to then locate a number of facilities in such a manner as to minimize the total weighted distance, where it is assumed that each demand is served by their closest facility.

Consider the following notation:

$i =$ index of demand areas $(1, 2, \ldots, n)$
$j =$ index of potential facility sites $(1, 2, \ldots, m)$
$d_{ij} =$ shortest distance or travel time from demand area i to potential facility site j
$a_i =$ amount of demand in area i
$p =$ number of facilities to be located
$Y_j = \begin{cases} 1, & \text{if facility at site } j \text{ is located} \\ 0, & \text{otherwise} \end{cases}$
$X_{ij} = \begin{cases} 1, & \text{if demand } i \text{ is served by facility } j \\ 0, & \text{otherwise} \end{cases}$

With this notation, we can define the notion of efficiency between a demand area i and a facility located at site j as follows:

$$a_i d_{ij} \tag{11.1}$$

This represents the total demand in area i, a_i, multiplied by the associated assignment distance/time, d_{ij}. If we incorporate the allocation decision about which demand is served by what facilities, the following weighted assignment distance results:

$$a_i d_{ij} X_{ij} \tag{11.2}$$

If demand area i is served by a facility located at site j, then $X_{ij} = 1$ in (11.2) and indicates the product of demand multiplied by associated travel distance/ (or time). Summing this value across all demand areas and all potential facilities gives:

$$\sum_{i=1}^{n} \sum_{j=1}^{m} a_i d_{ij} X_{ij} \tag{11.3}$$

This, then, is a system efficiency measure, equaling the total weighted travel distance associated with a particular allocation scheme defined by the values of X_{ij}. Of course we wish to optimize this accessibility measure.

Given that each demand area is to be served, a constraining condition is that each area is allocated to a facility. This can be structured as follows for demand area i:

$$\sum_{j=1}^{m} X_{ij} = 1 \tag{11.4}$$

In allocating demand areas to facilities, we must ensure that no allocation occurs unless a facility is actually sited. This can be assured mathematically using the following inequality for demand area i and facility j:

$$X_{ij} \leq Y_j \tag{11.5}$$

If $Y_j = 0$, then X_{ij} must be zero because of the zero bound on the right-hand side of the inequality. Alternatively, if $Y_j = 1$, then X_{ij} can equal zero or one. That is, an allocation assignment is possible.

If we assume that a specified number of facilities are to located, p, then this can be assured mathematically as follows:

$$\sum_{j=1}^{m} Y_j = p \tag{11.6}$$

This condition, given the binary requirements on Y_j, ensures that exactly p of the Y_j variables will equal one. Note that any number of located facilities can be considered in this way, depending on budgetary limitations, or even a range of located facilities. These functions and inequalities can be brought together to specify the following location-allocation problem:

$$Minimize \sum_{i=1}^{n} \sum_{j=1}^{m} a_i d_{ij} X_{ij} \tag{11.7}$$

Subject to:

$$\sum_{j=1}^{m} X_{ij} = 1 \quad \text{for each } i = 1, 2, \ldots, n \tag{11.8}$$

$$X_{ij} \leq Y_j \quad \text{for each } i = 1, 2, \ldots, n \text{ and } j = 1, 2, \ldots, m \tag{11.9}$$

$$\sum_{j=1}^{m} Y_j = p \tag{11.10}$$

$$Y_j = \{0, 1\} \quad \text{for each } j = 1, 2, \ldots, m \tag{11.11}$$

$$X_{ij} = \{0, 1\} \quad \text{for each } i = 1, 2, \ldots, n \text{ and } j = 1, 2, \ldots, m$$

The objective, (11.7), is to minimize total weighted assignment distance/time. Constraints (11.8) are allocation conditions requiring each demand area i to be served by a facility. Constraints (11.9) restrict allocations made for a given demand i to only sites j that have been chosen for housing a facility. The sense of the objective (minimize) and constraints (11.8) and (11.9) dictate that each demand will be allocated to their closest located facility. Constraint (11.10) specifies that p sites will be selected for facility placement. Finally, binary requirements are imposed in constraints (11.11). Note that it is only necessary to maintain the binary properties on the Y_j variables when solving this problem in practice. Since each demand must be allocated exactly once, and is restricted to assign to only those sites that have been selected for a facility, the objective function ensures that demand assignments will be made entirely to the closest facility, if there is a single closest facility. An assignment variable for a given demand may be fractional in an optimal solution only when there is a tie for the closest located facility to that demand area. This particular location-allocation model is known as the **p-median problem** (PMP) and was originally described by Hakimi (1964, 1965) and mathematically formulated by ReVelle and Swain (1970). The PMP is an integer-linear programming problem and commercial software packages, like LINGO, can be used to solve moderately sized application instances.

11.2.1 Heuristic Solution

The p-median problem does, unfortunately, have potential shortcomings when applied in practice. There are $nm + m$ variables and $nm + m + 1$ constraints, where n is the total number of demand areas and m is the total number of potential facility sites. If a problem contains 1,000 demands areas and 100 potential facility sites, there would be over 100,000 variables and constraints. Although this would not be considered very large within the context of many geographical planning problems, it starts to stretch the limits of many commercial optimization packages. That is, there is a practical limit on the size of an applied p-median problem if it is to be optimally solved using a commercial package. Of course, permissible problem size limits have increased over time as general purpose integer/linear optimization software has become faster and capable of solving larger problems, but limits remain. So, we can summarize by stating that, if we want to solve a relatively large p-median problem application, brute-force enumeration discussed in Chapter 10 is out of the question, as are commercial solvers.

The limitation posed by general-purpose software in solving location models like the p-median problem has prodded researchers to explore different types of solution approaches. The bulk of the research on solving the p-median problem has been devoted to the development of a vast variety of heuristics. As discussed in Chapter 3, *heuristics* are solution approaches that are crafted based on some type of search strategy. There is no guarantee that they will find the optimal solution, but good heuristic designs are likely to perform well in terms of speed and quality of the solution(s) identified. Heuristics are used when an optimal approach either does not exist, the problem is too large to solve optimally, or the heuristic can save considerable time and/or money in identifying a solution.

A well-known heuristic developed for the p-median problem is that designed by Teitz and Bart (1968), commonly referred to as an **interchange heuristic**. This is a neighborhood search/substitution approach that begins with a randomly generated configuration of p sites, and an associated allocation of each demand area to its closest facility. Of course, such a starting solution will probably not be very good in terms of minimizing objective function (11.7), but it will at least be feasible. That is, all constraints, (11.8) through (11.11), will be satisfied. The heuristic strategy can be thought of as an attempt to find improvements to the starting solution using a process called *swapping* or *interchange*. When an improvement is found, it is adopted and the search continues, but is focused on finding improvements to the newly adopted solution. Thus, the process yields a path of *adopted solutions*, where each one, in turn, is an improvement over the previously adopted solution. When the search fails to find any improvements, the heuristic stops and the best solution is reported.

The *interchange heuristic* for solving the p-median problem is as follows:

Step 1: Generate at random a starting solution of p sites. Let the set of p sites be designated as set S.

Step 2: Let C be defined as the set of all candidate sites not in S. Set $Flag = $ No.

Step 3: If the set C is empty, go to step 6. Otherwise pick a candidate site $k \in C$ and go to step 4.

Step 4: Remove site k from the set C. Calculate if candidate site k can be used to replace, one at a time, each site $j \in S$ and yield an improvement in total weighted distance, (11.7). If any exchange of k for a $j \in S$ results in a reduction of total weighted distance, then go to step 5. Otherwise, go to step 3

Step 5: Set $Flag = $ Yes; Make the exchange of k with the $j \in S$ that yields the greatest improvement in weighted distance. Candidate site k has now been added to the solution set S and one of the sites in S has been dropped. This means that S is a new improved solution. Go to step 3.

Step 6: A cycle has been completed. If $Flag = $ Yes, go to step 2, otherwise stop. S is a local optimal solution.

The interchange heuristic is effective because it is able to focus on the selection of p sites, as the optimal allocation is easy to derive given p facilities. To overcome bias associated with a given starting solution, this heuristic is usually restarted a number of times, each time with a different random starting pattern of facility sites. The best solution generated after a number of restarts is then identified as the best overall solution. Of course, no matter how many restarts are relied on, the solution found can only be characterized as a *local optima*. It could be that it is a global optimal solution, but this cannot be assured or confirmed. Empirical evidence suggests that solutions identified using the interchange heuristic are likely to be of high quality when a significant number of random restarts have been applied.

11.3 GISCIENCE

Uncertainty and **error** associated with digital information are unavoidable facts of life. It would be unrealistic to believe that such error and uncertainty did not somehow impact modeling results. First, the data about the earth is collected in a digital format and stored in a data model using GIS; the data model represents an abstraction that may be easy to manipulate, but may not be an accurate format in which to support a location or location-allocation model.[1] Second, models themselves are abstractions of some planning reality. In fact a specific planning model may not be easily supported by a general GIS data model. Third, data collection effort introduces potential errors and uncertainty as well. Finally, there can be uncertainty in the communication of results. These issues will now be discussed in more detail.

The *abstraction* of Earth was discussed in Chapter 2, highlighting that there were various approximations relied on to represent Earth in a digital environment. Of course it goes beyond simply representing Earth, as there are also human decisions regarding how to model spatial variability (e.g., raster vs. vector) and what phenomena are measured and recorded in the database. Related to this is the fact that there are vagueness and ambiguity issues as well. Spatial objects in GIS are exact and precise, yet on the surface of the earth they may not be. As an example, the coastline constantly changes due to tides, waves, erosion of soil, and so on, and the same is true for rivers and streams. This vagueness in boundary definition is not part of our reported information in GIS, however. Further, objects may be viewed ambiguously by different people due to perception, cognition, culture, or scale.

Models are also an abstraction of reality. That is, models take a complex issue and attempt to define it mathematically. In our case, the mathematical statement is generally specified in terms of decision variables, an objective function(s), and constraining conditions. In the process of specifying the model, many assumptions are made, irrelevant or unimportant factors are

---

[1] For example, a large city in the United States experienced difficulty in using its GIS database to route EMS vehicles during emergencies. The routing algorithm was set up to minimize turns, as making turns tended to reduce the travel speed of the ambulance. Unfortunately, most opposing streets at intersections did not match up exactly, and had a slight distance offset in the GIS. Thus, any intersection resulted in what the algorithm considered to be a turn. Until the source of the problem was identified and the algorithm was modified to ignore these small digitizing errors, the digital map could be used.

excluded, and various interactions are ignored. The hope is that the derived model incorporates the important and relevant variables, attributes, and influential conditions. However, there is always a chance of omissions and limited knowledge/understanding.

The third uncertainty and error issue identified was associated with data collection. There is no doubt potential for various types of measurement error. Instruments can be one source of such error. For example, temperature readings might be off or precipitation levels inaccurate. Discussed in Chapter 2 was that data might be generated through map scanning or digitizing. The maps themselves might shrink or stretch, could contain spills or other disfigurations that suggest the existence of an object, or could simply show misplaced, exaggerated, or otherwise altered objects due to cartographic license (artistic design). If data are generated using GPS, as another example, then it may be that locational coordinates are only known within $+/- 30$ m, yet are reported as precise coordinates. As a final example, consider the classification of remotely sense imagery with respect to vegetation. Classification is usually based on identifying the dominant type of vegetation. However, for a 30×30 m cell, as an example, it could be that multiple vegetation types exist. Thus, the reported attribute is misleading, or uncertain to some degree.

Let us now turn our attention to the p-median problem detailed in the previous section. Upon closer scrutiny, we can identify a number of data uncertainties in practice. The demand for service, a_i, is typically an expected or potential measure. Thus, by definition it is uncertain. Distance, d_{ij}, too, could be uncertain or in error. What is the metric relied on? In Chapter 6, many potential distance metrics were discussed, including Euclidean and network based measures. Are either actual travel paths? They may or may not be, depending on the application context, or also could simply be expected distances or travel times.

The final uncertainty issue mentioned was associated with the communication of modeling results. Given that various aspects of spatial data are potentially uncertain or in error, how does this relate to planning and management solutions derived using mathematical models? An important GIScience area of work has been attempting to deal with uncertainty and error in spatial and aspatial information. Often, this has been approached through the use of visualization-based techniques. As we have seen in the text thus far, geographic visualization of modeling results is also very effective in communicating identified plans. However, a deeper understanding requires more than just the depiction of variable values. As an example, the traditional **spider plot** of a p-median problem solution is illustrated in Figure 11.1. What is shown are facility location decisions, as well as allocation decisions. This is informative, but what about attribute values (demand) and associated allocation quantities? How certain are these values and locations? The challenge is to reach a better understanding of the problem for decision making, so communication of additional information is important.

The point here is that uncertainty and error are possible because of a number of potential causes, and may be intentional or unintentional. Nevertheless,

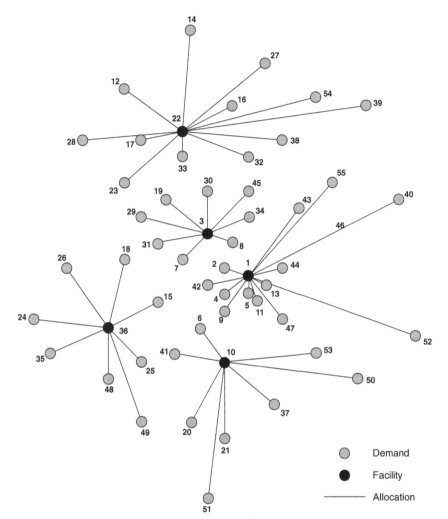

Figure 11.1   Spider plot of location and allocation decisions.

they have potential implications for modeling and, more importantly, for the reliability of the associated analysis. GIS offers some potential to mitigate or minimize the negative effects of error and uncertainty, but this remains an area in need of further research.

11.4   MODELING APPLICATION

In this section, the p-median problem is utilized to site recycling centers, with the intent of identifying the best multiple-facility siting configuration and allocation scheme. The decisions are whether or not a potential recycling center site j is selected, Y_i, as well as which center serves a neighborhood i,

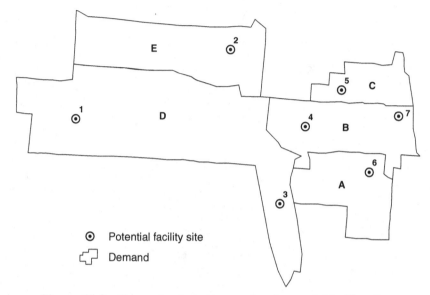

Figure 11.2 Demand units to be served and potential facility sites.

X_{ij}. This location-allocation problem makes sense for recycling center siting because relative costs to locate a kiosk are essentially the same at the various potential sites. Although there is a practical limit as to how many kiosks the city can afford, it is also possible to solve the model over a range of p values, and assess how accessibility changes relative to the value of p.

The model is applied to the area shown in Figure 11.2. There are five neighborhoods (labeled A, B, C, D, and E) and seven potential recycling centers. Demand, or expected recyclable waste, in tons per month is given in Table 11.1 along with expected travel distances (miles) between neighborhoods and potential centers. Given budgetary considerations, it is decided that two recycling centers are to be located, or specifically, $p = 2$.

TABLE 11.1 Demand and distance information

			Potential Facility Sites						
		a_i	1	2	3	4	5	6	7
Demand	A	31	1.89	1.21	0.48	0.51	0.65	0.17	0.58
	B	24	1.79	0.92	0.64	0.26	0.26	0.32	0.38
	C	38	1.97	0.95	0.97	0.50	0.19	0.57	0.28
	D	46	0.62	0.68	0.88	0.92	1.19	1.37	1.54
	E	26	0.81	0.36	1.21	0.99	1.13	1.51	1.54

Given the spatial and aspatial information needed in the p-median problem, the algebraic specification of the model can be stated:

Minimize $58.59X_{A1} + 37.51X_{A2} + 14.88X_{A3} + 15.81X_{A4} + 20.15X_{A5}$

$+ 5.27X_{A6} + 17.98X_{A7} + 42.96X_{B1} + 22.08X_{B2} + 15.36X_{B3} + 6.24X_{B4}$

$+ 6.24X_{B5} + 7.68X_{B6} + 9.12X_{B7} + 74.86X_{C1} + 36.10X_{C2} + 36.86X_{C3}$

$+ 19X_{C4} + 7.22X_{C5} + 21.66X_{C6} + 10.64X_{C7} + 28.52X_{D1} + 31.28X_{D2}$

$+ 40.48X_{D,3} + 42.32X_{D4} + 54.74X_{D5} + 63.02X_{D6} + 70.84X_{D7}$

$+ 21.06X_{E1} + 9.36X_{E2} + 31.46X_{E3} + 25.74X_{E4} + 29.38X_{E5}$

$+ 39.26X_{E6} + 40.04X_{E7}$

Subject to:

$$X_{A1} + X_{A2} + X_{A3} + X_{A4} + X_{A5} + X_{A6} + X_{A7} = 1$$
$$X_{B1} + X_{B2} + X_{B3} + X_{B4} + X_{B5} + X_{B6} + X_{B7} = 1$$
$$X_{C1} + X_{C2} + X_{C3} + X_{C4} + X_{C5} + X_{C6} + X_{C7} = 1$$
$$X_{D1} + X_{D2} + X_{D3} + X_{D4} + X_{D5} + X_{D6} + X_{D7} = 1$$
$$X_{E1} + X_{E2} + X_{E3} + X_{E4} + X_{E5} + X_{E6} + X_{E7} = 1$$

$X_{A1} \leq Y_1, X_{A2} \leq Y_2, X_{A3} \leq Y_3, X_{A4} \leq Y_4, X_{A5} \leq Y_5, X_{A6} \leq Y_6,$

$X_{A7} \leq Y_7, X_{B1} \leq Y_1, X_{B2} = Y_2, X_{B3} \leq Y_3, X_{B4} \leq Y_4, X_{B5} \leq Y_5,$

$X_{B6} \leq Y_6, X_{B7} \leq Y_7, X_{C1} \leq Y_1, X_{C2} \leq Y_2, X_{C3} \leq Y_3, X_{C4} \leq Y_4,$

$X_{C5} \leq Y5, X_{C6} \leq Y_6, X_{C7} \leq Y_7, X_{D1} \leq Y_1, X_{D2} \leq Y_2, X_{D3} \leq Y_3,$

$X_{D4} \leq Y_4, X_{D5} \leq Y_5, X_{D6} \leq Y_6, X_{D7} \leq Y_7, X_{E1} \leq Y_1, X_{E2} \leq Y_2,$

$X_{E3} \leq Y_3, X_{E4} \leq Y_4, X_{E5} \leq Y_5, X_{E6} \leq Y_6, X_{E7} \leq Y_7$

$Y_1 + Y_2 + Y_3 + Y_4 + Y_5 + Y_6 + Y_7 = 2$

$Y_1 = \{0, 1\}, \ Y_2 = \{0, 1\}, \ Y_3 = \{0, 1\}, \ Y_4 = \{0, 1\}, \ Y_5 = \{0, 1\},$

$Y_6 = \{0, 1\}, \ Y_7 = \{0, 1\}$

$0 \leq X_{ij} \leq 1 \quad \text{for all } i, j$

This model instance has seven siting decision variables and 35 allocation decision variables. There are five allocation constraints, 35 constraints limiting assignment to open facilities and one constraint specifying the number of facilities to be sited ($p = 2$ in this case). As structured, this is a mixed-integer linear programming problem because no integer requirements are imposed on the X_{ij} variables. As noted previously, these variables should naturally be binary, unless there is a tie between the closest located facilities to a specific demand. This problem can be specified using LINGO, as depicted in Figure 11.3. Note that the model is described using sets for demand, sites and allocations (representing all possible demand-site assignments). The form of the model is presented so that it follows the structure of the algebraic statement. The data for this model is specified at the bottom of the LINGO file. Note that comparison of the LINGO structured model to the algebraic statement is possible using "LINGO→Generate→Display model" pull-down menus (or Ctrl+G) in LINGO.

Solving the problem, we find that locating recycling centers at sites 2 and 5, with associated allocations shown in Figure 11.4, results in the lowest total weighted travel distance (or greatest accessibility), having an objective value of 74.25 (requiring 31 iterations for LINGO to solve).

```
! p-Median Problem;
MODEL:
SETS:
 Demand /A,B,C,D,E/  : a;
 Sites /1 .. 7/ : Y ;
 Allocation(Demand,Sites) : d, X ;
ENDSETS

! The objective, minimize cost of travel measured as weighted distance;
MIN = @SUM( Allocation(i,j): a(i) * d(i,j) * X(i,j));

! Each demand must allocate once to an open facility;
@FOR( Demand(i):
 @SUM( Sites(j): X( i,j)) = 1; );

! Assignment is restricted to those sites selected for facilities;
@FOR( Demand(i):
 @FOR( Sites(j): X(i,j) < Y(j) ); );

! Open exactly p facilities;
@SUM( Sites(j):  Y(j) ) = p ;

! Integer restrictions on the variables;
@FOR( Sites(j): @BIN(Y(j)); );

! Input data and parameters;
DATA:
 p =  2;
 a =  31, 24, 38, 46, 26;
 d =  1.89, 1.21, 0.48, 0.51, 0.65, 0.17, 0.58,
      1.79, 0.92, 0.64 0.26, 0.26, 0.32, 0.38,
      1.97, 0.95, 0.97, 0.50, 0.19, 0.57, 0.28,
      0.62, 0.68, 0.88, 0.92, 1.19, 1.37, 1.54,
      0.81, 0.36, 1.21, 0.99, 1.13, 1.51, 1.54;
ENDDATA
END
```

Figure 11.3 *p*-median problem structured in LINGO.

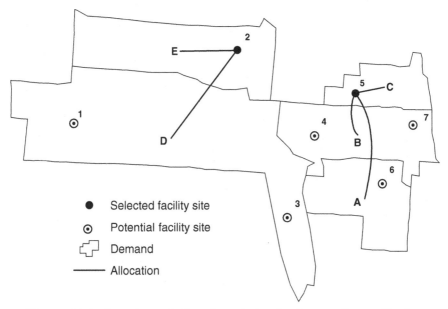

Figure 11.4 Location and allocation solution for the recycling application.

The interchange heuristic can also be applied to solve the recycling center problem. Adopted solutions are shown in order of their acceptance in Figure 11.5. The heuristic begins (step 1) by randomly selecting two facilities ($p = 2$), 1 and 3, so $S = \{1, 3\}$. Thus, $C = \{2, 4, 5, 6, 7\}$ in step 2 and $Flag =$ No. The result is an objective value, (11.7), of 116.68. In step 3, site 2 is selected for evaluation, replacing either facility 1 or 3 in step 4. If site 2 replaces facility 1, the objective is 106.98. Alternatively, if site 2 replaces facility 3, the objective is 133.57. Thus, site 2 replacing facility 1 is an improvement. The exchange is made in step 5, so $S = \{2, 3\}$ and we return to step 3 with $C = \{4, 5, 6, 7\}$. This evaluation and/or exchange process continues until $C = \{\}$, or rather, when C is empty. This signifies the end of cycle 1. Since $Flag =$ Yes (an improvement was found in this cycle), we return to step 2 and set $Flag =$ No. Cycle 2 now begins. In cycle 2, no improving interchanges are found, so the heuristic stops when $C = \{\}$. The heuristic now terminates, and a local optima solution is found. In this case, the local optima involves locating recycling centers at sites 2 and 5 and allocations as shown in Figure 11.4, giving a total weighted distance of 74.25.

A few points are worth noting about the interchange process. Figure 11.5 indicates the progression of adopted solutions. In particular, the process found a solution that was a significant improvement over the initial randomly generated solution (by almost 60%). Of course, during the process many non-improving solutions were considered, but only improvements are actually

Cycle 1

$S = \{1, 3\}$
$Flag$ = No
$C = \{2, 4, 5, 6, 7\}$
Objective = 116.68

$S = \{2, 3\}$
$Flag$ = Yes
$C = \{4, 5, 6, 7\}$
Objective = 106.98

$S = \{2, 4\}$
$Flag$ = Yes
$C = \{5, 6, 7\}$
Objective = 81.69

$S = \{2, 5\}$
$Flag$ = Yes
$C = \{6, 7\}$
Objective = 74.25

Cycle 2

$S = \{2, 5\}$
$Flag$ = No
$C = \{1, 3, 4, 6, 7\}$
Objective = 74.25

Figure 11.5 Interchange heuristic summary for five-demand, seven-site recycling center siting problem.

adopted. It so happens that in this case, for this problem, the optimal solution was actually found. This is only known because we were able to solve the problem exactly using LINGO. Without this knowledge, we would not have any basis for assessing the quality of the identified local optima. As mentioned previously, it is not necessarily the case that an optimal solution is found when the interchange heuristic is applied in practice. Further, we likely would begin the heuristic with different randomly generated solutions a significant number of times, then adopt the overall best solution found.

11.5 ADVANCED TOPICS

The p-median problem has been used in locating a number of different facilities, including courts, post offices, salt piles for road deicing programs, parks, and transit garages. In some instances, however, potential facility sites are not restricted to predefined sites, but, rather, can be located anywhere in continuous space. This location-allocation problem variant is known as the **multifacility Weber problem**. Thus, one issue to be discussed as an advanced topic is the formal specification of the multifacility Weber problem, along with possibilities for solving this problem. A second advanced topic deals with the introduction of facility capacities and fixed costs. The last topic addressed in this section deals with issues of data uncertainty in applying a location model like the p-median model.

11.5.1   Continuous Space Siting

Virtually all location models have been defined within the context of both a continuous space domain and a discrete problem domain. In section 11.2, we presented a formulation of the p-median problem where we assumed that potential sites were discrete and finite in number. Here, we relax the assumption concerning facility placement and assume that facilities may be sited anywhere in continuous space. The counterpart to the discrete p-median problem, but using a continuous space domain, is known as the *multifacility Weber problem* (where the Euclidean distance metric is used). This problem is an extension of the single-facility location problem introduced in Chapter 6, known as the Weber problem. Like the p-median problem, the multifacility Weber location problem is based on the assumption that demand is represented by a set of points.

The specification of the multifacility Weber problem relies on the following notation:

$$i = \text{index of demand areas } (1, 2, \ldots, n)$$
$$j = \text{index of facility sites } (1, 2, \ldots, p)$$
$$a_i = \text{amount of demand in area } i$$
$$(x_i, y_i) = \text{coordinates of demand } i$$
$$p = \text{number of facilities to be located}$$
$$\bar{X}_j = \text{x-coordinate value of facility } j$$
$$\bar{Y}_j = \text{y-coordinate value of facility } j$$
$$U_{ij} = \begin{cases} 1, & \text{if demand area } i \text{ is allocated for service to facility } j \\ 0, & \text{otherwise} \end{cases}$$

The major changes here are that this notation specifies the coordinates of facilities as decision variables and alters the allocation variables. This should not be any cause for concern as notation is only what we define it to be. This is the inherent flexibility of mathematical communication. Given this, Euclidean distance between a demand area i and a facility j is:

$$\sqrt{\left(x_i - \bar{X}_j\right)^2 + \left(y_i - \bar{Y}_j\right)^2} \tag{11.12}$$

With this notation, a continuous space location-allocation problem is as follows:

$$\text{Minimize} \quad \sum_{i=1}^{n} \sum_{j=1}^{p} a_i U_{ij} \sqrt{\left(x_i - \bar{X}_j\right)^2 + \left(y_i - \bar{Y}_j\right)^2} \tag{11.13}$$

Subject to:

$$\sum_{j=1}^{p} U_{ij} = 1 \quad \text{for each } i = 1, 2, \ldots, n \tag{11.14}$$

$$U_{ij} = \{0, 1\} \quad \text{for each} \quad i = 1, 2, \ldots, n \quad \text{and} \quad j = 1, 2, \ldots, p \tag{11.15}$$

$$\bar{X}_j, \bar{Y}_j \geq 0 \quad \text{for each } j = 1, 2, \ldots, p$$

The objective, (11.13), minimizes the total weighted assignment distance, and is a nonlinear function of location and allocation decision variables. Constraints (11.14) require each demand area to be allocated to a facility. Constraints (11.15) present the associated integer and nonnegativity restrictions on decision variables.

Again, this model, (11.13) through (11.15), is known as the multifacility Weber problem and was first described in Cooper (1963). Due to the obvious nonlinearity of the objective, (11.13), this is a difficult problem to solve. Heuristics have therefore been essential for solving this problem. Perhaps the most well known is the alternating heuristic detailed in Cooper (1964). An exact approach does exist for solving this problem, based on a transformation into a large-scale set partitioning problem. Unfortunately, it is limited in application to problems of less than 150 demand points.

11.5.2 Service Capacities and Fixed Costs

One complication with the p-median problem is that it does not specifically address issues of capacity and variable fixed costs. The basic assumption is that each facility will have the capacity to handle the demand that is assigned to it. Further, it is assumed that each facility is essentially the same cost to build. Neither assumption may hold true in different planning contexts. What if a site has a confined area and this translates to a limited capacity to handle demand? Or, what if an existing factory has a limit on capacity that has been reached and the company wants to know whether it is better to add capacity to that existing factory or, for logistics reasons, site a new factory in a different region? Finally, what if the costs vary significantly between potential facility sites? In such cases, the p-median problem is inadequate for addressing the planning context, and a different location-allocation model is needed.

To formulate a model with capacities and fixed costs, consider the following notation:

$i =$ index of demand areas $(1, 2, \ldots, n)$
$j =$ index of potential facility sites $(1, 2, \ldots, m)$
$a_i =$ amount of demand in area i
$c_{ij} =$ cost to ship to demand i from facility j
$f_j =$ fixed cost to build a facility at site j
$b_j =$ capacity of facility j
$Y_j = \begin{cases} 1, & \text{if facility at site } j \text{ is located} \\ 0, & \text{otherwise} \end{cases}$
$Z_{ij} =$ amount of demand i served by facility j

With this notation, we can structure a fixed charge and capacitated location-allocation problem:

$$\textit{Minimize} \quad \sum_{i=1}^{n}\sum_{j=1}^{m} c_{ij}Z_{ij} + \sum_{j=1}^{m} f_j Y_j \qquad (11.16)$$

Subject to:

$$\sum_{j=1}^{m} Z_{ij} = a_i \quad \text{for each } i = 1, 2, \ldots, n \qquad (11.17)$$

$$\sum_{i=1}^{n} Z_{ij} \leq b_j Y_j \quad \text{for each } j = 1, 2, \ldots, m \qquad (11.18)$$

$$Y_j = \{0, 1\} \quad \text{for each } j = 1, 2, \ldots, m \qquad (11.19)$$

$$Z_{ij} \geq 0 \quad \text{for each } i = 1, 2, \ldots, n \text{ and } j = 1, 2, \ldots, m$$

This location-allocation model minimizes all costs associated with facility siting and shipment to customers (demand). The first component of objective (11.16) specifies shipment costs. The second term represents the fixed costs of the sites that have been selected for a facility. Constraints (11.17) ensure that located facilities satisfy the demands of all customers. Constraints (11.18) maintain two properties. The first is that no shipments can be made from a facility j unless it is located. The second property is that the total demand served by facility j is less than or equal to its capacity. Constraints (11.19) impose zero–one and nonnegativity restrictions on specific decision variables.

This model is the **fixed-charge capacitated location-allocation problem**, where f_j is the fixed cost or charge associated with establishing a facility and b_j is the capacity of service for facility site j. If all facility sites were selected (e.g., $Y_j = 1$ for all j), then what remains are the allocation decisions of the transportation problem. If the fixed-charge term is removed from the objective and the location siting variables are removed from constraints (11.18), then the remaining problem structure is exactly that of the transportation problem (Chapter 4). Also worth noting is that several extensions to this fixed-charge capacitated location-allocation problem are possible, including addressing multiple commodities, expansion costs, direct and indirect shipments, and so on.

11.5.3   Accounting for Uncertainty and Error

Issues associated with **uncertainty** and **error** were discussed earlier in this chapter. We return now to uncertainty in the context of the p-median problem, recognizing that demand estimates reflect uncertain quantities and as a result might lead to questions of reliability when interpreting model results. Specifically, a_i typically represents a likely or expected level of demand. In waste recycling, as an example, the estimated level of recycling is based on household and neighborhood characteristics. Given this, the estimate may be erroneous or inaccurate. How, then, can we reduce uncertainty associated with the use of the demand estimate? What if we have a number of demand estimates, each representing some sort of scenario? As an example, method 1 might represent a best-case scenario where each household in a neighborhood recycles waste to the greatest extent possible, method 2 might represent a scenario were only more educated and affluent households in neighborhoods recycle, and method 3 might represent a worst-case scenario where only minimal recycling takes place. We now have a number of potential demand estimates, and addressing uncertainty would mean that we should consider all reasonable scenarios. With this in mind, it is possible to extend the p-median problem to account for multiple demand scenarios.

Demand for each area, given different scenarios, can be defined in the following manner:

k = index of scenarios
a_{ik} = demand in area i under scenario k
w_k = relative importance weight given to scenario k

Using this added notation along with the notation presented for the p-median problem in section 11.2, (11.7) to (11.11), we can formulate the following **scenario-based** p-median model:

$$\text{Minimize} \quad \sum_k w_k \sum_{i=1}^{n} \sum_{j=1}^{m} a_i d_{ij} X_{ij} \qquad (11.20)$$

Subject to:

$$\sum_{j=1}^{m} X_{ij} = 1 \quad \text{for each } i = 1, 2, \ldots, n \tag{11.21}$$

$$X_{ij} \leq Y_j \quad \text{for each } i = 1, 2, \ldots, n \text{ and } j = 1, 2, \ldots, m \tag{11.22}$$

$$\sum_{j=1}^{m} Y_j = p \tag{11.23}$$

$$Y_j = \{0, 1\} \quad \text{for each } j = 1, 2, \ldots, m \tag{11.24}$$

$$X_{ij} = \{0, 1\} \quad \text{for each } i = 1, 2, \ldots, n \text{ and } j = 1, 2, \ldots, m$$

The objective, (11.20), incorporates multiple scenarios as it minimizes the to-tal of weighted assignment distance/time associated with each scenario. The model constraints, (11.21) through (11.24), are exactly the same as for the p-median problem. The use of weights, w_k, enables varying levels of impor-tance to be established for different scenarios. Typically, $\sum_k w_k = 1$, so if $w_1 = 1$ and all others equal 0, then scenario 1 would only be considered and would be equivalent to the p-median problem using demand values associated with scenario 1. When two or more weights are positive, the model will iden-tify noninferior location-allocation solutions on the trade-off frontier. This model can be classified as a robust optimization model as it attempts to find a solution which is a top performer under different demand scenarios. Robust optimization is one such technique that can be used when data uncertainty exists.

11.6 SUMMARY

Accessibility is an important feature of an effective service system. Good sys-tem access is the result of planning, and not likely if left to chance. Location-allocation models were introduced in this chapter as a way of simultaneously addressing both location and allocation decisions in the planning process. Of course, the models presented here can all be extended in a number of ways, and have been in the literature.

A major emphasis in research has focused on solving location-allocation models, particularly the p-median problem. The evolution and maturity of GIS has in fact lead to more complex extensions of this model, but also significantly larger application instances. Given this, improved solution approaches continue to be sought. Church (2008) provides a review and in-troduces approaches for solving the p-median problem using exact methods. Murray and Church (1996) discuss meta-heuristics for solving the p-median problem. Recent research has exploited spatial proximity relationships in mathematical formulation and in structuring solution processes, and this can be enhanced through the use of GIS. Finally, there has been considerable work focused on addressing error and uncertainty, and a good summary is provided in Murray (2003).

11.7   TERMS

accessibility

allocation

weighted distance

p-median problem

interchange heuristic

error and uncertainty

spider plot

multifacility Weber problem

Fixed-charge capacitated location-allocation problem

scenario-based or robust optimization

11.8   REFERENCES

Church, R. L. 2008. BEAMR: An exact and approximate model for the p-median problem. *Computers & Operations Research* 35:417–426.

Cooper, L. 1963. Location-allocation problems. *Operations Research* 11:331–343.

Cooper, L. 1964. Heuristic methods for location-allocation problems. *SIAM Review* 6:37–53.

Hakimi, S. L. 1964. Optimum location of switching centers and the absolute centers and medians of a graph. *Operations Research* 12:450–459.

Hakimi, S. L. 1965. Optimum distribution of switching centers and some graph related theoretic problems. *Operations Research* 13:462–475.

Murray, A. T., and R. L. Church 1996. Applying simulated annealing to location-planning models. *Journal of Heuristics* 2:31–53.

Murray, A. T. 2003. Site placement uncertainty in location analysis. *Computers, Environment and Urban Systems* 27:205–221.

ReVelle, C. S., and R. Swain. 1970. Central facilities location. *Geographical Analysis* 2:30–42.

Teitz, M. B. and P. Bart 1968. Heuristic methods for estimating the generalized vertex median of a weighted graph. *Operations Research* 16:955–961.

11.9   EXERCISES

11.1. The city manager of Tomorrow has determined that there is some limit to how many of the recycling centers can be operated. Overall, there is enough money to staff five recycling centers, and enough money to rent space at up to four shopping centers. This means that at least one of the facilities must be placed on a municipal lot. Can you propose a model extension to address these requirements?

11.2. There are four city council people who will vote to adopt or reject the plan for recycling centers in city of Tomorrow. Can you think of issues in which specific council members will either support or reject your plan? Are there additional constraints that might be added that will make the solution more desirable in the eyes of the council people? One of the shopping centers is interesting in having a recycling center on its parking lot, and states that it will not charge any rent. Such a proposal is not actually free, as it still involves the cost of operation. Can you suggest a method in which you can determine the impact on system operation, should the city take the shopping center owner up on its offer?

11.3. Suppose that Company X wants to locate three warehouses from which product is supplied to customers instead of direct from the factory, taking into account fixed costs and capacities. Company X decides that it wants to begin the development of such a system, one facility at a time. There are many reasons for this decision. First, this spreads out development costs over a period of years. Second, this allows it to develop its first warehouse and start operations, enabling it to work out any system problems before the other two warehouse are fully built. Third, it allows the company to further compare costs and services between warehousing and direct shipment from the factory before fully developing the warehouse system. The big problem is to determine the order in which warehouses should be built. Can you suggest a strategy in deciding the order in which to develop the warehouses? Why do you think your plan is desirable?

11.4. Many heuristic strategies have been developed to solve the p-median problem. Besides the method discussed in this chapter, one such technique is the *greedy drop* approach. It starts with all sites as a part of the solution, and then drops the site that results in the least increase in weighted distance. Once that facility is dropped, the heuristic identifies the next site that, when dropped, has the least impact on weighted distance. The heuristic continues until p facilities remain. Can you think of a simple strategy that might be efficient at solving a p-median problem?

11.5. Company X likes the model developed in section 11.5.2, except for one property found in solutions. Sometimes a customer in the optimal solution is supplied by several locations (*e.g.,* two different warehouses). Company X says that customers like dealing with one supply location, and should always get their shipments from the same place. This is called *single sourcing*. Formulate a new model for Company X that ensures that each customer is supplied from only one source.

11.6. Several approaches have been used to reduce the number of constraints and variables in the *p*-median problem formulation. Are there assignment variables that will never be used? Constraints (11.9), so called *Balinski constraints*, require one constraint for each assignment variable. Can you structure a constraint that uses one constraint for each facility and forces assignments to only those sites that have been selected for a facility?

11.7. What happens in the progression of adopted solutions for the interchange heuristic when alternative random initial solutions are utilized? Note there are 20 other possible combinations.

11.8. Suppose that there are distance restrictions limiting the maximum distance a demand can be allocated to a facility. Can you modify the LINGO formulation to limit possible allocations to less than 0.5 miles?

CHAPTER 12

CONCLUSION

12.0 INTRODUCTION

An introductory text on location analysis cannot possibly cover every important and/or noteworthy topic in business site selection, GIS, and modeling. We certainly have not in this text, due to space limitations, but have tried to seek a balance between all three elements. Our intent was to establish a foundation for students and professionals to understand the importance of modeling and GIS within the context of applications and research. The future of location science lies at the interface of GIS, optimization, and application-specific problem domains. That said, there are several issues in need of further discussion. First, there are many classes of location models beyond those covered here. Second, considerable depth and variety exists within each location model class. Third, our discussion of specialized techniques used in the solution of models was often somewhat limited. Finally, there are significant existing challenges in location modeling and GIS. We discuss each of these topics in the remainder of this chapter.

12.1 CLASSES OF LOCATION MODELS

Location models are defined in the literature based in terms of spatial domain (e.g., network, continuous space, hybrid, etc.), type of facility (e.g., point, line, area, etc.), metrics (e.g., covering, median, cost, etc.), number of sited facilities (e.g., one or multiple) and special structure or constraints (e.g., hierarchical, capacitated, etc.). These basic properties can be used to classify specific types of problems. In the 1970s, popular classifications were public- and private-sector distinctions, as well as continuous space and network-based models. Although these categories remain valid today, models are often classified in terms of the underlying intent. For example, obnoxious location models deal with siting dangerous or unwanted facilities, and median models address issues of access in minimizing total weighted distance in locating facilities. Reviews of the literature usually focus on a given class of model with respect to basic intent, or within the context of domain (e.g., continuous or discrete space). In this text we have introduced a variety of different models that span a number of problem classes. For example, Chapter 11 introduced two multifacility location-allocation problems: the p-median problem and the fixed-charge plant location problem (capacitated and uncapacitated). Both types of models are location-allocation in intent, but their objectives are not the same so are classified differently. Table 12.1 presents a number of model classes that exist in the literature. Of those listed, the first six model classes have been discussed in this textbook. Although we attempted to introduce a number of the problem classes, there are some notable exceptions that we did not have the space to address. Two examples are *hub location problems* and *resilient design problems*.

12.2   CLASS VARIETY AND EXTENSIONS

The previous section highlighted that there are a range of location model classes. Not only are there many classes, but within a given class there numerous varieties and extensions of models. That is, our discussion of a particular class in this text has necessarily been limited, as it was not possible to review all problem variants and extensions given space limitations. In what follows the intent is to provide a better appreciation of the variability of potential models within a class. The median model class identified in Table 12.1 is utilized for the discussion of class variety and extension. The p-median problem is defined as follows:

> Locate a fixed number of facilities, p, in such a manner as to minimize the total weighted distance of serving all customers, when each customer is served by its closest facility.

Although there have been a number of instances where the p-median problem has been applied to help determine the location of a set of facilities, there has been a continued interest to redefine the problem (and associated models) in order to address issues beyond the original intent. Table 12.2 identifies 10 variants of the p-median problem, each representing an extension to handle nuances encountered in application. For example, traffic congestion can vary throughout the day, and therefore the time to travel to a facility will vary. The stochastic p-median problem addresses temporal variation by dividing the day into a number of discrete time periods, and accounting for demand

TABLE 12.1 Representative location model classes

Model Class	Definition
Median	Locate one or multiple facilities in order to minimize weighted distance (Chapter 6, Weber, and Chapter 11).
Line-based facility	Locate a route or corridor across a terrain or along a network (Chapter 7).
Covering	Maximize coverage given p-facilities or minimize cost in order to completely cover all demand (Chapter 9).
Area-based facility	Acquire land for same intended use (Chapter 8).
Obnoxious facility location	Locate one or more facilities in order to disperse them from each other or from demand (Chapter 10).
Fixed-charge plant location	Locate one of more facilities in order to minimize facility and interaction costs (Chapter 11).
Center	Locate one or multiple facilities in order to minimize the maximum distance that any user is from their closest facility.
Tree-based facility	Locate a tree structure (continuous space or network) to maximally connect and minimize cost (e.g., Steiner tree).
Hub and spoke	Locate one or more hub facilities along with connections so as to optimize transport or travel between a number of origin–destination pairs.
Competitive	Locate one or more facilities in order to marginalize competitors market share, knowing that they are attempting to do the same.
Resilient design	Locate facilities so that risk of disruption is taken into account.
Hierarchical	Locate a facility system that has defined levels that are interrelated (e.g., clinics and hospitals; elementary, middle and high schools; etc.).
Flow capturing	Locate facilities in order to capture customer flow, where flow is based on travel patterns of potential customers.
Combined route and access point models	Locate a route (e.g., public transit bus), along with access sites along the route (e.g., bus stops) to optimize service.
Combined network design and facility location	Expand a network as well as locate facilities so that the combined system is as efficient as possible.
Reserve design	Select sites in order to protect endangered species, as well as to reduce the risk of species loss.

TABLE 12.2 Select median models

Problem Name	Definition	Assignment
p-median	Locate *p*-facilities in order to minimize weighted distance.	Closest facility assignment
Stochastic *p*-median	Locate *p*-facilities in order to minimize weighted distance when a number of travel time states exist.	Closest facility assignment in each travel time state
Vector assignment *p*-median	Locate *p*-facilities in order to minimize weighted distance.	Closest facility assignment for V_1% of each demand, second closest facility assignment for V_2% of each demand, V_3% to the third closest facility, etc.
Congested *p*-median problem	Locate *p*-facilities in order to minimize weighted distance, when taking into account that some facilities may be busy and users must then be served by further facilities that are available.	Users are served by their closest available facility
Hierarchical *p*-median	Locate sets of interacting facilities (e.g., hospitals and clinics) in order to minimize weighted distance.	Closest assignment of demand to the lower service level facility, assignment of demand to higher-level facility either through lower-level facility or directly from demand area.
Shortest-path median problem	Find the shortest route from an origin to a destination where the weighted distance of users to the route is minimized.	Assignment of demand to the closest stop or node on the chosen route
Capacitated *p*-median problem	Minimize weighted distance when facilities have a capacity.	Closest facility assignment
Transportation *p*-median	Minimize weighted distance.	Allocation of demand is based on a transportation problem
r-Interdiction *p*-median	Maximize weighted distance resulting when *r* of *p*-existing facilities is destroyed or rendered inoperable.	Closest facility assignment
r-interdiction median problem with fortification	Minimize weighted distance while fortifying a limited number of facilities, where unprotected facilities are subject to an intentional strike of up to *r*-facilities.	Closest existing facility assignment after fortification and interdiction
p-median scheduling and location problem	Locate *p*-facilities and determine their operating schedules in order to minimize weighted distance, assuming that demand varies over predefined time periods.	Closest open facility assignment in each time period

across time periods. The objective is to then locate facilities in such a manner as to minimize total weighted travel, given that a demand in a period of time will be served by the closest facility in that period. To describe all of the extensions noted in Table 12.2 is not our intent here. Rather, we aim to shed light on the fact that models within classes are often varied and/or extended in many ways, resulting in a richer model. Suffice it to say that a number of very important model extensions have been undertaken with the purpose of making the p-median problem fit circumstances found in real-world applications.

From the previous discussion and Table 12.2, it should be clear that the literature associated with the median class of location models is quite large. The fact is that this holds true for each of the model/problem classes introduced in this text. Whether it is a standards-based covering model or a dispersion model, one can find a rich literature focusing on model extensions designed to handle specific real-world nuances.

12.3 SOLUTION APPROACHES

Discussed in various places in the text was that many encountered optimization models can be difficult to solve in practice. In Chapter 3 we discussed two basic approaches for solving a model: exact and heuristic. An *exact method* is an approach that guarantees an optimal solution to a problem. A *heuristic* is a technique that gives a solution to the model, but it is not possible to prove or verify anything about the quality of the solution. Of course, we would always prefer an optimal (or exact) solution to a problem, but this may be either impossible to obtain or require too much computational time/effort. If a model cannot be easily solved, then our options are to reformulate the model to make it more amenable to exact solution or develop an efficient heuristic.

It should not be surprising, then, that considerable interest and effort has been devoted to the development of solution approaches for location models. In fact, any class or particular model within a class has generally witnessed substantial research devoted to exact and heuristic solution approaches. To illustrate this point, we return to the p-median problem. Formulated in Chapter 11, the p-median problem was structured as an integer linear programming model. Two solution approaches were discussed. An exact approach was to use commercial optimization software to solve the model, and was demonstrated using LINGO. We also described a heuristic solution approach called *interchange* for solving this model.

Because of the importance of this problem, it has been the subject of tremendous research directed at methods to efficiently solve difficult and/or large problem instances. Table 12.3 lists a number of directions that have been taken to solve the p-median problem. They range from creating sophisticated heuristics to the development of different model formulations. Recall that there are $nm + m$ variables and $nm + m + 1$ constraints, where n is the total number of demand areas and m is the total number of potential facility

TABLE 12.3 Select research focused on solution of the *p*-median problem

Solution	Approach	Description
Exact (model reformulation), with solution by general purpose optimization software	Hybrid: Smaller model formulation, helping to solve larger problems	A model that combines two forms of allocation constraints, (12.1) and (12.2)
	COBRA: A model that reduces needed variables and constraints by taking advantage of spatial structure	A model that combines variables and constraints based on spatial properties
	BEAMR: A model that can be used in two modes, exact or approximate, reducing problem size	A model that eliminates variables and associated constraints that do impact the identification of the optimal solution
Exact	Lagrangian relaxation with subgradient optimization embedded into a branch and bound algorithm	Based on solving a dual model generated by the relaxation of one or more model constraints. The procedure searches for optimal values of Lagrange prices, and guarantees optimal results because it is embedded in a branch and bound algorithm.
Heuristic	Vertex substitution (or neighborhood search)	A substitution-based algorithm, like interchange
	Lagrangian relaxation with subgradient optimization	A lagrangian based process without a branch and bound algorithm
	Tabu search	A substitution-like approach that always makes a change, regardless of improvement, keeping track of the progression of changes and avoiding "tabu" moves
	Variable neighborhood search	S substitution heuristic that involves a search neighborhood that varies in size
	Heuristic concentration	Based on using a heuristic to identify core and concentration sites, then using the hybrid exact model to select from the concentration set
	Simulated annealing	Based on an analogy to tempering glass or metal, where configuration perturbations are tested and compared to a Boltzman distribution
	Genetic algorithm	Based on a genetic encoding and biological inspired operators, such as mating and mutation

sites in the formulation of the p-median problem detailed in Chapter 11. In technical terms, this is considered quite large for a given problem instance, so there have been attempts to produce a model formulation that is smaller and easier to solve. In fact, reformulating any model is quite common, and this was demonstrated in this text for the standards-based dispersion problem in Chapter 10 (involving neighborhood, pairwise and clique constraints).

The original p-median model formulation that was first presented in ReVelle and Swain (1970) relied on the following constraints to ensure that no allocation of demand was made to a facility unless it was sited:

$$X_{ij} \leq Y_j \quad \text{for each } i = 1, 2, \ldots, n \text{ and } j = 1, 2, \ldots, m \qquad (12.1)$$

where X_{ij} equals one if demand i is served by potential facility j and zero if not, and Y_j equals one if potential facility j is selected as a site and zero if not. These were constraints (11.9) in Chapter 11, and they are often referred to as *Balinski* constraints due to their structure and the relationship to conditions imposed by Balinski (1965) for plant location. In terms of the number of variables and constraints, the conditions imposed in (12.1) dominate the problem formulation, as there are nm constraints of this type. As a result, these conditions have been recognized by researchers as offering potential for model reformulation. One alternative is the so-called *Efroymson and Ray* constraint,from Efroymson and Ray (1966), for the plant location problem:

$$\sum_i X_{ij} \leq nY_j \quad \text{for each } j = 1, 2, \ldots, m \qquad (12.2)$$

Easily discerned is that this form only requires m constraints to impose the necessary allocation conditions. That is, this is a valid constraint set that can replace constraints (12.1) in the p-median problem formulation. Why not use them then? The answer is simple: Because in practice, the structural properties associated with constraints (12.2) are such that their use makes the problem substantially more difficult to solve using exact methods. So, the structural properties of constraints (12.1) are good, but require many constraints. In contrast, the structural properties of constraints (12.2) are poor, but there are relatively few constraints. Complicating matters further is that structural properties can be affected by the number of constraints of a given type used in a model.

Beyond the two classic approaches for imposing allocation restrictions, three interesting alternatives have been developed and are summarized in Table 12.3. The first involves the combined use of constraints (12.1) and (12.2), a hybrid of sorts (Rosing, ReVelle and Rosing-Vogelaar 1979). The second model (COBRA) is based on a spatial property that allows certain variables to be combined, thereby reducing the number of variables and constraints (Church 2003). The third model form (BEAMR) is based on another geographic principle, given that a complete model contains many variables which are in all probability superfluous to the problem at hand (Church 2008). BEAMR is based on identifying which variables are likely to be superfluous and eliminating these variables from the resulting model. In solving BEAMR, it is easy to tell whether enough variables have been included to find the optimal solution.

Besides using general-purpose optimization software, there has been considerable interest in developing special-purpose software to solve the p-median problem optimally (exact). A second exact approach reported in Table 12.3 involves the use of Lagrangian relaxation. Most of these methods have been based on structuring a *dual* model that is generated by relaxing one or more of the constraints, and appending them to the objective with an associated Lagrange variable (or dual price). Relaxed models are less restricted and can be solved to generate a lower bound on the solution to the actual problem. The idea is to use this relaxed model to produce a bound, and thereby the capability to calculate the *gap* from optimality associated with a specific solution and the bound. There are many variants of this approach based on how prices are modified, as well as how the process is embedded in a branch and bound routine.

A third category of solution approaches reported in Table 12.3 for the p-median problem is heuristics. These approaches have followed a renaissance of sorts in the development of heuristics to solve difficult combinatorial problems. These include heuristic approaches that have some physical or biological analogy to ones that attempt to break away from local optimums and more fully explore solution space. Examples include interchange, tabu search, simulated annealing, and heuristic concentration, among others.

The point to be emphasized here is that most model classes have been the subject of considerable research in terms of designing efficient and robust solution methods, just as has been done for the p-median problem.

12.4   FINAL THOUGHTS

The field of location science can be defined more broadly than the selected subjects included in this book. However, the future lies at the interface between GIS, modeling, and an application domain, like business site selection. Products like Google Earth and car navigation systems can bring a rich variety of data to our fingertips. It is now customary to look through the lens of a satellite or at an aerial photograph of a region on Web sites such as Google Earth, as well as access a variety of spatial data with a portable navigation device. For example, given GPS coordinates, it is possible, using the "never lost" navigation of Hertz rental cars, to identify the closest McDonald's restaurant.

Location-based services is a field in its infancy that takes advantage of such information in providing greater access to business data for customers. This means that in the future, potential customers will no longer need to observe a store or go to the phone book to find out about a potential business or service, but may be steered toward a store because of a query or need. That said, the climate for business is changing, and so must the strategies for making location decisions. For example, an out-of-sight location may now be made more desirable because it can be viewed in a navigation/mapping system and the potential customer can be directed to it. It is also conceivable that stores might increase their effective market area by selling a good on the Internet and then having the customer pick it up at a local store. It is now possible to develop business site location models that integrate the effectiveness of location-based service information, and even address the potential for Internet sales within a site-selection model. This type of development will impact a number of businesses, including banking, restaurants, specialty shops, and medical services. New models and solution approaches are needed for this emerging problem domain.

There also exist significant challenges associated with the integration of location models in terms of GIS functionality. Often, applications are fed data extracted from GIS, and after solution of the model, the results are then imported back into GIS for display and further analysis. Such loosely coupled systems often fail to take full advantage of true spatial detail, particularly within GIS. It seems reasonable that future models will be defined so that they capture spatial relationships to a greater extent. This means that such models are likely to be larger in size, more complex, and no doubt more computationally difficult to solve. However, there is also much potential to take greater advantage of GIS representation and functionality in problem solution, and may in fact enable problems to be more efficiently solved, both by exact and heuristic methods.

Finally, GIScience, and GIS as a platform of choice for spatial analysis, represent more than just increased location model detail and greater computational burdens. We are already witnessing evidence of advancing theoretical understanding and enhanced modeling. In particular, researchers are already developing and applying new location model constructs as well as extending existing models in ways not previously possible. Merging the model with the system in which the data are stored and organized will continue to increase opportunities for improved location decision making.

12.5 REFERENCES

Balinski, M. L. 1965. Integer programming: Methods, uses, computation. *Management Science* 12:253–313.

Church, R. L. 2003. COBRA: A new formulation of the classic p-median location problem. *Annals of Operations Research* 122:103–120.

Church, R. L. 2008. BEAMR: An exact and approximate model for the p-median problem. *Computers & Operations Research* 35:417–426.

Efroymson, M. A., and T. L. Ray. 1966. A branch–bound algorithm for plant location. *Operations Research* 14:361–368.

ReVelle, C. S., and R. Swain. 1970. Central facilities location. *Geographical Analysis* 2:30–42.

Rosing, K. E., C. S. Revelle, and H. Rosing-Vogelaar. 1979. The p-median and its linear programming relaxation: An approach to large problems. *Journal of the Operational Research Society* 30:815–823.

GLOSSARY

$\binom{n}{p}$ Expression related to the total number of combinations possible in selecting p items from a set of n items ($n > p$). Specifically, $\binom{n}{p} = {}^{n!}/_{p!\,(n-p)!}$, where $n! = n\,(n-1)\,(n-2)\,(n-3)\cdots 1$.

absolute suitability (screening/filtering)   Type of *suitability analysis* where a location is classified either as suitable or not suitable.

accessibility   Relative capacity or capability to travel from one location to another. That is, some locations are more accessible than others from a given location.

adjacency   Topological property associated with two spatial objects (e.g., cells or polygons). Objects are adjacent if they share a common point or boundary.

aggregation   Process or technique involving the creation of one new object from several input objects.

allocation   Process of determining what demand is served by which facility.

analytic hierarchy process   Approach to dividing problem components into a logical hierarchy and determining importance weights for a set of objectives or criteria.

anti-covering   Standards-based dispersion problem, where the goal is to find the maximum weighted number of facilities, and their location, such that no two facilities are within a stipulated minimum distance or travel time of each other.

area-distance   The cost of a route or path in terms of both distance and width (area).

breakpoint formula   A mathematical approach for demarcating a trade area, identifying the point between two retail sites where a customer would be indifferent to store choice based on travel distance and attraction, measured in terms of population.

buffer   An object representing a buffer zone created by a topological transformation of an input object (point, line, polygon, or raster cell) using a specified width or travel time, which can be regular or irregular in shape.

carrying capacity   Maximum number of individuals of a given species that can be supported throughout the year at a given site.

central place theory   A theory of the placement of retail and administrative centers across space, originally proposed by Christallar. Based on certain economic and spatial assumptions, including range and threshold.

choropleth map   A thematic map displaying data by area using color or shade intensities to depict different classes or magnitudes.

clique   Set of potential facility sites that are simultaneously proximal to each other, or rather, within a prespecified spatial restriction limit.

competition   The existence of two or more retail establishments that attempt to capture as much market as possible.

complete coverage   A configuration of facilities that is able to serve all demand within a maximal distance, time, or other standard.

constraint set   A set of mathematical equalities and or inequalities that must be satisfied in order for a solution to be considered feasible.

containment   Topological property associated with two spatial objects. One object contains another if the object is entirely within the other object.

contiguity   Topological property associated with a set of spatial objects (e.g., cells or polygons). The set of objects is contiguous if it is possible to traverse across space from one object to any other in the set without leaving the set.

continuous space vs. discrete space   The domain representing all potential facility sites in a model can be defined as either discrete individual locations (e.g., points) or can be defined as any location (e.g., anywhere along a line, in a plane or on a spherical surface, etc.).

continuous variable A decision variable in an optimization model that can take any value along a continuum (e.g., greater than or equal to zero).

coordinate system A referencing approach measuring relative position in the x- and y-direction from an established origin in two-dimensional space. Often used to refer to locations in three-dimensional space, as well.

coordinate transformation A mathematical function of process used to transform one coordinate system into another coordinate system.

corridor A path connecting an origin and a destination, with a defined width.

cost-distance The cost of a route or path in terms of distance.

covering Concept associated with facility service, and the notion that service is provided if an area can be reached within a specified maximum distance, time, cost or other metric standard from the facility.

data measurement type There are four commonly recognized types: nominal, ordinal, interval, and ratio.

data transformation The process of creating one data type from another data type (e.g., transforming nominal data into ratio-scaled data).

descriptive vs. prescriptive The process of understanding why a facility is located at a given place, as compared to the process of identifying what the best location is for the facility.

Dijkstra algorithm An exact, iterative approach for solving the shortest-path problem.

dispersion The property of a locational pattern of facilities where the intent is to spread out the service facilities, in contrast to clustering.

distortion errors Errors that arise when using a discrete network to represent all possible movements across a continuous surface.

error and uncertainty Recognition that spatial information in a digital environment (GIS) has many associated errors and imprecision due to abstraction, simplification, and measurement issues.

Euclidean distance Straight-line distance between two points in a Cartesian plane.

exact A process designed to identify an optional solution to a problem.

fixed-charge capacitated location-allocation problem A location-allocation problem where facilities are to be sited in order to minimize assignment and facility costs in serving all demand in a region. Each facility has a limit on the total amount of demand that can be served.

geoid   An approximate representation of the shape of the earth in a digital environment, taking into account spheroidal irregularities.

GeoVisualization   Techniques and software designed to visually explore spatial data, spatial phenomena, and spatial models.

GIS (geographical information system)   Hardware, software, and procedures that support decision making through the acquisition, management, manipulation, analysis, and display of spatially referenced information.

gravity model   A mathematical specification of the interaction between to locations based on an analogy to Newton's law of gravitational attraction, taking into account population and distance.

great circle distance   The distance between two points on a sphere, accounting for the curvature of earth.

heuristic   A process design to identify a good, if not optional, solution to a problem.

Huff model   A mathematical specification of the probability that a customer will shop at competing stores or retail centers based on a derivative of the gravity model.

integer variable   A variable that is constrained to be integer in value (e.g., $0,1,2,\ldots$).

interchange heuristic   An approach for solving the p-median problem. It is a neighborhood search/substitution approach that begins with a randomly generated configuration of p sites, and an associated allocation of each demand area to its closest facility, then iteratively considers swaps of selected facility sites with unselected facility sites. Sites are interchanged when total weighted distance is improved.

interpolation   A method of estimating a data value for a given location, based on data values measured at other locations.

interval data   Attribute data measured on a continuous scale, although the scale does not have a calibrated zero (i.e., an arbitrary zero).

knapsack model   A model that is based on selecting items that have a benefit and a cost. The objective is to select those items that maximize the sum of benefits, while keeping the costs of selected items within an allowable budget. The knapsack model has been used in land acquisition modeling.

land-use acquisition   The problem of determining which parcels or units of land to acquire in order to support a given purpose or use (e.g., purchasing land for a park).

laws of location science   Basic geographical properties associated with spatial decision making. Some locations are better than others for a given purpose

(LLS1). Spatial context can alter site efficiencies (LLS2). Sites of an optimal multisite pattern must be selected simultaneously rather than independently, one at a time (LLS3).

line   A spatial object represented in a vector-based GIS defined by a series of coordinate pairs (two-dimensional space) connected by a straight line segment: $\{(x_1, y_1), (x_2, y_2), (x_3, y_3), \ldots, (x_n, y_n)\}$. The resulting line may be curvilinear.

linear function   A mathematical equation that is based on the sum of linear terms, where each term is either a constant or a scalar times a variable.

location (descriptive and prescriptive)   The process of understanding why a facility is located at a given place, as compared to the process of identifying what the best location is for the facility.

location science   A field of study involving the location of activities across a spatial domain in order to optimize one or more objectives.

location set covering problem   A standards-based coverage problem where the goal is to identify a configuration involving the fewest facilities necessary to provide suitable service to all demand in a region.

map algebra   Rules and operational procedures applied to an attribute layer(s) (input) to produce a new layer (output).

map projection   A mathematical model used to convert three-dimensional reality into two dimensions for the purposes of representation on a map, or within a GIS.

mathematical expression   A combination of mathematical terms.

maximal coverage   A facility configuration that achieves the highest coverage possible.

maximal covering location problem   A standards-based coverage problem where the goal is to identify a configuration of p facilities that provide suitable service to the greatest amount of demand possible in a region.

minimize the numbers of facilities vs. minimize the cost of facilities   When the cost of locating a facility is somewhat constant, then minimizing the number of located facilities is equivalent to minimizing the cost of located facilities.

model   An abstraction of a real-world problem as a set of mathematical statements.

modeling language   A special programming environment that aids in building and solving an optimization model.

modifiable areal unit problem (MAUP)   Recognition that spatial information for a given region can vary in terms of scale and definition of the underlying reporting units, and as a result there is potential for obtaining differing analytical results.

multifacility Weber problem   A location-allocation problem involving the siting of p facilities in continuous space in order to minimize total weighted distance, where distance is measured using the Euclidean metric.

network representation   The process of representing a space as a collection of connected nodes and arcs.

nominal data   Attribute data that represent a name, class, or category (also referred to as categorical type).

nonlinear function   A function composed of one or more nonlinear terms, where a nonlinear term involves the product of several variables, a variable raised to some power other than 1 or 0, or the use of a trigonometric or logarithmic function.

nonnegativity conditions   Requirements imposed on model variables, where variables are constrained to be greater than or equal to zero.

normalized weights   Set of weighting values for attribute layers or objectives whose sum is equal to zero.

objective   A mathematical function or measurable metric used to assess the goodness of a model solution.

operations research   A field of applied mathematics that involves modeling everyday business, management, and engineering problems using methods of optimization, statistics, simulation, game theory, and decision theory.

ordinal data   Attribute data that are nominal but ranked (also referred to as ranked type).

O.R. (Operations Research)   A field of applied mathematics which is focused on decision making and simulation.

overlay   Data manipulation function in GIS involving the creation of a data layer from two or more data layers.

path   A route connecting two points, an origin and a destination.

path alternatives   Paths that differ in some way, but have the same origin and destination.

perimeter   Resulting exterior edge of acquired parcels in an area based location model. More generally, it is the boundary of a geographical object.

planning revolution   The period starting in the early 1960s in which planners conceived of using large-scale models to analyze and support decision-making in a wide variety of applications, from environmental management to transportation planning.

p-**median problem**   A location-allocation problem where p facilities are to be sited in order to minimize total weighted distance in serving all demand in a region.

point   A spatial object represented in a vector-based GIS defined by a coordinate pair (two-dimensional space): (x, y).

polygon (or area)   A spatial object represented in a vector-based GIS defined by a series of coordinate pairs (two-dimensional space) connected by a straight line, with the last coordinate pair connecting to the first coordinate pair: $\{(x_1, y_1), (x_2, y_2), (x_3, y_3), \ldots, (x_n, y_n)\}$.

probabilistic coverage   A standards-based location model that takes into account that facilities (or servers) may not be available some of the time, so coverage is viewed in uncertain (or probabilistic) terms.

range   The distance beyond which customers are unlikely to travel to a retail site for goods or services.

raster GIS   A GIS data format that consists of cells of regular size, where the attribute value of a cell is assumed to represent the entire cell.

ratio data   Attribute data that are measured on a continuous scale with a calibrated zero.

r-**based network**   A network defined for a raster, where the arcs defined for a given cell are directed to all cells within r-rings of cells about that cell. An $r = 1$ ring of cells is the set of cells that form a continuous loop around the center cell and share an edge or a corner with the center cell. An $r = 2$ ring of cells is the set of cells that form an outer loop around a center cell and share an edge or a corner with the $r = 1$ ring.

rectilinear distance   A distance metric (also called Manhattan or grid distance) accounting for travel in terms of vertical and horizontal displacements between two points.

Reilly's law   A gravity-based model of retail attractiveness for customers choosing between two competitors.

relational DBMS   A database management system with the ability to access data organized in tabular files that are related by key fields.

relative suitability (scoring)   Type of *suitability analysis* where a location is classified within a range of values, indicating greater or lesser desirability of a location for an intended use.

saturation   High or excessive concentration of retail or market services in an area.

scan order   Path through a raster model associated with storing attribute values for each cell. Common scan orders are row by row, Morton, Peano, and row prime.

scenario-based or robust optimization An optimization model that uses data to represent different possible outcomes, so that the solution that is identified is sensitive to the possible outcomes and the underlying uncertainty.

selective inclusion The process of selecting elements based on one or more criterion.

separation The distance or time that separates the closest pair of points or facilities in a pattern or configuration.

service area The region or zone that is served by a given facility.

shape model A land acquisition model that optimizes one or more shape metrics (e.g., contiguity, compactness, etc.).

shortest-path problem A problem of finding the path of least distance, beginning at a prespecified origin and ending at a prespecified destination.

skeleton (medial axis) Refers to central location of a polygon, and is the locus of the centers of circles that are tangent to the polygon at two or more points, with all such circles being contained in the polygon.

spatial representation A method or approach to represent spatial objects in a model or database. Two popular approaches are the vector and raster representations of space.

sphere A commonly assumed shape of the earth, generated by rotating a circle around one of its axes.

spheroid A commonly assumed shape of earth. It is an object that is shaped like a sphere, but is not perfectly round. A shape that is generated by rotating an ellipse around one of its axes.

spider plot Method of illustration for a location-allocation problem showing selected facility sites and associated assignment of demand to facilities (see Figure 11.1).

SQL Structured (or standard) query language. A syntactic structure for identifying objects in a database relying on: SELECT <columns> FROM <tables> WHERE <conditions>.

standards-based service Facility service that is measured in terms of a standard (e.g., the capability of responding in 10 minutes).

suitability analysis A process of systematically identifying or rating potential locations with respect to a particular use.

Thiessen polygons (Voronoi diagram) Given a set of points, a Thiessen polygon depicts the area that is closer to one point than any of the other points.

threshold A distance or value beyond which a land unit is either too far or too costly to use. In central place theory, a *threshold* represents the needed market size to be economically viable.

threshold model   A model that involves picking all land units that fall within a specified threshold.

trade area (market area)   The region or zone surrounding a given retail site for which that retail site attracts the preponderance of its customers.

transformation   Approach based on utility theory for converting nominal, ordinal, and/or interval data to ratio data.

transportation problem   A problem associated with minimizing transportation costs when allocating resources form a set of distinct sources to meet demand distributed among a set of distinct destinations.

vector GIS   A GIS data format based on the representation of space as a collection of objects (points, lines, polygons, etc.).

Weber problem   Single-facility, Euclidean distance, point-based location problem, where the facility can be located anywhere in continuous space.

weighted distance   Sum over all areas of demand for service, multiplied by the distance to be traveled to an area's service facility.

weighted linear combination   Specification of attribute values across layers as a linear function with weights associated with each attribute, resulting in a new single new value.

Weiszfeld algorithm   Iterative solution technique for solving the Weber problem (single-facility Euclidean distance location problem).

INDEX

Printed in the United States
By Bookmasters